PARALEGALS

Progress and Prospects of a Satellite Occupation

QUINTIN JOHNSTONE
AND
MARTIN WENGLINSKY

EMERGING PATTERNS OF WORK AND
COMMUNICATIONS IN AN INFORMATION AGE, NUMBER 2

GREENWOOD PRESS
WESTPORT, CONNECTICUT • LONDON, ENGLAND

Library of Congress Cataloging in Publication Data

Johnstone, Quintin.
  Paralegals : progress and prospects of a
satellite occupation.

  (Emerging patterns of work and communications
in an information age, ISSN 0882–3316 ; no. 2)
  Bibliography: p.
  Includes index.
  1. Legal assistants—United States. I. Wenglinsky,
Martin. II. Title. III. Series.
KF320.L4J64 1985   340′.023′73   85–9889
ISBN 0–313–24945–8 (lib. bdg. : alk. paper)

Library of Congress Catalog Card Number: 85–9889
ISBN: 0–313–24945–8
ISSN: 0882–3316

First published in 1985

Greenwood Press
A division of Congressional Information Service, Inc.
88 Post Road West
Westport, Connecticut 06881

Printed in the United States of America

10 9 8 7 6 5 4 3 2 1

CONTENTS

LIST OF TABLES

ACKNOWLEDGMENTS

In carrying out this study we are most grateful to a number of individuals and organizations for their assistance. Financially, we were aided by Yale University and Quinnipiac College as well as by a most timely grant from The Ford Foundation. Parts of the manuscript were read and very helpful comments made by William Fry, Anthony Kronman, Albert Reiss, Richard Schwartz, Lea Nordlicht Shedd, William Statsky, and Stanton Wheeler. Two student research assistants, Rebecca Friedkin and George Voss, made valuable contributions, and throughout the study Jill Zarnetske provided highly competent secretarial assistance. Also, Gene Coakley of the Yale Law Library staff was of great help on many occasions, and Frank Papale, Janice Cirillo, and Lisa Hartmann of the Quinnipiac Computer Center provided valuable assistance in data analysis. Without the cooperation of many paralegals and lawyers this project would have been impossible, and we are particularly indebted to those we interviewed and to the paralegals who responded to our questionnaire. Although their identities are kept anonymous, the time they gave and the information and insights they made available to us are deeply appreciated.

PARALEGALS

INTRODUCTION

Recently a new occupation has emerged in the United States to help provide legal services to consumers of such services. Those working in this rapidly expanding occupation commonly are referred to as paralegals, the term adopted in this study, and they assist lawyers in the wide range of tasks that lawyers are responsible for in representing clients. This book takes a broad look at the paralegal occupation, an occupation that has been largely ignored by scholars, and explores its development, operations, and future prospects. The occupation has now progressed to the point that a comprehensive examination of it is merited.

Paralegals are law office employees who have not been admitted to practice law but who perform legal tasks also performed by lawyers and who are under the general supervision and control of lawyers. Paralegals are so dependent on lawyers and lawyers exert sufficient dominance over them that in effect the paralegal occupation is a satellite of the lawyers' profession. This has created problems and will create more problems in the future. Any expansive consideration of paralegals must also give close attention to lawyers, an occupation that functionally and organizationally is interlocked with paralegals.

Paralegals are now found in many law offices of all kinds and are part of the lawyer support staff in offices employing them. Most law offices with paralegals clearly distinguish their paralegals from other kinds of support personnel, but it is a sign of the newness of the occupation that designations are not always clear and functions are mixed so that ambiguity exists in some offices as to who is and who is not a paralegal.

Employment by American law offices of unadmitted personnel to perform lawyerlike tasks is not new, but what is new is the coalescing of this nonlawyer group into a separately recognized occupation with its own organizations and influence. Also new are the rapid increases that have occurred recently in numbers of persons working as paralegals.

There are no precise statistics on the total number of paralegals in the United States. No census has been taken; and there is no universal accreditation requirement for paralegals, such as licensing provides for lawyers, that enables easy identification of those in the occupation. Perhaps the best possible estimating approach to determine the total number of paralegals is to develop a working paralegal to lawyer ratio that seems to have some validity and then project this nationally or regionally based on available data on numbers of lawyers. Using this procedure we believe a ratio of one paralegal to eight lawyers has some validity and applying this ratio to the American Bar Foundation estimate of approximately 650,000 lawyers in the United States as of early 1984[1] gives a paralegal population of approximately 81,000 as of that year.[2] Using the same procedure for New York City gives a New York City paralegal population of 5,000.[3] It should be emphasized that at best these are only very rough estimates. More exact figures are available for numbers of paralegals nationally in certain categories of law offices. As of 1983, a survey of personnel in the 200 largest American law firms showed 5,717 paralegals and a paralegal to lawyer ratio of 1:5.6.[4] In 1981, there were 2,800 paralegals working in local legal aid in the United States and these offices had a paralegal to lawyer ratio of 1:2.2.[5] For New York City, samples of law offices that were selected for this study show paralegal to lawyer ratios varying from 1:9.3 for the small firms to 1:3.5 for the large ones, with ratios for other types of offices falling in between.[6]

Data on the extent to which the total paralegal population has increased in recent years is even more conjectural. All the evidence points to tremendous growth since the late 1960s but that evidence includes little in the way of precise figures.[7] Some indication of this growth is what has happened recently in large firms, where the number of paralegals in the 200 largest American law firms increased from a reported total of about 2,000 in 1975 to over 5,700 by 1983, with the paralegal to lawyer ratio for these firms changing from 1:7.6 in 1975 to the 1983 1:5.6 ratio.[8] Data on growth in numbers of lawyers is more complete and accurate. In 1960 there were a quarter of a million lawyers,[9] by 1970 this number has increased to 325,000,[10] and by 1984 to 650,000. By 1990 the lawyer population in the United States will probably exceed three quarters of a million. It is significant that the recent rapid increase in the number of paralegals has occurred simultaneously with a very substantial increase in the number of lawyers.[11] These concurrent occupational expansions have taken place even though many beginning lawyers have been having difficulties in finding jobs as lawyers.[12]

The introduction of paralegals as a major occupational group in providing legal services faces law offices with a choice of far-reaching consequence that can alter the nature of legal practice for both practitioners and consumers. It is a choice between more or less bureaucracy in the way law offices are structured and operated. On the one hand, those who favor a strongly professional model of law practice and see legal representation as a set of delicate, individualized, and often momentous handcrafted activities are likely to see paralegals as a passing fad, an intrusion on the proper way law should be practiced, or, at least, as a relatively inconsequential accretion to law office support staffs, a brush with modern ideas of efficiency that does not change the nature or quality of legal work or the role of lawyers. On the other hand, those who see law practice as inevitably becoming far more bureaucratized to serve larger and often more complex caseloads with need for a much greater degree of efficiency are likely to see paralegals as highly desirable lawyer adjuncts, without necessarily realizing the profound alteration in law practice that such a personnel change may introduce. It is well for both traditional and nontraditional lawyers to consider the major bureaucratization decision they face, a decision that will be made again and again in law office after law office in the years ahead. Each decision will be made because of particular personalities and the exigencies of particular practices but all responding to circumstances that the legal profession currently faces.

Research on paralegals is but one way of studying law office bureaucratization but it is a particularly useful way of doing so. It enables the contrasting and complementary features of bureaucratic and professional organizations to be seen more clearly in the context of law practice, and identical issues concerning these organizations become well-exemplified in attempts by law offices to resolve such problems as how to reduce costs, how to control work quality, and how to expand the volume of services without increasing personnel expense. The study of paralegals also provides an excellent vantage point for observing law office routinization and the development of bureaucratic systems and procedures for more effective routinization of legal work, as paralegals are commonly utilized in very routine work settings. Many private firms are finding that routinization enables them to handle a more profitable volume of cases and many public sector law offices are discovering that routinization is essential to deal with the massive volume of matters that by law they are mandated to handle.

Expanded reliance on paraprofessionals has been going on in other professions than law and its scope as a transforming force is an indication that it is much more than a fad. Paraprofessionals have become particularly important in medicine, with physician extenders,[13] x-ray and laboratory technicians, and nurse practitioners, among others, who have changed medicine from being individual practitioner based to being largely hospital based, with elaborate technology and extensive support staffs making possible a bureaucratic division of labor that challenges the collegial relation of physicians as the foundation for institutional dominance. Paraprofessional occupations tend to come on the scene or expand rapidly in membership when the fields they serve arc in major growth spurts. Some have developed as adjuncts to operate and manage new technology, not a major factor, however, in the development of paralegals.

The first four chapters that follow concentrate successively on what paralegals do, who they are, what their organizations are, and what their controls are. These chapters also consider in some detail such other matters relevant to paralegals as law office systems for performing routine work, law office personnel policies and practices, and paralegal education. The final two chapters make some general observations about paralegals and their place in delivery of legal services, relying extensively on descriptive data from the first four chapters. Chapter five is a sociological analysis that emphasizes the significance of professionalism and bureaucracy in the emergence and evolution of paralegals as a separate occupation. Sociologists have been among the most astute observers of occupations and there is a rich sociological literature on professions and on occupations aspiring to be professions. Much of this literature is concerned with the medical profession[14] but important studies have been published on the legal profession as well.[15] Chapter five applies to paralegals some of the major concerns and basic concepts that have characterized occupational sociology. The last chapter, chapter six, draws some additional conclusions about paralegals, discusses trends and the possible future of the occupation, and makes some recommendations as to how the paralegal occupation can be improved and can help strengthen the legal services delivery system.

So as to enable a look at the occupation and its context in some depth, the focus throughout is heavily on paralegals and law offices in New York City, the largest center of legal work in the United States. Every major type of law office is well-represented in this great center and the study stresses comparisons among types of law offices in use and assimilation of paralegals. The organizational side of providing clients with legal services is highly diverse and to understand paralegals and the many ways law offices have adapted to them requires consideration of the different settings in which paralegals work. The profusion of different kinds of law offices in New York City is further supplemented by the city's relatively well-developed set of paralegal organizations, including a local association of paralegals and a number of paralegal schools. Although our field research was centered on New York City, we have sought at appropriate points to bring to bear information about paralegals and their organizations in other parts of the nation, principally by drawing on the literature about paralegals. This literature is fairly extensive and appears mostly in law reviews, publications of bar associations and paralegal associations, and in teaching materials developed for paralegal school instruction.

The types of law offices compared in this study are these: large private law firms, medium-sized private law firms, small private law firms, corporate law departments, government law offices, and legal aid offices. This breakdown was adopted because it is one lawyers and paralegals are familiar with and commonly follow in referring to various kinds of legal work units. It also provides a useful and enlightening basis for making important distinctions in such matters as how and for whom law is practiced and how offices are organized and staffed, including how paralegals are utilized and what kinds of paralegals are employed for what kinds of work. Large private law firms are defined herein as those with more than fifty lawyers, medium-sized law firms as those with ten to fifty lawyers, and small firms as those with under ten lawyers, including offices operated by solo practitioners. In determining a firm's size, if the firm had lawyers regularly based outside New York City—in a suburban or Washington branch, for example—only lawyers regularly based in New York City were included.

During the course of the study paralegals in a number of New York City law offices were asked to fill out and return a written questionnaire submitted to them. A copy of the questionnaire appears as Appendix A. We received 409 usable questionnaires, a return rate of 55 percent. Not all questions were answered in some of the usable returns. As identifying and locating paralegals was a major problem, questionnaires were submitted through employers, with the request that a copy be given to all paralegals in the office. This was done after it was ascertained that an office did employ paralegals and the office had agreed to cooperate. The procedure followed was considered far preferable to circulating questionnaires to paralegals named on membership lists of local or national paralegal associations, the procedure usually followed in previous surveys of paralegals. Most employers contacted agreed to cooperate,[16] but quite universally made it clear to their paralegals that filling out and returning the questionnaire was entirely discretionary with each paralegal.[17] In the great majority of offices, paralegals were clearly designated and their position as paralegals clearly recognized as such within the office. Where doubt existed as to classification, we left it up to the employer to determine who were paralegals and should receive questionnaires.[18] At most offices to which questionnaires were distributed, selected lawyers and paralegals were also interviewed.[19] Approximately 200 persons were interviewed in connection with this study.[20]

Samples of law offices at which questionnaires were distributed were not all drawn in the same manner. Medium- and small-sized firms, of which there are thousands in New York City, were selected by a random sampling drawn from the *Martindale-Hubbell Law Directory*, a comprehensive listing of American lawyers by state and city.[21] The remaining offices were selected because we knew they employed paralegals and were assured of their cooperation. Most of them are large offices with comparatively large paralegal staffs. They include three large Wall Street-type firms, six corporate law departments, four government agencies, and six legal aid offices. Each of the three large firms is highly prestigious and represents principally corporations and individuals of great wealth. The corporate law departments are units within giant corporations and each corporation is engaged in a very different business from any of the others. Two of the government law offices are prosecutors' offices doing exclusively or predominantly criminal work; each of the other two provides a much wider range of services to its government client. The legal aid offices include one very large office and five small ones. Collectively, at the time of our interviews, they employed 95 percent of all legal aid paralegals in New York City.[22] The large legal aid office is unusual in that most of its work is criminal defense, it being the public defender for New York City in addition to representing poor people in a large volume of civil matters.[23]

Clarification of some important terms as used by us should be noted at this point, terms not always carrying the same meanings in discourse about law. The term *legal services* as used herein refers to legal work performed by anyone, not just by legal aid organizations; nor do we use the term *legal services* as a synonym for legal aid. Lay advocates also are distinguished by us from paralegals. Lay advocates are lay persons who perform legal work for others but are not supervised or controlled by lawyers; paralegals perform such work under the supervision and control of lawyers.[24] However, in our use of the term *paralegals*, we do not include law student summer clerks or summer interns working in law offices. These clerks and interns tend to be sufficiently unique in such respects as career expectations, occupational status, and group identifications that they should not be included with paralegals.[25] It should also be noted that paralegals in this country commonly are called legal assistants. This is the term preferred by the American Bar Association and by some paralegals and is frequently used in the literature.[26]

NOTES

1. The estimated total number of lawyers in the United States as of 1984 is 649,000, the number found for 1980 is 542,205. American Bar Foundation, *The 1984 Lawyer Statistical Report: A Profile of the Legal Profession in the United States* (1984).

2. The determination of a paralegal to lawyer ratio of 1:8 is based on a very rough approximation drawing on such data as is available and recognizing that most American lawyers are employed in small private law offices, offices in which, on average, there apparently is a larger number of lawyers per paralegal than in other kinds of offices. For sources of available data on paralegal to lawyer ratios, *see infra* notes 4–6 and 21. The text estimate of approximately 81,000 paralegals in 1984 is fairly consistent with an estimate of 80,000 paralegals in 1979 made by one source, C. Bruno, *Paralegal's Litigation Handbook* xiv (1980). The Bruno book does not, however, state how the 80,000 number was ascertained. The United States Department of Labor has estimated the number of paralegals in 1980 to have been 31,500, but has a separate category for law clerks and estimates their number in 1980 to have been 32,700. U.S. Dept. of Labor, Bureau of Labor

Statistics, *Supplement to 1982–83 Occupational Outlook Handbook* 79 (Dec. 1982). The Department estimates that in 1990 there will be between 65,800 and 75,300 paralegals and between 42,600 and 48,000 law clerks. *Ibid.* The distinction between paralegals and law clerks in these estimates is not clear.

Paralegals are and long have been more important numerically in English solicitors' offices than in American law offices. The paralegal to solicitor ratio in English solicitors' offices is approximately 1:2, but paralegals have been decreasing in number and solicitors increasing. Johnstone and Flood, Paralegals in English and American Law Offices, 2 *Windsor Yearbook of Access to Justice* 172–75 (1982). On paralegals in English solicitors' offices, also *see* Q. Johnstone and D. Hopson, *Lawyers and Their Work* ch. 12 (1967); and R. Abel, Lawyers in the United Kingdom 75–77 (unpublished first draft, 1983, prepared for the Working Group for Comparative Study of Legal Professions of the International Sociological Association Research Committee on Sociology of Law). English barristers' offices also have paralegals, called barristers' clerks, of whom there are fewer than a thousand. The role of barristers' clerks is generally quite different from that of paralegals in American law offices or English solicitors' offices. These important aides to barristers negotiate for new work coming to their principals, including setting and collecting fees, and do much of the office management and administration. The ratio of barristers' clerks to barristers is about 1:6. On these barristers' aides, *see* J. Flood, *Barristers' Clerks, The Law's Middlemen* (1983).

3. The American Bar Foundation statistical report found 39,851 lawyers in New York City. American Bar Foundation, *supra* note 1.

4. These figures are derived from a 1983 firm-by-firm survey of the 200 largest American law firms, *National Law Journal*, September 19, 1983, at 4. Size of firms is based on number of lawyers. The survey reports data on number of paralegals as not available for 5 firms, hence only 195 firms are included in the text paralegal and ratio figures. One New York City firm employed 127 paralegals, the most of any firm listed. A similar survey showed, as of early 1979, 115 paralegals employed by the 25 largest Connecticut law firms and a paralegal to lawyer ratio in these firms of about 1 to 5, 3 firms not included because of incomplete data. *Connecticut Law Tribune*, Jan. 15, 1979. These Connecticut firms average far fewer lawyers per firm than do the 200 largest in the nation. A 1983 survey of 500 private law firms in the United States and Canada, excluding solo practitioners, shows a paralegal to lawyer ratio of 1:4, with the ratio higher in Canada than in any section of the United States, almost 1:2, and somewhat higher in small firms than large ones. Anderson and Ruth, A Comparison of Staff Salaries, *National Law Journal*, Nov. 21, 1983, 15 at 17.

5. These figures are for the 323 local programs funded by the Legal Services Corporation. Erhlich, Save the Legal Services Corporation, 67 *American Bar Association Journal* 434, at 435 (1981). The 323 programs operated in 1,450 main and branch offices throughout the United States. Legal Services Corporation, *Annual Report 1981*, at 8.

6. Paralegal to lawyer ratios for the other samples of New York City offices were medium-sized private law firms, 1:7.9; corporate law departments, 1:4.3; government law offices, 1:8.6; and legal aid, 1:5. Sampling and ratio calculations for the small- and medium-sized firms are described *infra* note 21. For the other types of offices, ratios were determined as of 1980–81 from the numbers of par-

alegals and lawyers then working in the offices from which questionnaires were received.

7. In very few offices with paralegals where we conducted interviews for this study was there evidence brought to our attention that paralegals were employed in these offices prior to the late 1960s. Another indication of the tremendous recent expansion in numbers of paralegals is that today there are about 350 schools turning out paralegals for initial entry into paralegal employment but until the late 1960s there were no such schools.

Undoubtedly, prior to the latter 1960s, there were secretaries and law student clerks in some law offices who today would be called paralegals based on the kind of work they performed. In an earlier period there also were some law offices that employed other categories of lay persons, in essence paralegals, for highly specialized routine tasks. *See*, for example, the description of lay examiners of mortgage documents in Johnstone and Hopson, *supra* note 2, at ch. 7 (1967).

8. The 1975 figures are derived from survey statistics in *National Law Journal*, Sept. 18 and 25, 1978. Only 170 firms are included in the 1975 computation because for 30 firms no paralegal figures were available.

9. American Bar Foundation, *The 1971 Lawyer Statistical Report* 8 (1972).

10. *Id.*

11. On the reasons for recent increases in the lawyer population, *see* Johnstone, The Future of the Legal Profession in Connecticut, 55 *Connecticut Bar Journal* 256, at 261–62 (1981). For a somewhat different view on these increases, *see* Pashigian, The Number and Earnings of Lawyers: Some Recent Findings, *1978 American Bar Foundation Research Journal* 51.

Total receipts from legal services received by all entities providing legal services in the United States went up from $10.9 billion in 1972 to $35.5 billion in 1982 and it has been estimated that by 1993 it will be $124.4 billion. Business Trend Analysts, Inc., *The U.S. Market for Legal Services* 9 (1984).

12. There is little reliable data on difficulties beginning lawyers are encountering in finding law jobs or in numbers who cannot satisfactorily establish themselves in the occupation and hence drop out. It is asserted in a 1984 article that one-quarter of all 1982 law school graduates were still looking for jobs in 1984 or had opted for nonlegal positions. A Divided Profession: The Law's Two Worlds, *National Law Journal*, Aug. 6, 1984, at 42. Similar beginning lawyer placement problems are also discussed in The Classes of 1981: 90% Found Legal Jobs, *National Law Journal*, Aug. 9, 1982, at 2; Law Firm Recruiting: A National Slowdown, *National Law Journal*, Sept. 27, 1982, at 6; Glaberson, Lawyers' Job Market: Hard Times for Some, *New York Law Journal*, July 21, 1982, at 1. *See also* Conference Proceedings, Are There Too Many Lawyers?, 6 *Canada-United States Law Journal* 98 (1983).

13. There is a particularly close analogy of paralegals to physician extenders in their occupational roles and occupational evolution. Widespread use of physician's assistants and other types of physician extenders developed in the 1970s at about the same time that paralegal use was rapidly expanding. On different types of physician extenders and their contributions to health care, *see* G. Appel and A. Lowin, *Physician Extenders: An Evaluation of Policy-Related Research* (1975). Also *see* Sapadin, A Comparison of the Growth and Development of the Physician Assistant and Legal Assistant, *Journal of the American Association for Paralegal*

Education, Retrospective 1983, at 137 (1983); and Schneller, The Design and Evolution of the Physician's Assistant, 3 *Sociology of Work and Occupations* 455 (1976), now entitled *Work and Occupations*.

14. *See*, for example, H. Becker, *Boys in White* (1961); C. Cox and A. Mead (eds.), *A Sociology of Medical Practice* (1975); and E. Freidson, *The Profession of Medicine* (1970).

15. *See*, for example, J. Carlin, *Lawyers on Their Own* (1962); J. Heinz and E. Laumann, *Chicago Lawyers: The Social Structure of the Bar* (1982); H. O'Gorman, *Lawyers and Matrimonial Cases* (1963); D. Rosenthal, *Lawyer and Client, Who's in Charge?* (1974); D. Rueschemeyer, *Lawyers and Their Society* (1973); and E. Smigel, *The Wall Street Lawyer* (2d ed. 1969).

16. One large law firm and two corporate law departments refused to cooperate in distributing questionnaires to their paralegals, although interviews with lawyers or supervising paralegals were conducted at each of these offices. For small- and medium-sized firms the cooperation rate was somewhat lower, in some instances because once they had informed us that they employed paralegals, principals in the firms who could authorize questionnaire distribution could not be contacted. Solo practitioners were the most difficult to reach.

17. There was obvious reluctance on the part of employers to appear as exerting any coercion on their paralegals to fill out questionnaires, although follow-up reminders were sent employees by some employers. In at least one office, the employer cleared distribution of the questionnaire with the union to which the paralegals belonged.

18. We did make it clear, however, that law student summer clerks or interns were not to be included as paralegals. On this type of summer employee of law offices, *see infra* note 25. In a very limited number of offices, mostly small offices, doubts arose as to whether persons doing a substantial amount of typing and other secretarial work, in addition to lawyer-like work, should be considered secretaries or paralegals. The tendency seemed to be for employers not to classify most of these in-between types as paralegals.

19. These interviews were open-ended and generally lasted thirty minutes to an hour each.

20. Employers usually determined who should be interviewed. The lawyers selected were almost invariably persons who worked closely with paralegals or were responsible for hiring or policy setting for paralegals within the office. In larger offices, employers generally made an effort to select a representative sample of paralegals in terms of amount of experience and type of work performed. If the office employed a lay paralegal supervisor, we usually interviewed that person. Since the advent a few years ago of periodicals that provide extensive and often critical news coverage of what is going on at individual law offices, law offices seem particularly wary of outsiders probing into their internal affairs.

21. To determine which small- and medium-sized firms employed paralegals, a random sample of firms was contacted by letter and those replying that they had paralegals on their staffs were then contacted by telephone for permission to distribute questionnaires and to interview. Five hundred letters were sent to persons identified in a random sample drawn from *Martindale-Hubbell* listings of lawyers who appeared from their listings to be working in New York City law firms of fifty or fewer lawyers. To the 500 letters, 340 written responses were received and

another 58 were returned by the Post Office because the addressees were untraceable. Telephone contacts were attempted when replies to initial letters were not received and some added responses were obtained through these contacts. This entire procedure was time-consuming and onerous, particularly in relation to solo practitioners, of whom many in the sample were difficult or impossible to contact and a number of whom turned out to be retired or deceased. Responses to the letter inquiries resulted in identification of 263 small firms and 73 medium-sized firms; 68 of the small firms and 58 of the medium-sized ones reported that they employed paralegals. All the small firms that responded, including those with and those without paralegals, employed a total of 99 paralegals and 924 lawyers, for a paralegal to lawyer ratio of 1:9.3. Totals for all medium-sized firms, including those with and without paralegals, were 196 paralegals and 1,544 lawyers, for a paralegal to lawyer ratio of 1:7.9. In the tables that appear in subsequent chapters, questionnaire responses under medium-sized firms are included for two additional firms not selected at random. One of these is a legal clinic and the other a prepaid operation functioning under a union contract, significant forms for providing legal services not picked up in the random sample. These two firms, at the time of our interviews, employed a total of 21 paralegals and 70 lawyers, and we received questionnaire responses from 13 of the paralegals.

22. Of the five New York City legal aid offices not included in our sample, as of the time of our interviews, one employed no paralegals and the others employed a total of eight paralegals.

23. In securing data of and about New York City paralegals, special emphasis was given to legal aid because of the exceptional diversity of tasks and degree of responsibility so often assumed by legal aid paralegals. On the other hand, due to difficulties in locating them and securing employer cooperation, small-firm paralegals received less attention from us than their probable number in the overall paralegal population might seem to call for.

24. The term *lay advocate* is not used consistently in the legal services field. On the nature of lay advocates as perceived by an important legal training center for lay persons, *see* Powers, Legal Advocacy: An Expanding Field, *New Roles in the Law Conference Report* 147 (1982). On meaning of the term *lay advocate*, *see also* Fry, The Future of Paralegals and Advocacy, *id.*, 230, at 231. On the use of and need for lay advocates in providing legal services to the poor, *see* Sparer, Thorkelson, and Weiss, The Lay Advocate, 43 *University of Detroit Law Journal* 493 (1966).

25. Large law firms, in particular, hire substantial numbers of law students full-time during the summer to do legal work, usually students from top law schools prior to their last year in law school, as part of the firms' lawyer recruitment process. The main purpose of this summer employment is for the hiring firm to determine if there is mutual interest in the students, upon completing law school, becoming lawyers with the firm. If such interest exists, offers are usually extended by the employing firm at the end of the summer to students with only one more year of law school to complete.

26. Today the terms *paralegal* and *legal assistant* generally have synonymous meanings. Other terms occasionally used to denote paralegals include *paralegal assistants*, *subprofessionals*, *legal specialists*, and *paralegal technicians*. On paralegal definitional problems, *see* K. Strong and A. Clark, *Law Office Management* 83–84

(1974); and Haskell, Issues in Paralegalism: Education, Certification, Licensing, Unauthorized Practice, 15 *Georgia Law Review* 631 at 632 (1981). In 1977, the United States Department of Labor defined paralegal assistant as follows:

PARALEGAL ASSISTANT. Law Clerk; Legal Aide. Researches law, investigates facts, and prepares documents to assist lawyer: Researches and analyzes law sources such as statutes, recorded judicial decisions, legal articles, treatises, constitutions, and legal codes to prepare legal documents such as briefs, pleadings, appeals, wills, contracts, deeds, and trust instruments for review, approval and use by attorney. Appraises and inventories real and personal property for estate planning. Investigates facts and law of case to determine causes of action and to prepare case accordingly. Files pleadings with court clerk. Prepares affidavits of documents and maintains document file. Delivers or directs delivery of subpoenas to witnesses and parties to action. May direct and coordinate activities of law office employees. May prepare office accounts and tax returns. May specialize in litigation, probate, real estate, or corporation law. May search patent files to ascertain originality of patent application and be designated patent clerk.

United States Department of Labor, *Dictionary of Occupational Titles* 76 (4th ed. 1977).

A major association of paralegals has defined legal assistants in this way:

Legal assistants are a distinguishable group of persons who assist attorneys in the delivery of legal services. Through formal education, training, and experience, legal assistants have knowledge and expertise regarding the legal system and substantive and procedural law which qualify them to do work of a legal nature under the supervision of an attorney.

National Association of Legal Assistants, Model Standards and Guidelines for Utilization of Legal Assistants, 11 *Facts and Findings*, no. 1, at 6 (1984).

1

THE WORK OF PARALEGALS

PARALEGAL WORK TASKS

Paralegals are hybrids, in part performing traditional lawyer tasks[1] and in part tasks commonly performed by secretarial and clerical support staff. Law offices often see paralegals as partial substitutes for lawyers, although paralegals may in addition perform considerable work also assigned to secretaries and clerical personnel. In their lawyerlike work, however, it is unusual for paralegals to be assigned tasks that call for a high level of professional skill or knowledge as to which lawyers have had special education and training and believe they have special, even unique, understanding and competence. These tasks include legal research and drafting, except at an elementary level; advocacy before courts and administrative agencies; and legal characterization and evaluation of client problems and development of solution strategies.

When paralegals are assigned legal research, it usually consists of such relatively simple procedures as citation source checking, shepardizing, or seeking easily ascertained and understood answers from unambiguous provisions of statutes or regulations.[2] An important exception to this limited legal research pattern is that paralegals who are attending law school frequently are given more difficult and demanding legal research assignments. By the end of their first semester, and certainly by the end of their first year, most law students have developed considerable capacity at legal research in the usually resorted to American legal source materials. Many lawyers feel that other paralegals, whether or not they have been to paralegal school, do not have equivalent legal research capabilities. To the extent that paralegals draft legal instruments, this ordinarily involves fairly simple types of drafting work, such as legal form completion by filling in blank spaces on printed forms or limited adaptation of model office forms to particular transactions. Paralegal oral advocacy before adjudicatory bodies is limited principally to the rather informal administrative agency hearings involving government benefits for poor persons in which the hearing officers frequently are not lawyers and where pleading and evidentiary rules applied generally in litigation are not rigorously imposed. In most offices where they are used, paralegals also are not relied on for diagnosing client legal problems or proposing how they should be solved, these being exclusively lawyer functions. Legal characterization of client concerns, developing strategies for dealing with opposing parties, and counseling clients on what can and should be done commonly are perceived by lawyers as falling within their special ambit of competence.[3] These matters usually are seen as calling for so much knowledge of the law, judgment about client affairs, and sensitivity to client satisfactions that only lawyers should deal with them. Another task of importance that many law offices restrict to their lawyers and will not authorize their paralegals to perform is negotiation with adverse parties on such issues as claim settlements and contract terms. Hard bargaining and negotiating on key issues are seen as often requiring considerable legal knowledge and it is also felt that a lawyer has more authority and credibility in the negotiation process than does a paralegal. Paralegal negotiating with adverse parties and paralegal counseling of clients also may constitute the unauthorized practice of law.

The most frequent task assignments to most paralegals fall under the general rubric of fact acquisition: investigation, assembly, analysis, or reporting on data pertaining to client problems.[4] Although the line of demarcation is not a clear one, facts to lawyers are distinguished from legal rules and concepts as disclosed in such authoritative source materials as statutes, judicial opinions, and administrative regulations. So fact acquisition commonly is differentiated from legal research, even though some facts or fact assumptions normally are prerequisites to seeking answers to legal problems by resort to legal source materials. The variety of factual matters that can become relevant to the work of lawyers in dealing with client problems is almost endless, and the activities of paralegals in fact investigation and submission are also extremely varied. Examples of these activities are client and witness inquiries and interviewing; searching for and perusing documents; examining the situs where events occurred; and organizing and summarizing data by physical assembly, identification marking, indexing, or descriptive summaries. The fact work of paralegals may require extensive telephoning or correspondence; discussions with people of all kinds, both friendly and unfriendly, in most any location; and examining and organizing masses of documents in the examiner's office or some other office. Tables 1 and 2 point up the heavy emphasis on fact acquisition in the work of paralegals in all types of law offices. Large-firm paralegals are particularly involved in obtaining data from masses of documents, reflective of extensive paralegal use by the big firms in heavily documented litigation. Tables 1 and 2 also point up the considerable legal

Table 1.
Most Time-Consuming Work Task

	Large firms	Medium-sized firms	Small firms	Corporate law departments	Government law offices	Legal aid	All offices
Legal drafting	8%	23%	24%	10%	19%	2%	15%
Legal research	8	3	6	12	11	6	7
Acquiring information directly from others	2	10	3	15	19	43	14
Acquiring information from books, records, and files	20	11	6	24	10	2	13
Organizing masses of documents	46	14	9	10	4	0	17
Keeping clients' books and records	1	6	3	2	0	0	2
Keeping employers' books and records	1	4	0	0	0	0	1
Attending court or taking of depositions	1	0	0	0	1	4	1
Supervision of paralegals and other office staff	3	2	0	7	1	2	2
Running errands	0	5	6	0	0	2	2
Typing	0	2	9	0	0	0	1
Other[a]	4	7	6	10	2	6	6
Multiple response[b]	7	13	27	10	30	30	18
No response	0	0	0	0	4	2	1
	(N=92)	(N=115)	(N=33)	(N=41)	(N=81)	(N=47)	(N=409)

[a]The other responses include one choice from the questionnaire, office or personnel management.
[b]The question requested a single choice for most time-consuming tasks, but 72 respondents indicated two or more choices. The most common choices were acquiring information from others, 44; acquiring information from books, 39; legal drafting, 29; organizing documents, 23; and legal research, 17. The remaining choices were each selected by 7 to 12 respondents.

Table 2.
Second and Third Most Time-Consuming Work Tasks[a]

	Large firms	Medium-sized firms	Small firms	Corporate law departments	Government law offices	Legal aid	All offices
Legal drafting	8%	21%	15%	17%	17%	21%	16%
Legal research	20	11	12	10	10	6	12
Acquiring information directly from others	16	23	15	24	25	19	21
Acquiring information from books, records, and files	40	25	18	27	20	21	27
Organizing masses of documents	27	14	9	32	11	4	17
Keeping clients' books and records	8	15	0	5	0	9	7
Keeping employers' books and records	3	5	15	5	5	0	5
Attending court or taking of depositions	12	8	6	2	10	11	9
Supervision of paralegals and other office staff	11	6	6	5	2	2	6
Running errands	4	10	15	10	14	9	10
Typing	0	1	6	2	0	0	1
Other[b]	10	17	6	22	4	13	12
Multiple responses[c]	4	10	12	7	2	17	8
No response[d]	11	17	24	5	40	30	21
	(N=92)	(N=115)	(N=33)	(N=41)	(N=81)	(N=47)	(N=409)

[a]Responses sum to more than 100% because the table includes responses for both the second and third most time-consuming work tasks.

[b]The other responses include one choice from the questionnaire, office or personnel management.

[c]The question requested one choice for each of the second and third time-consuming tasks but 32 respondents indicated two or more choices. The most common choices were acquiring information from others, 10; legal research, 9; and attending court, 8.

[d]Includes respondents who did not indicate second and third major tasks, and those who indicated three or more tasks as most important. Some respondents included in the body of the table did not indicate third most time-consuming task.

drafting and research activity of paralegals, however rudimentary most of this work may be.

Table 3 shows a desire by paralegals to take on work that in many offices is reserved to lawyers, work that the paralegals feel competent to perform. This includes particularly legal research and tasks requiring paralegals' presence at hearings and the taking of depositions.[5] Quite clearly, many paralegals wish to do more professionally important work than is assigned them, presumably because they consider it more interesting and prestigious, and based on their office or paralegal school experience believe they are capable of doing it. Table 3 further shows a paralegal interest in moving into support staff supervisory and management roles, another form of work upgrading. Processing masses of documents, a common but particularly boring and simplistic form of paralegal work, has a low priority among those who currently are not assigned this kind of work. Keeping clients' and employer's books also has a low priority. Surprisingly, there is some interest in running errands, probably reflective of a desire to put more variety into the workday by getting out of the office.

Most law office fact acquisition is focused on obtaining and processing data directly relevant to the legal problem at hand. But facts frequently are also required to give lawyers an understanding of the setting in which the problem arises. A problem may not be understandable without a great deal of knowledge about particular business practices, scientific principles, or other contextual phenomena that no one in the law office has. To provide the requisite background, a quick data buildup may be necessary, information coming from such sources as textbooks, scientific or trade journals, government reports, and discussions with experts. Medical malpractice, patent infringements, and antitrust violations are examples of matters in which such background buildups are particularly common, although they may be necessary in any major deal or big litigated case. A fairly frequent paralegal assignment is this search for, and assembly of, background information.

A variety of clerical tasks are, of course, needed for the operation of modern offices, law offices included. These tasks range from simple chores requiring the most modest abilities, other than a high boredom tolerance level, to tasks demanding a substantial degree of literacy and manual dexterity. Illustrative clerical tasks are filing, photocopying, proofreading, billing, typing, simple bookkeeping, and operating word processing equipment. All law office personnel, even lawyers, at least occasionally perform some clerical tasks; but, as has been indicated, many paralegals are given substantial clerical work to do, usually incidental to their other duties.

Whether performing lawyer craft skill type work, such as legal research and legal drafting, or doing fact acquisition or clerical tasks, most paralegal work is very routine. There normally is a continuing flow of similar matters that the paralegal is expected to deal with in much the same way, with

Table 3.
Duties Not Currently Performed which Respondents Feel Competent to Perform and Would Like to Perform[a]

	Large firms	Medium-sized firms	Small firms	Corporate law departments	Government law offices	Legal aid	All offices
Legal drafting	21%	15%	9%	22%	11%	2%	14%
Legal research	35	29	21	24	21	23	27
Acquiring factual information directly from others	36	17	12	12	6	0	16
Acquiring factual information from books, records, files	12	9	3	17	11	2	9
Keeping clients' books	2	8	3	2	11	0	5
Keeping employer's books	4	2	0	2	10	2	4
Organizing, indexing, or filing masses of documents	0	3	3	10	11	4	5
Attending hearings or taking of depositions	34	26	24	37	28	15	28
Supervision of paralegals or others	32	17	3	15	16	30	20
Running errands outside office	5	1	0	10	7	2	4
Office or personnel management	14	11	3	17	14	13	12
Other[b]	12	8	12	5	19	11	11
No response or none	20	45	52	22	46	45	38
	(N=92)	(N=115)	(N=33)	(N=41)	(N=81)	(N=47)	(N=409)

[a]Percentages sum to more than 100% due to multiple responses.
[b]Other duties listed most frequently are negotiation, 14; client counseling, 11; proofreading, 7; maintaining library, 5; and typing, 4.

little exercise of discretion or choice on the part of the paralegal. An office system often has been evolved for paralegal disposition of repeat tasks and adherence to the system is expected. Repetition and fixed work procedures characterize operation of the system. If difficulties arise—for example, something unusual comes up that does not seem to fit within the system— directions from the supervisor or other superior may be required. To be sure, paralegal tasks rarely are as repetitive and routinized as tasks on a factory assembly line, but there is a resemblance to such factory work, although with less division of labor, as the paralegal normally performs a greater variety of procedures than does the assembly line worker. In many law offices, the flow of repeat work is not heavy enough or steady enough to keep a paralegal indefinitely busy with one set of tasks or one system, with the result that it is common for a paralegal to be familiar with a series of tasks and to work within more than one system.

Although most paralegal work can be characterized as repeat and routine, not all of it is of this nature. Many paralegals are given assignments that are novel or require innovative and creative approaches on their part. These assignments often are special projects and are likely to be given to a paralegal who has become a close personal assistant to a particular lawyer, has special training or competence in a field of relevance to the office, or has exhibited unusual ingenuity and intelligence on the job. Another type of less routine work assignment sometimes given to paralegals, particularly in large law offices, is the supervision or coordination of the work of other paralegals. There also are smaller offices in which paralegals double as law office administrators. Most law office supervision and management jobs, however, go to lawyers or to law office administrative specialists with no paralegal experience.[6] Law office management is often a part-time lawyer activity and is frequently carried on through committees of partners or other senior staff lawyers.

An occupational group whose work in some offices resembles or overlaps that of paralegals is legal secretaries. A legal secretary, as we use the term and as commonly used in the legal profession, denotes a law office employee assigned personally to a lawyer or upper-level administrator, who performs clerical duties for the person to whom assigned—including typing, filing, and reception, but who often is given additional duties of considerable responsibility. These added duties may include, for instance, simple legal drafting chores, in addition to document typing; some fact investigation, especially over the telephone; and assembly and preparation of factual reports. Legal secretaries are considered either top clericals or, as is true of most paralegals, as paraprofessionals, with higher status than clerks but lesser status than lawyers. In a few offices, we found secretaries who were called secretary-paralegals, although no questionnaire returns were received from such persons. We also found instances of secretaries who had gone to paralegal school with the expectation of broadening their roles and increasing their value as secretaries.

In contrast to offices in which paralegal and secretary roles are merged, far more frequently paralegals and their employers clearly separate paralegal and secretarial positions. Many offices we visited, in their job descriptions and job titles, draw sharp distinctions between paralegals and secretaries and discourage or even prohibit transfer of their secretaries to paralegal positions. The question of typing we found a significant symbol of this status differentiation, and with surprising frequency paralegals are told that they are not expected to type or even that they should not type. Some paralegals, in our interviews, stressed that they do no typing, as if to underscore their superiority to secretaries. Others told us that they occasionally type some of their own work efforts in order to meet emergency deadlines, but do so rather surreptitiously so as not to be seen as cheating on the status ban. Questionnaire responses on typing by paralegals are summarized in table 4. A rather small minority of paralegals type their own work—17 percent overall, but paralegal typing of others' work is unusual—only 2 percent overall. This is indicative of how clearly paralegals are being distinguished from secretaries within law offices.[7] The comparatively few paralegals who do any considerable amount of typing, even for themselves, is some evidence that many employers regard their paralegals as similar to professional staff. The incidence of paralegal typing in small-sized firms suggests that in a number of these offices paralegal positions may be in transition from traditional secretarial positions.

It is rare for a law office staff to include personnel other than lawyers, administrators, paralegals, secretaries, librarians, receptionists, and clerks. In unusual circumstances or in very large or highly specialized offices, representatives of other occupational groups can be found as full-time employees, not classified as paralegals or as one of the other more usual law office occupations. Examples of these atypical law office employees are accountants, economists, and social workers.

It is common for lawyers and their support staffs to classify their work by substantive or procedural fields of practice, and larger law offices are often internally organized along specialty field lines, with a separate department or other unit for each major field of office specialization. There are many of these specialty fields but among the most common are litigation, corporate and securities, taxation, estates and trusts, real estate, matrimonial, and criminal. Corporate departments in larger private firms are often the catchall for matters that do not clearly belong in other departments. In large prosecutors' offices, the organizational breakdown may be in terms of different kinds of criminal matters or trials and appeals. Some fields normally involve extensive litigation, criminal and antitrust for example; and persons working in these specialties frequently are litigation specialists whether they refer to themselves as such or not. Table 5 shows

Table 4.
Typing by Paralegals

Considerable typing reported	Large firms	Medium-sized firms	Small firms	Corporate law de-partments	Govern-ment law offices	Legal aid	All offices
Of own work	8%	21%	33%	17%	12%	23%	17%
Of others' work	1	3	15	0	0	0	2
Of own and others' work	0	1	9	0	0	0	1
No considerable typing reported	91	75	42	83	88	77	79
	(N=92)	(N=115)	(N=33)	(N=41)	(N=81)	(N=47)	(N=409)

the most common fields of paralegal practice as reported on our questionnaire returns. It indicates the extensive involvement that paralegals as a
group have with the litigation process, including the heavily litigated fields
of criminal law and antitrust. It also indicates heavy paralegal concentration
in private law firm corporate and securities work, large firm and corporate
law department antitrust work, and legal aid and govenment law office
criminal work—the latter restricted principally to the public defender's and
prosecutor's offices. Paralegals, according to table 5, do the most real estate
and estates and trusts work in middle- and small-sized law firms.

There are various principal alternatives used for allocating work to paralegals: specific assignments by a particular lawyer, specific assignments by
any lawyer in need of help, specific assignments by a nonlawyer paralegal—
usually a paralegal supervisor—and automatic routing. Table 6 sets forth
how our questionnaire respondents reported work was assigned to them.
Automatic routing means that it is office practice for all matters of a
particular kind to be referred to a designated paralegal; and it may signify,
as well, that considerable autonomy has been delegated to the paralegal
as to how these matters will be handled. Assignment by any lawyer in need
of help implies a pool or floater arrangement and a less personal lawyer-
paralegal relationship, with the lawyer less likely to assume the role of
mentor to the paralegal than if assignments come from a particular lawyer.
Automatic routing assignments are most frequent in legal aid, some indication of considerable paralegal autonomy in legal aid offices, also verified in some of our interviews. Paralegal assignments by a particular lawyer
are most common in large firms, evidence that each paralegal in these
offices often works primarily or exclusively for one lawyer. The relative
frequency of large-firm paralegal assignments by a nonlawyer paralegal
supports our interview findings that it is in the large firms that paralegals
are most often supervised by other paralegals. The high incidence of paralegal assignments by any lawyer in need of help, very common in medium-
and small-sized firms and corporate law departments, points up the importance in many settings of paralegals being able to adjust to the demands
and work styles of different lawyers, lawyers who may even be working in
different legal specialty areas.

As an adjunct occupation to lawyers, paralegals are normally supervised
by lawyers, frequently associates or other junior lawyers, although in larger
offices their supervisors sometimes are other paralegals or lay administrators.[8] Table 7 shows how varied are the methods of paralegal supervision.
Certain other features disclosed by the table also stand out, most particularly that each type of office uses a mix of methods, the frequency with
which supervision occurs only after work is completed, and the fairly common practice of combining supervision with educating or informing the
supervisor on the content of the paralegal's work. In this latter instance,
the supervisor is usually a lawyer who will be incorporating the paralegal's

Table 5.
Major Areas of Legal Work[a]
(Each respondent was asked to indicate not more than two such areas)

	Large firms	Medium-sized firms	Small firms	Corporate law departments	Government law offices	Legal aid	All offices
Litigation	72%	35%	48%	56%	35%	4%	43%
Corporate and/or securities law	25	23	18	12	5	0	16
Real estate	2	19	15	7	5	6	10
Estates and trusts	2	19	9	0	0	2	7
Matrimonial	1	7	9	0	1	9	4
Criminal	0	0	9	0	36	47	13
Pensions, employee benefits	0	2	6	0	2	11	3
Antitrust	32	1	3	41	0	0	12
Taxation	2	8	3	0	1	0	3
Torts and negligence[b]	0	1	3	0	10	4	3
Patents, trademarks, copyrights[b]	0	4	18	5	0	0	3
Other[c]	2	15	9	15	14	34	13
Three or more responses[d]	1	3	12	2	1	0	3
No response	0	2	0	2	10	2	3
	(N=92)	(N=115)	(N=33)	(N=41)	(N=81)	(N=47)	(N=409)

[a]Percentages sum to more than 100% because up to two responses were requested.

[b]Frequently cited "other" responses, these categories were not on the questionnaire.

[c]Other common responses were welfare and social security rights, 11 (10 in legal aid offices); bankruptcy, 8; and banking law, 6.

[d]The question requested no more than two choices but 11 respondents indicated a total of 37 choices. The most frequent choices were litigation, 7; estates and trusts, 6; corporate and/or securities law, 5; and matrimonial, 4.

Table 6.
How Work is Assigned

	Large firms	Medium-sized firms	Small firms	Corporate law de-partments	Govern-ment law offices	Legal aid	All offices
By a particular lawyer	45%	17%	21%	22%	32%	6%	26%
By any lawyer in need of help	17	40	52	34	14	23	28
By a nonlawyer paralegal	16	3	0	10	14	2	8
By automatic routing	3	13	6	12	19	36	14
By social worker	0	0	0	0	0	2	0
Multiple responses[a]	15	24	15	17	11	28	19
No response	3	3	6	5	11	2	5
	(N=92)	(N=115)	(N=33)	(N=41)	(N=81)	(N=47)	(N=409)

[a]The question requested one choice but 76 respondents indicated two or three choices. The most frequent of these multiple responses was by any lawyer, 52; followed by automatic routing, 50; a particular lawyer, 46; and a nonlawyer paralegal, 24.

Table 7.
Ways in Which Work is Usually Supervised[a]

	Large firms	Medium-sized firms	Small firms	Corporate law de-partments	Govern-ment law offices	Legal aid	All offices
Regularly, on a fixed schedule	1%	4%	0%	15%	10%	23%	8%
In irregular conferences	40	39	52	24	26	38	36
For accuracy, only when completed	36	51	42	34	37	17	39
For thoroughness, only when completed	32	43	36	37	33	26	35
For accuracy, during course of work	12	12	6	20	14	21	14
For thoroughness, during course of work	11	9	15	17	20	15	13
To ascertain if work is completed	17	24	21	12	16	17	19
When something goes wrong	13	14	18	17	19	26	17
To educate supervisor on content of work	24	17	27	37	23	45	26
Other[b]	16	12	6	7	4	6	10
No response	1	2	3	0	11	9	4
	(N=92)	(N=115)	(N=33)	(N=41)	(N=81)	(N=47)	(N=409)

[a]Percentages sum to more than 100% due to multiple responses.
[b]The most common other response was that work is completely or usually unsupervised, 32.

work effort into his own work product and uses the supervisory session as a means of ascertaining what the paralegal has come up with as well as of suggesting how the paralegal's performance can be improved. Supervision after work completion to educate the supervisor is common as well in senior lawyers supervising of junior lawyers and in many other professional relationships.

ROUTINE WORK OF PARALEGALS

Routine work so dominates the occupational life of most paralegals that the nature of this work and the utilization of paralegals in performing it merit separate consideration and emphasis. As law offices become larger and more specialized, the volume of routine work is expanding and paralegals increasingly are being relied on for the performance of routine tasks. The highly repetitive character of routine work makes it well-suited to paralegals. Persons with limited background or training in law often can learn to perform effectively quite demanding tasks if the work is sufficiently repetitive and the required procedures sufficiently clear. Division of labor differentiating work assignments of lawyers and paralegals and of different paralegals can make it still easier effectively to use persons of limited background for routine tasks.

Lawyers are being urged by specialists in law office management, both from within and without the profession, to develop better systems for more efficiently performing routine work.[9] By systems is meant what in other disciplines may be known as programs or formalization,[10] comprehensive procedures or rules of operation for conducting routine work.[11] Those advocating improved law office systems usually recommend that the systems be in writing; be carefully developed for important categories of work; and include, as needed, instruction manuals, checklists, and forms. Many systems for law office use have been created and are being increasingly relied on. Some of these systems make use of modern computer technology to enhance their efficiency,[12] and further reliance on such technology can be expected as equipment is improved, its cost reduced, and lawyers become more accepting of mechanical automation techniques.

Most lawyers and law offices have developed unwritten practices for performing repeat work, practices that have grown up with experience, have evolved from ad hoc responses to particular cases, may be largely in the mind of one key person in the office, and are perpetuated and passed on to subordinates and successors by oral instruction. Rather than such informal approaches to repeat-type work, advocates of systems believe that better results can be obtained by carefully planned comprehensive programs worked out in advance and put in writing. Systems can be tailored to the needs and preferences of a particular office, as is often desirable;

but some systems may even prove useful, with little or no adaptation, to most any office that is heavily involved in the kind of work to which the system pertains. Formal written systems can be expensive to prepare, but when justified by sufficient volume of repeat work, can reduce training and supervision time, enhance output quality, and expand the scope of matters that can be entrusted to paralegals.

Essential for competent systems work by paralegals is that the paralegals understand what is expected of them, follow directions meticulously, know when to seek advice from superiors on questionable matters, and to the extent that they are delegated discretion to make decisions on their own, make choices consistent with client objectives. A carefully developed system for work performance can be useful not only for paralegals but for any other law office staff members having important work assignments within the system. Even offices that employ no paralegals and in which routine work is mostly performed by lawyers may find that formal written systems increase work efficiency and quality.

Given the variety of high-frequency matters that law offices deal with, there are innumerable different high-volume routine work situations in which paralegals are assigned important responsibilities. Among the more common of these, in which each of many offices has a high-volume flow of the particular kind of matter, are document processing in heavily documented complex litigation; government benefits; sale or loan closings, such as closings on home purchases; estates, including post-mortem decedent's estate administration and pre-death estate planning; preparing and maintaining required corporate documentation, sometimes referred to as corporate housekeeping; and divorce. We found instances in which all of the work on some of the above kinds of matters was performed by a paralegal, with typing a possible exception. More frequently, the work is shared between a lawyer and one or more paralegals, the lawyer in some cases only reviewing the paralegals' work or being available for instructions when an unusual problem arises.

To provide a better insight into just what paralegals do in routine work situations, to show the variety of such situations, and to give a feel for law office routine work settings, examples of high-volume routine matters that paralegals frequently work on are discussed in some detail below. The data is drawn from interviews conducted as part of this study. Examples selected all involve fairly common types of volume matters handled by law offices that rely heavily on paralegals. To be sure, not all law offices that take these kinds of matters use paralegals in working on them, but many do, and the heavier the volume in any particular office, the greater the likelihood of extensive paralegal use. Many similar examples of high-volume routine matters exist in New York City and elsewhere, such as personal injury actions,[13] tenant evictions, small debt collections, bankruptcies, im-

migration and naturalization proceedings, and routine patent documentation.[14] However, the types of matters described below adequately illustrate
the nature and variety of high-volume routine paralegal work.

Document processing in heavily documented complex litigation. These
kinds of cases, typified by antitrust proceedings brought against big corporations by government or private business interests, also include occasional major cases in such fields as employment discrimination, patents,
international unfair pricing, and income taxation. The cost of bringing these
cases, and particularly defending them, can be tremendous, document
processing being a major cost item. Defense of the government antitrust
case against the International Business Machines Company, dismissed in
1982, reputedly cost the company over $100 million, mostly for outside
law firm fees and company employee time spent on the case. The recent
antitrust proceeding that led to breakup of the American Telephone and
Telegraph Company was another extraordinarily costly case. The scope
and cost of document work in most heavily documented litigation has been
considerably enhanced by liberal legal authorization and lawyer use of
pretrial discovery procedures. Current use of these procedures has come
in for no little criticism because of their added cost to clients and the delays
they cause.[15]

Repeat work in heavily documented litigation consists of searching through
great numbers of documents; screening out those that are relevant and
noting significant portions; organizing document files; and, where there is
sufficient volume, abstracting relevant documents and entering the abstracted data on a computer.[16] Computer use is likely if there are over
10,000 relevant documents. Relevant documents frequently are photocopied and pertinent notations made on the photocopies. Document processing is often carried out in response to legal demands by subpoena made
of one litigating party by the other. In such instances, paralegals doing
document work usually must be carefully instructed on those provisions of
the subpoena for which they have search or analysis responsibility.

A number of offices at which we interviewed regularly do considerable
document work in large-scale litigation, but one of these offices in particular
fairly typifies the work in this field. This office has a separate unit engaged
in document processing in response to antitrust case subpoenas. The unit
was formed two years prior to our interviews when a large antitrust case
came into the office, a case, incidentally, requiring far less preparatory
work than the massive IBM antitrust litigation. At the peak period for
document work in this case, the office had forty paralegals doing document
screening, plus a smaller paralegal staff doing analysis for entry of abstracted information into a computer. In relation to this one case, paralegals
in the office went over approximately ten million pages of documentation
during the screening process. Month after month many of the paralegals

went through boxes of documents, reading page by page looking for points of relevance in response to a subpoena. The subpoena was divided into several parts, and each screener searched for information relative to but one part of the subpoena. The tedium of these jobs was eased somewhat for a few of the paralegals when they were sent for a week or so at a time to screen active files at client field offices in various regions of the country.

Even more tedious than screening documents is document numbering and stamping as confidential, a process preceding screening that screeners are also assigned. One bright and ambitious paralegal who had just finished a long stint at numbering and stamping told us that the work was degrading but he recognized that it had to be done and rationalized his being assigned to it by saying that some of the other paralegals could not be trusted to do it properly, even stamping in the wrong place and obliterating important document wording.

Once documents are screened, they are photocopied and the photocopies sent to paralegal analysts for abstracting. The abstracting process consists of underlining relevant language or entering code words on each photocopy. Abstracted pages are then sent to a computer group that enters the abstracted information on computers. Computer personnel are not considered paralegals by the office.

Because the relative volume of screening and analysis work is not constant, some paralegals are moved from one function to the other as need arises. There is reluctance on the part of paralegals to move from screening to analysis because the latter is considered lower status, most of the analysts being up from the ranks and many not college graduates, whereas most of the screeners are college graduates, many with added paralegal school training.

The office in question, at the time of our visit, had a total of seventy-five employees engaged in document processing in heavily documented litigation, including paralegals, lawyers, supervisors, and clerks. There were three lay supervisors, one each for document screening, analysis, and computer entries, but only two lawyers for the entire document processing operation. One lawyer was top supervisor and paralegal consultant for the screeners and the other had overall responsibility for legal aspects of document processing, working closely with lawyers who would try the case and those engaged in other aspects of trial preparation. The supervisors made assignments and reviewed work, the review consisting principally of spot checks. Given the great volume of documents being dealt with, spot-checking was considered adequate even though, as a result, much paralegal work went through the process unreviewed. The lawyer assigned to screener supervision also conducted periodic three-day training sessions for new screeners and prepared a manual for each litigated case the screeners worked on. Each manual sets forth screening procedures and some background on the nature of the litigation. During the course of screening, memoranda were distributed revising procedures. In some cases, revisions were so frequent as to create paralegal antagonism.

Divorce. Throughout the United States divorce matters are among the most common types of legal work brought to lawyers, with nationally well over one million divorces being granted each year. There are many law offices specializing in matrimonial work, mostly or solely divorce, and some offices consistently handle a high volume of divorce cases, relying heavily on paralegals for disposition of these matters. The vast majority of divorce cases is uncontested. This means that by the time the matter comes before a court for determination, the defendant is not opposing the plaintiff, whatever differences the parties may earlier have had over the divorce or its terms. In some cases, the defendant spouse has disappeared, the plaintiff does not know defendant's whereabouts, and the divorce is not only uncontested but the defendant may not even know it is being sought.

Although the consequences of divorce can be great for one or both parties and the process of legal termination can generate intense emotional feelings, most divorce matters are comparatively simple from a legal and evidentiary point of view. Assembling and presenting essential facts is the principal law office function in most divorce cases, troublesome issues of law not often arising. Experienced paralegals in volume divorce operations are usually capable of obtaining needed factual information and can, as well, prepare the necessary documents for the ordinary uncontested case and even for many cases that are contested. Some document filing with the court is required in each divorce case, documents such as pleadings, motions, affidavits, and orders. However, an experienced divorce paralegal can also prepare many or all of these documents, relying on standardized office forms as guides. Hearings in divorce cases are before courts and paralegals do not have rights of audience before courts, but in New York uncontested divorces are normally obtained by document submission only, without court hearing.

Very large volumes of divorce cases are handled by many law offices that concentrate on representing the poor or near-poor, most especially legal aid societies but also some of the larger prepaid legal service offices that represent lower-income employees under plans paid for by large institutional employers. In their disposition of divorce matters, it is commonplace for such offices to make extensive use of paralegals. We interviewed divorce personnel at five offices that represent principally or entirely the poor or near-poor. Characteristically, each office of this kind has a separate divorce or matrimonial unit to which divorce matters are assigned. The units that we encountered are small, with one to four lawyers each, plus paralegals and one or two typists or word processors. Several units have more paralegals than lawyers, one having five paralegals and one lawyer. One office supplements its regular divorce unit staff with four to six law student interns, part-time during the school year, full-time during the summer. The students are principally assigned to interviewing and legal research. Some units will take only uncontested divorces, referring contested cases to other units within the office or to outside counsel. All of these units we encountered are geared to mass dispositions, one unit having obtained the amazing total of 1,000 uncontested divorces for clients in a single year with only one lawyer and two paralegals, no supplemental help except for typing and word processing.

Intake interviewing in some offices is by attorneys only, but in others paralegals do much of the initial client interviewing. Paralegals in these units also draft many of the pleadings and other essential documents, following standard office forms. At least after the initial interview, paralegals do much of the client contact work as well, including responses to clients as to how personal or family problems accentuated by the divorce proceedings should be dealt with or in just listening to very troubled clients unburden themselves of their problems. One office has social workers available to whom divorce clients are referred when emotional or family crises seem particularly serious. Paralegals occasionally accompany clients to court in contested divorce cases to help explain the proceedings and to provide moral support in what to the clients are strange and threatening surroundings. Difficult child custody and child support issues also can arise in divorce practices. One of the divorce units whose personnel we interviewed makes a specialty of battered women cases whether or not divorce is being sought or even contemplated by those who have been maltreated. Another unit handles adoptions in addition to divorces. In many offices, divorce matters are assigned to paralegals as their cases, and active paralegal caseloads of forty to sixty such cases at any one time apparently are common.

Lawyers in these matrimonial units work on contested divorces, if their unit takes them; supervise and review paralegal work; and may take over unusually or exceptionally difficult cases, whether or not contested. Paralegals also rely on lawyers in their units as resource persons on legal and administrative problems; but several paralegals told us that they maintain close ties with some of the court clerks so as to keep up on legal and procedural changes pertaining to divorce. Also, as one divorce paralegal informed us: "It is good to show one's face at the court occasionally, as personal acquaintanceships can result in better service." Most attorneys in divorce specialty units are responsible for supervision and training of new paralegals but are so busy with their own cases that they are likely to do little review of work done by more experienced paralegals. They also are too busy to prepare instruction manuals, relying instead on ad hoc oral guidance when this appears necessary.

There are many law offices serving middle- and upper-income clients that also do substantial divorce work in which they make use of paralegals.

However, lawyers in these offices usually do more and paralegals less than is typical of lawyers and paralegals in the volume offices serving divorce clients among the poor and near-poor. This is so partly because in divorce proceedings involving more affluent clients considerable money and property frequently are at stake. Such financial concerns can make cases legally more complex and can lead to delicate negotiations with the other side that the lawyers believe require more skill, knowledge, and status than paralegals possess.

Government benefits. There are a number of government benefit programs that result in large volumes of claims, many leading to hearings before government administrative agency hearing officers. Among these programs are public welfare assistance, medicaid, medicare, food stamps, social security, supplemental security income (S.S.I.), veterans' benefits, and unemployment insurance. As the programs are directed mostly at aiding the poor, most work for claimants in the benefits field is handled by law offices that specialize in serving the poor, legal aid in particular. These offices conventionally turn over much of this benefits work to their paralegals. On the government side, benefits are administered by massive bureaucracies that inevitably make some errors and by personnel, not always of the best, that can be arbitrary in imposing regulations. As one claimant's attorney told us: "Our job is to force the agencies to do what they are supposed to do." The administrative problems of the agencies are made more difficult by the fact that those entitled to benefits or who think they are entitled to benefits are often unable to understand agency requirements or practices. In New York City, many of these people do not speak or read English fluently, an added obstacle to dealing with them effectively.

Offices that do a large volume of government benefits work for claimants usually assign these matters to a separate benefits unit composed of lawyers and paralegals. The larger units we visited each had two lawyers and four to six paralegals. A unit of this size can dispose of about 100 cases per month. Most cases involve welfare, social security, or supplemental security income claims. The work allocation between lawyers and paralegals is comparable to that in the divorce units of these same offices: lawyers act as supervisors of the paralegals, act as consultants to them when novel issues arise, and review their work for accuracy. Lawyers also handle the more difficult cases that come into the unit. Lawyer guidance of paralegals is oral, the lawyers, even those with supervisory responsibility, being too busy on other matters to prepare instructional materials.[17] Paralegals generally have their own caseloads, which may run as high as sixty at any one time, forty is common, but fifteen to twenty is considered optimal. It is obvious that the units are seriously understaffed. When experienced, benefits paralegals require little in the way of guidance and in some offices their work products receive little review. In handling their caseloads, benefits paralegals do much or all of the intake, maintain client contacts, assemble necessary factual information, and prepare documentation. They also try cases—represent parties in administrative hearings before hearing officers. It is in this trial or hearing function that the work of benefits paralegals differs in a major way from that of divorce paralegals or most other paralegals in law offices. Claimants in a high percentage of all government benefits cases are represented by paralegals at the hearing stage and half of the cases in the caseloads of many benefits paralegals go to hearing.[18] Hearing officers in these matters are often nonlawyers, as usually are the persons representing the government at the hearings. In some hearings, only claimants are represented; no one appears representing the other side. Appeals from rulings of the hearing officers are handled by lawyers, the appeals normally going to the courts. Appeals are infrequent.

The general consensus from their lawyer supervisors as conveyed to us was that claimants' paralegals perform well in government benefits hearings. The hearings tend to be informal and problems that arise are mostly factual, not legal. One lawyer expressed the view that she herself found these cases frustrating and exasperating to try because the lay hearing officers tend to take a nonlegal approach and tolerate lengthy testimony and argument on matters that lawyers consider irrelevant and become impatient with. Paralegals, on the other hand, seem to adjust well to the mood and tempo of the hearings and by and large get along satisfactorily with the hearing officers. Perhaps to be expected, relations between claimants' paralegals and their government agency counterparts are often hostile. Claimants' paralegals are particularly negative about their lay opponents in the agencies, and made charges to us that many of the agency people are uninformed, poorly prepared, and arbitrary. Less objectively, there were statements that these people "will not give you the time of day" and "they are SOBs." Some believe that the success of claimants' paralegals in agency hearings is partially attributable to the poor caliber of so many of the lay persons opposing them.

Sale or loan closings. Law offices commonly are called upon to perform a series of closing tasks in relation to the sale or mortgaging of real estate. This phase of conveyancing or financing has always been a staple feature of American law practice. These tasks are loosely referred to as closing work and are largely preparatory to passage of title or creation of a loan security interest at final settlement, known as the closing. At the closing, it is usual for the parties and their lawyers to meet together, any remaining differences are then sought to be reconciled, essential documents are presented for examination and delivered, and at many closings sale or loan moneys are paid. In some instances, closings are carried out by correspondence; no meeting together of the parties and their representatives takes place. Closings also occur for some long-term leases of real property and for some sales, mortgages, or long-term leases of very valuable items of personal property, such as major pieces of transportation equipment. Most closings are of a highly routine nature with similar procedures being followed in each type of transaction. However, some closing work is complicated by intricate financing or title arrangements or by outstanding claims of third persons not parties to the transaction being closed.

It is commonplace for law offices that do a big volume of closings to utilize paralegals extensively for this work. For the more simple kinds of transactions, such as representing buyers or sellers of single-family houses or individual condominium units, we found instances of law offices turning over all closing tasks to their experienced paralegals, including attendance at the final settlement meeting with the other side. In these more simple types of real estate sales transactions, paralegals may perform such tasks as preparing basic documents, following office forms; arranging for title insurance and verifying that the insurer will provide sufficiently broad coverage; arranging for payment of any overdue obligations that may constitute liens on the property; determining allocations between buyer and seller of expenses on the property, for example, property taxes, utilities, and fire insurance; ascertaining what furnishings or other items of personal property the buyer of the premises will be purchasing from the seller and at what prices; and preparing an agenda for the settlement meeting. In more general terms, the closing work of paralegals consists mostly of acquiring and processing factual information relevant to the transactions involved. Tasks, of course, may vary in detail depending upon whether the office is representing the transferor or transferee. Closing work can necessitate familiarity not only with required office procedures and forms but frequently, as well, familiarity with relevant personnel and practices of such outside organizations as banks, savings and loan associations, title insurance companies, and real estate brokers.

One paralegal, who had taken over the closing work of a senior associate who had recently left the law firm where she worked, volunteered during our interview that her duties are now so broad and she has so much discretion that in reality she is practicing law. Another real estate paralegal said that the firm has given her so much responsibility on closing matters and she handles so many closings that it is almost as though she were self-employed in a business of her own.

A frequent paralegal task in law offices representing parties in the sale of large rented office or apartment buildings is lease review. This may occur prior to final settlement between buyer and seller. It is important for buyers to know who the tenants are and what their leases provide, as leases normally continue in effect and are binding on buyers after the buildings are sold. Some large buildings have hundreds of tenants, there are differences in lease terms, and some of the leases or lease provisions may not be in writing. In the lease review process, an effort is made to assemble accurate versions of all outstanding leases on the building being sold, relying on copies of written leases and rent rolls, supplemented by such discussions with the landlord and tenants as seem necessary. Digests of all current leases of space in the building may also be prepared; and where there are doubts as to what leases provide, the apparent lease terms may be set forth in writing and the seller or tenants asked to sign a statement that these are accurate versions of the prevailing leases. This protects the buyer and clarifies what his obligations will be.

Another kind of closing task that paralegals in law offices representing large institutional mortgage lenders can be extensively involved with is mortgage review. Large institutional lenders in acquiring mortgages need to be certain that each mortgage is a valid security interest and meets all legal criteria for investment by these lenders. To provide this assurance, the documentation for mortgages being obtained by banks, insurance companies, and savings and loan associations is commonly sent to law offices for review. These offices may be in-house law departments or outside law firms. Some of the loans, such as those on large commercial or industrial properties, are for many millions of dollars; others, for example those on single family dwellings, are much smaller. Single-family dwelling mortgages may come to a law office in large volume from a lender originating many such mortgages or acquiring them in the secondary market. Paralegals are most likely to be used in the review of smaller mortgage loans and there have been times in the past when a few offices each employed as many as twenty to thirty paralegals to do this type of work.[19] The reviewers check over a package of documents for each loan to verify a variety of matters, including that all necessary documents are present and correctly phrased, that the property involved is correctly described, that the evidence of title is adequate, and that the mortgage secures a first lien on the property. Lawyers are available to supervise and to take over review of the bigger and more complex deals. With high interest rates restricting the volume of new mortgages and with some of the large institutional lenders reducing their mortgage holdings, there has been a decline recently in law office mortgage review work.

Estates. The administration of decedents' estates has long been another basic staple of American law practice, having assumed increased importance with the advent of high estate and inheritance taxes.[20] These taxes, along with intricate income and gift tax laws, have also increased the complexity of law office pre-death estate planning, a service that usually is accompanied by execution of wills or trusts. Administration of decedents' estates, the law office function in the general estates field for which paralegals are mostly used, is the process by which assets of decedents are identified, debts of decedents are approved and paid, applicable taxes computed and paid, and the balance distributed to heirs and devisees as determined by will or by laws of intestate succession. Estates of decedents are administered under close court supervision and each major step from will probate or heirship determination to final asset distribution requires judicial approval. The courts also resolve many of the disagreements that arise in the course of administration. In decedents' estates work, law firms usually represent the legal representative of the estate, an executor or administrator, but may represent creditors, heirs, or devisees. Small estates, those with assets of under $100,000, are usually fairly simple to administer. Very big estates can be extremely complicated and can raise difficult tax questions. Aspects of decedents' estate administration that can be time-consuming and troublesome to law offices in representing an executor or administrator are locating, evaluating, and managing estate assets; collecting debts owed the estate; finding buyers for estate assets that must be sold but have no ready market at a fair price; disposing of questionable creditors' claims against the estate; and dealing with emotionally distressed or contentious estate beneficiaries or representatives.

Paralegals in offices that do considerable estates work are commonly assigned such tasks as locating and inventorying assets, securing appraisals, arranging for the sale of estate assets, and arranging for stock transfers.[21] Asset searches may involve questioning relatives and examining such records of the decedent as canceled checks and income tax returns. In the course of asset inventorying, paralegals sometimes will go to the decedent's last residence and prepare a list of all items of value belonging to the decedent. Arrangements for storing these items pending their sale or distribution may also be necessary. In some cases, personal effects are sold at auction, with a paralegal arranging for the auction and attending the sale. Obviously, these various tasks can involve personal associations with the decedent's close relatives and friends shortly after the decedent's death, and many paralegals are excellent at handling these delicate situations with sympathy and tact.

Other estates tasks that paralegals perform in some offices are preparation of tax estimates, tax returns, and financial accounts. This work is also often assigned to fiduciary accountants, nonlawyer employees of law offices who specialize in estates work, usually have had formal training in accounting, and normally are paid above the usual paralegal salary scale. In some law offices, fiduciary accountants are considered to be paralegals; in others they are treated as a separate occupational group.

Corporate documentation. There are many requirements imposed on corporations by statute and government regulation as to how these organizations are to govern themselves and what government authorizations are required for them to carry on their businesses. To comply with these legal requirements it is necessary for corporations to prepare a variety of documents and keep them with their own records or file them with one or another government agency. The documents frequently are treated as perfunctory matters of form by the corporations and governments concerned and usually follow standard models with little or no originality. Law offices often are given responsibility for preparation and disposition of this documentation, with much of the work commonly assigned to paralegals. Prospects for paralegal involvement are increased if an office represents numerous corporations and the documentation follows quite repetitive patterns, as can occur in the law department of a very large corporation that has many subsidiaries or a law firm that represents many small independent corporations. Examples of documents for which paralegals may be responsible in performing this corporate housekeeping function are by-laws, minutes of boards of directors meetings, boards of directors action by unanimous consent without a meeting, articles of incorporation, and applications from foreign corporations to do business in a state.

Two law offices at which we interviewed illustrate rather well the use of paralegals for corporate documentation. One is the law department of a large multinational corporation, the other a law firm representing twenty-five small independent corporations. The large corporation in question has 200 subsidiaries, foreign and domestic. Routine documentation work is done by two paralegals, one working on foreign subsidiaries and one on domestic ones. Lawyers supervise the work of each and the paralegal assigned foreign subsidiaries uses as resource persons a group of in-house lawyers who specialize in the laws of particular foreign countries. All relevant instructions and forms are translated into English, as the paralegal is fluent only in English. Most of the work is following or adapting forms, and in-house forms for all the subsidiaries are as uniform as the laws of different countries and states permit. In the law firm, at the time of our interviews, one paralegal did routine documentation for twenty-five small corporations that considered it more efficient to send this work out than to have it done by their own employees. Presumably, all of these corporations were too small to have law departments. The paralegal operated with considerable independence in her minutes and by-laws work, and provided assistance to the lawyers in preparing some corporate tax returns. Her work, she said, was so routine that legal problems seldom arose. She frequently communicated with clients and was rather proud of the fact that she received more mail than anyone else in the office.

USE OF PARALEGALS BY DIFFERENT TYPES OF LAW OFFICES

To more fully understand the work of paralegals, it is helpful to be aware of how paralegals are used in different types of law offices. There are substantial distinctions among types of law offices and these distinctions can influence the extent and nature of paralegal use.

Differentiation among law offices is largely determined by the kinds of clients served and the range of services offered.[22] Many law offices are specialized by one broad category of clients. Some offices arc sct up to serve all the legal needs of their clients; others restrict the sorts of services their clients can receive from them. Client needs determine in large measure the expertise of a law office and also greatly influence the kind and quality of staff the office employs. Client ability and willingness to pay are important, too. Those most able to pay can often acquire the most competent law office personnel and the highest quality services. Wealth obviously is an important factor in who obtains and who provides top legal representation. However, those unable to pay are in many circumstances provided satisfactory, even quality, legal services through such means as legal aid, public defender programs, employer prepaid plans, and contingent fee contracts. Willingness to pay is also a significant consideration, and clients knowledgeable about law office costs, or sensitive to what they perceive as excessive fee demands, frequently seek lesser quality or amounts of services than they are capable of paying for, concluding that these will sufficiently serve their needs. More expensive services may be seen as retaining more competent lawyers than required or risking lawyer featherbedding. If clients are large organizations, they probably will have set up their own in-house law office as the best means of filling their legal service requirements. Types of law offices are to a degree competitive with one another, and one type through time may prosper at the expense of other types.

Some of the more significant features of each type of law office with which this study is concerned, including use of paralegals, are discussed below. The work and work environment of paralegals can vary considerably among types of offices.

Large firms. Most of these firms attract as clients principally organizations and individuals of substantial wealth for help with matters involving large sums of money. Their clients are primarily corporations that they represent in major litigation, the negotiation of big financial deals, new financing schemes, takeover bids, serious tax issues, adaptation to government regulations, and the myriad of other troublesome legal problems encountered by modern big business.[23]

Many big-firm corporate clients have their own law departments that send out to the big firms work that the departments are not satisfactorily staffed to handle inside, usually including litigation. At one time, large firms did nearly all the legal work for many of the major corporations. With the increase in number and size of law departments, this total servicing of corporate clients is much less common, and the big firms now do mostly specialty work for their larger corporate clients, with law department personnel monitoring the work of the firms and often, as with some major litigation, doing part of the work on a matter inside and sending the rest of it outside. Despite the growth of law departments in recent years, most of the large firms have likewise been expanding steadily both in the amount of work they handle and in staff size. As of 1983, the largest firm based in New York City had almost 400 lawyers, and 32 of the nation's 100 largest firms had their principal office in New York City.[24] Some of the big-firm growth has come from mergers with smaller firms and opening of branch offices domestically and abroad, mostly in major cities such as Washington, Los Angeles, and London.

Many lawyers look at the big firms as the most elite of American law offices. These firms represent wealthy and powerful clients, their lawyers receive top pay, the work they do is important and often intellectually challenging, they have the reputation of turning out work of high quality, and they regularly recruit their new lawyers from top-rank law schools.

The big firms are governed by their partners, senior partners usually having the greatest say in setting firm policy.[25] Committees of partners are delegated special responsibilities for such matters as internal education and training or long-range planning, and a small executive committee may coordinate and set policy within limits specified by the full partnership. A managing partner or lay office manager makes day-to-day decisions on administrative issues that arise.

Associates are junior lawyers, usually recruited out of law school or following a year of judicial clerkship, and nearly all of them are on the partnership ladder, with decision on partnership normally coming after five to eight years of apprenticeship as associates. Being selected as a partner is a rite of passage to which great significance is attached within the firm. It provides permanent tenure within the firm and status that carries with it both more power and enhanced remuneration. Competition for partnership is keen and is marked by long hours of intense work by these able and ambitious young lawyers.[26] Many associates never make partner and those turned down nearly all leave the firm. It is becoming increasingly common for associates to leave within two or three years and before even preliminary decisions have been made on their partnership prospects. Some find the grind and competition distasteful; some feel that the odds of their making partner are too long; some are enticed away by what they see as more attractive opportunities in law teaching, government service, a corporate law department, or a smaller firm. Being subject to very different inducements, paralegals rarely have the drive and work commitment of big-firm associates, even when sharing work with associates or taking over tasks of a sort formerly assigned to associates. Paralegals are often supervised by associates and motivational differences between associates and paralegals and greater time pressures on associates can lead to tensions. Problems of inadequate training and briefing of paralegals can also arise because neither associates nor partners feel they can afford to devote much time to instructing paralegals, especially those paralegals who do not readily grasp their assignments or who display serious writing or other skill deficiencies in the work they do.

Nearly all big firms employ paralegals in considerable numbers. As noted earlier, the paralegal to lawyer ratio of the 200 largest American law firms currently is about 1:5.6. The three big firms that we focused on in our interviewing had from thirty-five to sixty-four paralegals each at the time of our interviews. How rapid the big-firm growth in paralegal numbers has been is indicated in a study made by one of these three firms showing the firm's paralegal to lawyer ratio as 1:125 in 1970, 1:17 in 1975, and 1:5.6 in 1980. In most big firms, paralegals are heavily used in litigation, with much of the litigation work of paralegals consisting of processing masses of documents. The big firms are major litigators of heavily documented complex cases and, as has been seen, labor-intensive document processing has become an essential feature of these cases. Another litigation task often assigned big-firm paralegals is the indexing and digesting of depositions, transcribed statements of witnesses taken out of court and normally before trial.[27] Some depositions are very long, running to hundreds of transcribed pages. Indexing and digesting are particularly helpful to the lawyers when there are many depositions in a case. Sometimes paralegals also index and digest transcribed trial testimony. During trial, paralegals may be in court and responsible for organizing documents to be used as exhibits and locating them as needed for introduction into evidence. If a firm employs a dozen or more paralegals in litigation, an experienced paralegal often is appointed as supervisor or coordinator of the paralegals, with responsibility usually limited to litigation paralegals. These supervisors or coordinators commonly are responsible for paralegal work assignments, periodic evaluations, and recruitment. They also may act as intermediaries between lawyers and paralegals, and may be expected to attempt resolution of complaints either may have against the other. A paralegal supervisor's job can be a difficult one requiring both sensitivity and tact, and there are risks that paralegals will perceive their supervisors as having sold out to management and the lawyers will consider the supervisors as overly solicitous of paralegals. We encountered some remarkable young women successfully holding these positions who had moved up from the paralegal ranks.

The principal reason for big firms generally concentrating their paralegals on litigation is the relatively small amount of high-volume routine work sent them by their clients, other than for litigation, although there is some. Most big firms have an estates section that makes use of paralegals for many of the more routine tasks in estate administration and estate planning. One of the three big firms we focused on has a section doing mass closings on large items of personal property being leased or mortgaged and employs half a dozen paralegals for much of this very repetitive and routinized work. In another big firm we found paralegals doing some minor corporate housekeeping. To the extent paralegals are used elsewhere by big firms, it often is as personal assistants to individual lawyers doing odd jobs such as document collation in major closings, searching for file information in response to requests from auditors for companies that the firm represents, and occasional special projects such as library background research or statistical summaries. Paralegals, other than those who are law students, generally are not authorized to do legal research in the three firms, although some exceptions are made for citation and source checking.

There is another significant reason for the big firms not relying more on paralegals outside litigation. Their clients, although exerting pressure to hold down fees, do not want work product quality impaired and they can afford to pay for what they want. There is too much at stake monetarily to risk use of paralegals, they feel, unless it can be shown that paralegals can perform substantially as well as lawyers in the tasks being assigned. Paralegals can be particularly adept at fact investigation and analysis, but big-firm clients can often be relied on for whatever fact work is needed, major litigated cases excepted. Most of these clients are large organizations with data acquisition competence and many resource specialists quite articulate in communicating with lawyers. In brief, big-firm clients are paying top dollar and expect from the firms top-quality work of a sort they consider only lawyers, and only the best lawyers, generally can provide.

Small firms. In this category are included solo practitioners and multi-lawyer firms with fewer than ten lawyers each.[28] Most American lawyers in private practice work in small firms, with about half of all such lawyers practicing solo.[29] In New York City, small-firm lawyers probably predominate numerically among private practitioners, although accurate current statistical data is lacking. For the most part, small law firms in New York City, as elsewhere, represent very different kinds of clients from those represented by the big firms, and they usually work in different fields of law and with different kinds of legal problems. Small-firm clients are principally ordinary people of modest income and small local businessmen. These nonbusiness clients, generally able to pay for the services they receive, come to the small firms for such matters as divorces, home purchases, landlord-tenant problems, small debt collection, bankruptcy, wills and decedents' estate administration, personal injury claims, immigration problems, and criminal defense. Small-firm business clients come for help on such matters as incorporations, real property sales and mortgages, employee problems, taxes, and customer claims. Some small firms specialize, others take whatever comes along; but most lawyers in small firms specialize in one or a few fields of law, depending on client flow, profitability, and personal interest. Although business clients of small firms are mostly small local enterprises, a scattering of small firms develop reputations and narrow specialties attractive to big business clients. Litigation not requiring large support staffs is an example of this, for instance, defense of personal injury cases when claims are covered by large insurers.

Many small-firm practices economically are marginal, especially those of solo practitioners only recently admitted to the bar. It is comparatively easy to open a practice on one's own; it can be a long, arduous, and risky process to establish one that is economically viable. Furthermore, with the rapid increase in numbers of lawyers and the trend toward larger law offices that are more efficient and profitable, many small firms, especially solo practitioners, are having difficulty remaining financially successful even though long-established.

Being economically marginal, many small law firms cannot afford to hire paralegals, using lawyers or secretaries for work that elsewhere is performed by paralegals. Paralegals in small firms also tend to be less specialized than their big-firm counterparts, each of those in small firms commonly working in several fields of law. Multifield work is most likely when there is but one paralegal in the office, as frequently is the case. From what we observed in New York City, many small-firm paralegals are given more responsible work to do than what usually is assigned to paralegals in big firms. For example, we encountered instances of small-firm paralegals conducting initial screening interviews with prospective clients coming to the office, negotiating settlements in tort cases, and doing some advanced and rather difficult legal research even though they were not law students.

Small-firm litigation work can on occasion include sufficient documentation to require fairly extensive document processing, and we ran across two cases of this sort in each of which a paralegal was assigned for several months to document processing. One case was a small antitrust matter and the other an employment discrimination case. Most small-firm litigation, however, does not involve masses of documentation and when paralegals are used they are usually assigned such tasks as fact investigation over the telephone or interviewing in the field, drafting of motions and affidavits, maintenance of pending case dockets, and messenger work that may also entail filing and serving of documents. In real estate matters, if small-firm paralegals become highly experienced they may be given full responsibility to do closings of a routine character. If sufficiently experienced, they also may be given authority to do most of the work in simple decedents' estate administrations. For small-firm paralegals to become highly experienced in these sets of tasks, however, it usually is necessary for the firm employing them to have a continuing volume of repeat-type work of the kinds in question, something many small firms do not have. Many small law firms are unable to attract an adequate volume of repeat-type matters most suitable to use of paralegals.

Medium-sized law firms. These firms, numerous and highly important as legal servicing centers, received considerable attention in this study. More varied in what they do and whom they represent than the big firms; and better staffed and more affluent than the small ones, they provide an excellent cross-section of paralegal use by private law firms. Their clients come mostly from the spectrum in between the big firms and the small ones: major businesses but fewer giants than the big firms, individuals and families but fewer of modest means than the small firms. They often do all the legal work of their business clients, as many of these clients are too small to have law departments.

Many of the middle-sized firms are dominated by lawyers of ability with an entrepreneurial attitude toward the practice of law. They are aggressive and competitive in attracting clients; they have established high standards of performance for their offices; and they are seeking to emulate their models, the respected big firms, in hopes of expanding in size and moving their firms up and into top earning and status positions. The practice of law is sufficiently fluid that some will succeed and soon. How rapidly these firms can develop is illustrated by one of them at which we interviewed. It was then only eleven years old but had forty-seven lawyers and ten paralegals. The oldest lawyer was under fifty years of age.

Paralegal use by middle-sized firms in New York City is substantial and paralegals are used rather widely within the firms. Because they represent many businesses without law departments and many individuals and families, it is commonplace for middle-sized firms to have continued high-volume work flows of litigated cases and such other matters as real estate closings, decedents' estates, and corporate housekeeping. Paralegals are often relied on heavily in handling this volume work. In addition, table 5 discloses appreciable mid-size firm paralegal activities in other fields as diverse as matrimonial law, taxation, and patents, trademarks, and co-pyright. These firms do some heavily documented litigation, too, but generally of smaller cases than those taken by the big firms.

Two atypical medium-sized firms included in our study deserve special comment. They are a prepaid legal service operation and a legal clinic. Both depart in some respects from the usual medium-sized firm and are of particular importance as examples of new law office organizational forms that are becoming more common.[30] Both offices are nationally recognized models of their kind, although the prepaid office serves a lower-income clientele than many other prepaid operations. The prepaid office has been established pursuant to a union contract with a large employer and is operated by the union, paid for by the employer. The services it provides are among the benefits made available to union members as a result of the union-employer bargaining process. Union members are entitled to legal services by the office at no charge to them. Retirees are also included. The union members are mostly from a group of less-skilled, lower-paid employees and many can be categorized as working-poor or near-poor. The services that the office will provide are expressly limited but, other than not including criminal defense representation and nearly all personal injury claims, cover most kinds of legal problems that lower-income working people encounter.[31]

In organization, staffing, and much of what it does, the prepaid plan office bears some resemblance to a legal aid operation, but its funding arrangements are different from those of legal aid and its clients generally of somewhat higher income. If the prepaid program were not available, most of its clients would probably seek out small private law firms, as they would not be eligible for legal aid. Without free services, however, some no doubt would not seek any professional legal help at all. The prepaid office is in Manhattan at a central location with good access to public transportation, and at the time of our interviews had a staff that included forty-eight lawyers, seventeen paralegals, and a few social workers. It is a highly efficient operation geared to taking care of the legal needs of many individuals. There is little concern with test cases, law reform, or pushing any ideology other than individual client service. Paralegals are used because they are cheaper than lawyers and they are assigned where they can work with the greatest effectiveness, most particularly in client intake,[32] uncontested divorce, bankruptcy, and public benefits, including representation of claimants at administrative agency hearings. Paralegals are specialized by function or field. They do little or no legal research and they do no wills work.[33]

Legal clinics are private law offices that specialize in providing a narrow range of routine legal services, mostly or entirely uncontested.[34] They usually charge lower fees than generally charged by other firms in the area handling comparable matters, and they frequently rely heavily on advertising to attract a volume of work that enables them to hold down fees. Their clients consist almost entirely of ordinary persons desiring such common legal services as uncontested divorces, nonbusiness bankruptcies, simple wills, residential conveyances, name changes, and incorporation of small business enterprises. Legal clinics sprang up in all parts of the United States following the 1977 United States Supreme Court decision in Bates v. State Bar of Arizona,[35] a case that upheld the right of legal clinics to advertise. Some clinics have a chain of small offices scattered in local or regional commercial centers, and one Midwest-based clinic, the nation's largest, plans to open offices throughout the United States and may soon become one of the country's two or three largest law firms.[36] There have been instances of clinics encountering quality control problems and there have been charges that some smaller clinic operations engage in "bait and switch" tactics, drawing clients with expectations of low fees and then informing them that the problems presented are so complicated that higher than advertised rates must be charged. Aggressive clinic advertising has also irritated many more traditional lawyers, especially those who feel they are losing clients to clinics. The clinic form, concentrated uncontested routine work attracted by advertising, is here to stay; but the term *clinic* may be dropped by firms using this form in order to improve their image.

The clinic included in this study is a multioffice operation with a central administrative headquarters and small branch offices in neighborhood commercial areas. Each branch office is generally staffed by a lawyer and a secretary, and some of the secretaries are sufficiently experienced that they in effect are paralegals or paralegal-secretaries. It appears that a conscious decision has been made to attract clients by small offices conveniently located rather than by larger but less readily accessible offices. Clinics following the scattered small-office pattern are less likely to rely heavily on paralegals than clinics with fewer but more sizable offices better suited to task differentiation and extensive delegation of work to paralegals. As with many clinics, work of the one included in our study is heavily matrimonial, largely divorce. From our interviews, we were impressed with the excellent working relations between the clinic's lawyers and paralegals. In some offices of the clinic, where lawyer turnover has been higher than paralegal turnover, paralegals have become important transition and lawyer-training figures.

Corporate law departments. In amount and significance of work performed, corporate law departments are major providers of legal services in the United States.[37] The numbers of lawyers and support staff they employ have been increasing rapidly as more corporate enterprises establish law departments and law departments of other corporations are enlarged.[38] Each corporate law department does work for only one company or for a group of companies under common ownership or control. In effect, the client does its own legal work. The law department is usually located at the home office of the corporation but some large companies station some of their law department personnel at field office sites.

Growth in the importance of corporate law departments is due partly to the great expansion in legal services required by American business but also to many corporations retaining a much higher percentage of their legal work inside than they did formerly. As stated earlier in this chapter, outside firms are increasingly used by large corporations just for specialty work that inside law departments are not satisfactorily staffed to handle or to handle economically. This specialty work may be sent out because it arises too infrequently to justify hiring the requisite in-house expertise or, as often occurs with litigation, because it is centered at locations inconvenient and costly for in-house staff to reach. But occasionally corporate work is sent out because it involves such difficult and important issues as to merit a second opinion or, with less frequency today, because it is felt too much is at stake to trust assigning the matter to inside counsel.

The principal advantage of inside over outside counsel is cost. Legal work can generally be done for substantially less by corporate law departments, a recent study concluding that the cost of inside work is roughly half of that sent outside.[39] Another advantage of corporate law departments is that their staffs devote full-time to one employer and its activities and thus develop a better familiarity with company personnel, organization, and business policies than is usually possible with staff members at outside law firms. In many situations, such close ties contribute to efficiency of service and also assure that company policies will be carried out. Of course, many corporations are too small to afford house counsel so must send out their legal work, or, as they may with some matters, risk assigning it to inside lay personnel.

The governance of law departments is more concentrated in one or a few lawyers at the top than is generally true in large firms, and corporate management external to the department normally influences how and by whom the department is run. No comparable external intervention in private law firm operations exists. Law departments often have a more complex and differentiated formal hierarchy of lawyer positions than do law firms but the line between junior and senior lawyers is not as sharply drawn as between law firm associates and partners. Nor is it customary for law departments to have a cadre of nontenured up or out apprentice lawyers analogous to associates in law firms. Although it is changing as law departments take on more important work and exert control over lucrative matters going outside, among lawyers the prestige of house counsel does not match that of lawyers in the big firms.[40] In status, house counsel are a step below big-firm lawyers. Symbolic of this are the snide comments still heard of in-house counsel as kept lawyers or captive counsel.

Law departments of six large corporations with home offices in New York City were included in the paralegal questionnaire phase of this study. All but one of these departments employed more than fifty lawyers in its New York City office at the time of our interviews; the one exception was slightly below that figure. The business a company is engaged in, the places it does business, the amount and nature of its litigation, and the extent of its reliance on outside counsel are among the important variables determining what corporate law departments do. The six corporations from which paralegal questionnaires were received are engaged in a variety of businesses, including manufacturing, finance, energy, insurance, and communications. They operate over much of the nation and most of them do substantial business abroad. Several have a complex network of subsidiaries.

The extent of paralegal use by the six law departments differs considerably, with paralegal to lawyer ratios varying from about 1:20 to about 1:3, with 1:7 being more typical. This variation appears due in part to differences in the amount of routine work generated by the companies and assigned to their law departments. It also seems due to differences among general counsel in how much reliance they are willing to place on paralegals, which in turn may be influenced by how much pressure the department is under to cut costs.[41] The department in our study with the most paralegals uses them almost entirely for document processing in large antitrust cases to which the company is a party, thereby cutting expenses by having this work done inside and by relatively cheap lay help. Another department with considerable patent litigation had several paralegals assigned permanently to document processing in patent cases. Volume routine work also was the principal assignment of paralegals in the other departments, as all the departments had considerable work of this kind, although some clearly had more than others. Examples of such volume repeat work that we encountered being performed by law department paralegals were mortgage loan closings, mortgage review, corporate housekeeping for subsidiaries, arranging for payment where appropriate in response to wage garnishments of company employees, patent registration and docketing, and processing and paying accident claims against the company when it had assumed self-insurer responsibility. We did find, however, a few instances of less routine-type work in which considerable discretion was entrusted to experienced paralegals. In one of these cases a paralegal who had been with the company for thirty years was authorized to assemble and approve closing documentation on sizable loans. In another instance, law department paralegals acted as consultants to 200 branch offices of the company, responding to legal questions that came in from the branches. If the paralegals did not think they knew the answers, they referred the inquiries to one of the department lawyers. We also found some of the usual examples of law student paralegals being given substantial legal research responsibilities. Two companies, however, assigned to paralegals without law school experience the responsibility for periodically reviewing new statutes and regulations and alerting department lawyers to new developments that might be relevant to company affairs. For this work to be done thoroughly and accurately requires considerable legal knowledge, but errors in omission seldom could have serious adverse consequences for the company.

Government law offices. American government at all levels is a massive consumer of legal services. To a greater extent even than large corporations, government has its legal work performed by in-house lawyers.[42] Except for some small localities, it is unusual for government to contract out much if any of its legal work to private law firms. Many units of government centralize much of their legal services in one office, for example, a city law department, state attorney general's office, or the federal government's Department of Justice, although some agencies of the same unit of government may have their own legal staffs that are independent of the centralized office. The chief legal officials in the larger centralized government law offices are often persons of considerable local, state, or national political prominence; they are frequently well-connected in political party circles; and they may hope to use their present positions as springboards to higher political posts. Some chief legal officers are elected, but even if appointed they normally are replaced when new political administrations come to power. There also are government agencies in which most or all of the law office administrative and professional jobs are patronage positions with continued tenure subject to the vagaries of politics. However, even in government law offices with strong civil service systems for most employees, election results can cause sharp shifts in office policies.

Legal work for government is of two principal kinds: prosecuting persons charged with violating laws the government is responsible for enforcing and representing the government and its officials in the many other sorts of situations in which they need help from lawyers and lawyers' support staffs. Most government prosecutions are of persons charged with crimes but it is also common for government to prosecute persons charged with civil offenses. The nonprosecutorial work of government law offices includes such matters as defending government and its authorities in suits brought against them, advising government officials on their legal rights and obligations, negotiating and drafting agreements to which government agencies are parties, and drafting proposed statutes and regulations.

Included in this study are four large and important government law offices located in New York City, the largest one in staff terms employing over 500 lawyers. All four offices are marked by very extensive emphasis on litigation, a common characteristic of government law offices. In addition, all of the offices have high volumes of most kinds of matters they handle, they are under extremely tight budgetary restraints, and one consequence of their financial limitations is that they are inadequately staffed to handle properly all the work that comes their way. Their major staffing inadequacy is too few lawyers and principal support positions for lawyers, including paralegals. But some of the offices have staff quality problems as well: too many employees poorly motivated or lacking the skill and knowledge to work effectively. To a limited extent, the understaffing problem can be dealt with by restricting intake through screening out weak and less serious cases, as may be done with some criminal matters, for example. Liberal settlement or plea bargaining policies also can reduce work loads and staffing needs. Still another approach is assigning greater responsibility to junior lawyers and paralegals than might be preferred; and government legal service most everywhere is characterized by more responsibility being entrusted to lower-rank employees than is usual in private law firms. This kind of work spreading stretches budget dollars. It also may be used to ease the effect, at least temporarily, of inflexibilities in civil service systems that can delay filling of needed new positions. Despite these alleviating techniques, we observed serious instances of overburdening and under-performance in some of the government offices included in the study.

Much government legal work consists of criminal prosecutions; and in dealing with the tremendous number of criminal cases always pending in New York City, paralegals provide the prosecuting attorneys with a range of valuable support services. One of these is locating and contacting witnesses. Police reports usually give the names of witnesses, but accurate current addresses or telephone numbers are often lacking. When trial dates have been set, witnesses obviously must be notified and contacts with them in advance of trial may be necessary to complete the prosecution's investigation and properly prepare for trial. Finding witnesses, frequently many months or even years after the alleged criminal incidents, can be a difficult tracing procedure involving extensive telephoning and searches of police, welfare, employment, and other records. Some paralegals have developed great skill at this kind of witness tracing. In one office, paralegals also sit in on some witness interviews, thereby providing verification of what went on and what was said during the interviews. Another task that prosecutors frequently assign to paralegals, we were informed, is determining from police and court records, in and out of the city, prior arrest records of defendants and case dispositions where such records are found to exist. Paralegals also are used by some prosecutors to maintain calendars of upcoming court and motion dates, to subpoena documents, and to organize documents in larger cases. The police or FBI are usually responsible for investigations in criminal matters, but in some major cases supplemental investigation assignments may be given to paralegals. As do so many other law offices, prosecutors use law student paralegals for legal research, including, we noted, preparing memoranda for appeal briefs.

Although paralegals have become significant adjuncts in criminal prosecutions brought in New York City, we found certain spheres of civil work in which government law offices delegated somewhat greater authority to their paralegals than occurred in relation to criminal matters. The most striking examples of this were in case dispositions by the law department of a local government entity particularly hard-pressed financially. It should be said, however, that the cases, although numerous, generally involved rather small sums of money. One example is of tort cases against the government unit in question, running at the rate of almost 10,000 cases a year, and with most of the pleadings and motions in these cases prepared by paralegals, including non-law student paralegals. Some paralegals also analyzed files to determine if they were ready for trial. Lawyer supervisors were available for advice on doubtful points. Another example from the same office was a paralegal assigned to an overworked lawyer handling mostly landlord-tenant matters who had turned over case preparation and settlement negotiations to the paralegal in most eviction and rent collection cases involving properties taken by the city for nonpayment of taxes. In another law office involving a different unit of government, we encountered a paralegal doing a large volume of collection work for private claimants not paid wages or workers' compensation claims. The paralegal operated with relatively little supervision. His collection rate was low, however, as many of the debtors were out of business and judgment proof. We were not in a position to determine if the paralegals assigned were as effective as lawyers in performing these various kinds of traditional lawyer tasks, but it seemed clear that whether paralegals or lawyers were used, more help was needed than was made available. It is obvious that demands made of most government law offices commonly exceed what these offices have staff positions to provide. They are chronically shorthanded and make use of whatever help they can get.

Legal aid agencies. The principal providers of legal services to the large poverty segment of the American population are publicly supported legal aid and public defender organizations.[43] Only indigent and low-income persons are served by these organizations[44] and clients normally are taken care of without charge. The volume of matters handled by legal aid and defender agencies is tremendous given their comparatively small staffs. These mass dispositions are made possible by specialization in problems of the poor, a streamlining of operations, and more perfunctory treatment of some matters than they might receive in private law offices with full fees being paid.

The usual American pattern for providing legal services to the poor is for civil and criminal matters to be handled by different organizations: civil by legal aid agencies and criminal by public defender offices, with only one legal aid agency serving an entire community. The situation in New York City is more complicated. In that community, the New York Legal Aid Society is the public defender for both state and federal courts in the city and in addition provides representation in civil matters through a network of offices in different parts of the city.[45] There also are smaller legal aid agencies in the city that represent poor people in civil matters, most of these agencies operating only within one borough or other large section of the city. To a considerable degree, the smaller agencies offer the same services in civil matters as does the Legal Aid Society, giving clients some choice in where to seek help. At the time of our interviews of legal aid personnel, there were ten of these smaller organizations and they were funded principally by federal government grants.[46] The future of this federal funding is questionable and hence so is the future of these organizations.[47] The Legal Aid Society, on the other hand, receives only a relatively small percentage of its funding from federal sources, most of its public defender financing coming from local and state government[48] and much of its financing for civil representation coming from private sources, including sizable donations from the city's major law firms. When we interviewed at the Legal Aid Society, the Society employed almost 700 lawyers full-time, 550 of them in criminal defense work, and 120 paralegals.[49] At the same time, the ten smaller agencies employed about 120 lawyers and 40 paralegals.[50] Thus the paralegal to lawyer ratio in New York City legal aid at this time was approximately 1 to 5, compared to a ratio of about 1 to 2.2 nationally in legal aid agencies.[51]

The Legal Aid Society and the smaller agencies in 1981 were representing over 250,000 persons a year,[52] the great majority of them in criminal cases, the Legal Aid Society handling approximately 70 percent of all criminal defense work in the city, an astonishing concentration in one agency.[53] Legal aid civil representation is particularly heavy in government benefits and in family problems, especially uncontested divorce, matters usually handled with highly routinized procedures. Housing, including landlord-tenant controversies, and debt collection, representing mostly debtors, are other major fields of civil activity for the agencies.[54] As with government law offices, work of the agencies is marked by extensive emphasis on litigation, both in civil and criminal matters. Reductions in federal financial assistance to legal services for the poor will have little effect on numbers of persons represented by New York City legal aid organizations in criminal cases but could sharply reduce numbers of clients represented by these organizations in civil matters.[55]

In the course of this study, we interviewed and obtained questionnaires at most of the legal aid agencies in New York City, including both criminal and civil operations of the Legal Aid Society. In staff size, heavy emphasis on criminal work, and greater stability of funding, the Society differs from the smaller agencies. We also noted a difference in style, staff relations in the smaller agencies being more informal—a paralegal in one of these agencies referred to her office as "like a family"— and there seemed more ideological and emotional involvement in the smaller offices with policy issues of concern to the poor. The Society's orientation was more exclusively service to individual clients. There was, as well, a mood of gloom and frustration in the smaller offices caused by feared budget cuts and prospects of offices being shut down for lack of funds and many persons in need of services going unrepresented.

New York City legal aid organizations utilize paralegals for a broad and diverse range of tasks.[56] The high volume and specialized nature of so much legal aid work, plus budgetary constraints on the agencies, make paralegals appropriate for many tasks in legal aid offices. Also, more than any other type of law office, legal aid and defender organizations need personnel that can effectively communicate and identify with persons of culturally atypical or disadvantaged backgrounds, for example, ethnic minorities, those with little or no fluency in English, the chronically poor, the elderly, persons who have spent long periods in jails and prisons, those who are drug dependent, and persistent criminal offenders. Paralegals can often be found who are better at dealing with one or more of these groups than are lawyers, often because the paralegals have backgrounds similar to those of persons in one or another of these groups. In addition, legal aid organizations have discovered that many procedures they follow in client representation can satisfactorily be performed by nonlawyers and that there are no complaints when these tasks are delegated to paralegals. As tables 1 and 2 show, most of this work consists of acquiring factual information, especially acquiring it directly from others. In government benefits cases it also includes advocacy at administrative hearings. High volume and specialization enable the process to function effectively, although under-staffing can undermine quality and result in less than thorough representation.

Legal aid paralegals, as well as legal aid lawyers, usually work in units specialized in one major field of law or one important procedure, but one of the smaller New York legal aid offices has gone to more generalized assignments in which each lawyer, with paralegal help as needed, is expected to take on any kind of case accepted by the office. This office has found that many of its clients have multiple legal problems and has concluded that specialization of staff by client rather than substantive field of law is preferable, as it offers more opportunity for identifying and solving the totality of client difficulties.

Criminal defense work on a large scale has turned out to be particularly suitable to use of paralegals, as table 5 indicates. For example, the Legal Aid Society has a group of paralegals, called prison legal assistants (PLAs), stationed at ten pretrial detention centers in the city and who act principally as liaisons with defense lawyers. The prisons are inconveniently located for easy access by lawyers, and telephoning client inmates generally is not a feasible means of lawyer-client communication. Using the prison legal assistants as go-betweens is more efficient, as the PLAs are regularly at the detention centers and can readily arrange to talk with client inmates. They act as messengers for the lawyers and are useful as well in providing psychological support and useful information to client inmates. Relations between the PLAs and the prison staff are normally good, and the PLAs can be helpful in working out solutions to some of the complaints client inmates have about their treatment in prison. Another function that the Society utilizes its paralegals for is to secure data on certain clients prior to final case disposition when the attorneys believe a lenient sentence or diversion from incarceration may be justified and attainable. The paralegals in this Special Defender Services Unit make home visits, verify prior employment records, and obtain statements and other evidence relevant to appropriate sentencing or diversion from adjudication of guilt. Social workers in the unit supervise the paralegals and prepare reports incorporating findings of the paralegals. The reports are submitted to the court and in some cases the social workers appear before judges to answer questions about clients the unit has considered. Among other tasks pertaining to criminal matters that the Legal Aid Society assigns to paralegals are screening applicants for legal help, checking court records for previous criminal charges and dispositions, delivering and serving legal documents, securing continuances of court hearings, notifying witnesses of continuances, and obtaining data in support of bail applications.[57] Paralegals are also employed in the Society's Criminal Appeals Bureau, a unit that has approximately 1,000 cases pending on appeal at all times. Paralegals in this unit assist a managing attorney in completing files where necessary,[58] determining if there is a conflict of interest that precludes Society representation,[59] and maintaining dockets of cases on appeal. Little legal research is done by Society paralegals in the Criminal Appeals Bureau or elsewhere in the entire Society organization, and this includes paralegals who are or have been law students. The Society is averse to nonlawyers engaging in this kind of work.

EMPLOYER DISSATISFACTIONS WITH PARALEGALS

Employers, from their perspective, are experiencing some problems in use of paralegals, although we received relatively few reports of such problems in the course of this study. The overall satisfaction of most employers with their paralegals seems explainable in part by employer caution in assigning work to paralegals, paralegals rarely being assigned tasks if doubts exist about their capacity to carry them out. Nevertheless, we did hear some expressions of dissatisfaction with paralegals from their supervisors and others in authority.

One complaint, and one we heard primarily from large firms, was as to the quantity and quality of paralegal work. It was not that paralegals generally could not do the work assigned them, but that they were not sufficiently productive and too often their work was inaccurate. One big-firm associate who regularly supervises paralegals noted that before coming to work for a law firm few paralegals had ever before been required to be so accurate and that it is difficult for most paralegals to acquire the habit and self-discipline of being meticulously correct in the work they turn out. Particular concern was expressed by our informants about paralegals doing document review in big cases with masses of documents, dull work in which motivation is hard to sustain. Protracted time-wasting bull sessions by groups of paralegals were reported as a problem in two firms, and a paralegal supervisor told us that there had been occasional incidents of college dormitory-type behavior on the part of recent college graduate paralegals in her firm, including paper airplane contests in the hallways and juvenile acts of hiding the personal effects of fellow paralegals. Indicative of similar nonconformity with acceptable office conduct was the report that in another big firm, paralegals had come to work in college-style informal attire and had to be warned that this was quite inappropriate. There seems to be an expectation in the large firms that as so many of their paralegals come from class and educational backgrounds similar to those of their associates, the paralegals will easily fall into behavioral and motivational patterns similar to those of associates. In many instances this apparently is not happening.

Another difficulty in the use of paralegals that has generated employer concern in some law offices is friction between paralegals and other inside work groups, particularly junior lawyers and secretaries.[60] Such frictions are understandable as there is a degree of competition among these groups for work and for status recognition, and the advent of paralegals as an occupation inserted between professional and clerical workers in the office hierarchy increases possibilities for intergroup competition and animosity. Experienced paralegals often are particularly resentful of beginning lawyers, who seem to know so little, being brought in to positions above them; and they also find it hard to take when, as is not unusual, secretaries are paid more than they. Secretaries, on the other hand, tend to resent what they see as paralegal pretensions of being professionals.[61] Beginning lawyers, too, have their adjustment problems—finally having entered the profession after a long and demanding preparatory period, they frequently are oblivious to the subtle network of office relationships of which they are now a part and proceed arrogantly to offend both paralegals and secretaries. These intergroup tensions, however, seldom are more than minor irritants complicating work output and office management, but they could create more serious personnel problems if paralegals become better organized and more militant and begin to demand from their employers enhanced respect, status, and responsibility.

The high rate of paralegal turnover also is causing dissatisfaction and worry in some law offices. Especially if paralegal tasks require considerable on-the-job training or if particular paralegals have shown special aptitudes and been given more responsibility as a result, turnovers can be costly. At times, pay increases are enough to enable an office to hold onto its more valued paralegals, but many top paralegals have ambitions that make it impossible to retain them in their present positions. For some kinds of paralegal employment, however, high turnover seems to be causing little concern. Where replacement is easy and little training required, as with much document processing in large-scale litigation, high turnover rates are less damaging to the employer. There may even be employer advantages to turnovers in such circumstances as they can result in cost savings by avoiding pay increases based on seniority.

NOTES

1. Nelson, in his study of large law firms, considered the following tasks in his analysis of frequency of lawyer task performance: taking depositions, court appearances, legal research, administration, writing letters, negotiating with lawyers from outside the firm, conferring with lawyers from outside the firm, supervising others, writing briefs and memos, preparing motions, trial preparation, reviewing documents, drafting legal documents, talking to clients/lawyers, continuing legal education, and professional activities. R. Nelson, Practice and Privilege: The Social Organization of Large Law Firms 214 (unpublished Ph.D. dissertation, Northwestern University, Sociology, 1983). The most frequently performed tasks, as reported by big-firm lawyers in the Nelson sample, in order of performance frequency, are talking to clients/lawyers, conferring with lawyers from outside the

firm, writing letters, reviewing documents, negotiating with lawyers from outside the firm, and drafting legal documents. *Id.*

2. Source checking is verification of citation accuracy in briefs, articles, or other writings. This checking is usually done prior to publication or submission to a court or other body and normally involves physical examination of the books or other writings that are cited. Such matters are verified as the accuracy of book or case titles, authors' names, volume and page numbers, and whether or not commentary about the cited source is correct. Shepardizing is the process of determining from a comprehensive index, called a citator, the volume and page number in judicial opinions and professional journals at which previously published legal authorities have been referred to. These referred-to sources include other judicial opinions and such additional authorities as statutes, constitutions, and administrative regulations. A citator also enables one to locate where else particular legal authorities are published and their historic antecedents. The process is named after the publisher, Shepard's/McGraw-Hill. On shepardizing, *see* W. Statsky, *Introduction to Paralegalism* 466–70, 512–28 (2d ed. 1982). Both source checking and shepardizing can be simple routine tasks, but considerable knowledge of law may be required to determine the accuracy of commentary referring to cited sources or the relevance to the point being researched of cases or other authorities disclosed by a Shepard's citator. This commentary checking and determining of authority relevance are tasks likely to be taken over by lawyers, but if they are assigned to paralegals, lawyers will often carefully review the paralegals' work.

3. In current literature on dispute resolution, these lawyer functions are considered part of the process of dispute transformation. *See*, for example, Felstiner, Abel, and Sarat, The Emergence and Transformation of Disputes: Naming, Blaming, Claiming . . . , 15 *Law and Society Review* 631, at 645–46 (1980–81).

4. In a recent *American Bar Association Journal* survey of paralegals working in the offices of 525 ABA members questioned, the most common job duties of paralegals reported were preparing case chronologies or organizing documents, analyzing statistics or records, and fact investigating. Law Poll, 69 *American Bar Association Journal* 1626 (1983). In a recent study, a large sample of Chicago lawyers ranked fact gathering as the most important skill and area of knowledge in the practice of law. F. Zemans and V. Rosenblum, *The Making of a Public Profession* 125 (1981). The next four most important skills and areas of knowledge to the lawyers participating in this study were capacity to marshall facts and order them so that concepts can be applied; instilling others' confidence in the practicing lawyer; effective oral expression; and ability to understand and interpret opinions, regulations, and statutes. Despite the high priority lawyers give to fact gathering, in many offices they frequently delegate this task to paralegals.

5. For deposition-related work that a competent paralegal can perform, *see* Schaumburger, Role of the Legal Assistant, 10 *Facts and Findings* no. 2, at 19 (1983).

6. Law office administration is another rapidly expanding occupation. One indication of this is that in the decade prior to 1982, the Association of Legal Administrators increased its membership from 100 to 3,200. Ranii, New Roles for Firm Managers, *National Law Journal*, Oct. 25, 1982, at 1. On law office administrators and managers, also *see* B. Hildebrandt and J. Kaufman, *The Successful Law Firm* ch. 2 (1983); Akins, The Role of the Law Firm Administrator, 1 *Legal*

Economics no. 3, at 35 (1975); Guinan, Paralegals in Administration, *National Law Journal*, Jan. 2, 1984, at 14; and Heintz, The Administrator in the Larger Firm, 4 *Legal Economics* no. 2, at 31 (1978).

7. It may be, however, that especially in small firms, employers we contacted failed to identify as paralegals some of the secretaries they employ who do a substantial amount of paralegal work and might appropriately be classified as paralegals or at least as paralegal-secretaries.

8. In addition to paralegals who hold formal supervisory positions over a dozen or more other paralegals, paralegals in larger offices sometimes work in small teams on big cases with a more knowledgeable and experienced paralegal in each team being the informal supervisor with advisory or guidance authority.

9. On systems for law offices, *see* Kansas City Bar Association and University of Missouri-Kansas City Law Center in cooperation with the Kansas City Association of Legal Assistants, *Systems for Legal Assistants, Resource Manual* (1980); R. Kurzman and R. Gilbert, *Paralegals and Successful Law Practice* ch. 5 (1981); R. Ramo, *How to Create-A-System for the Law Office* (1975); K. Strong and A. Clark, *Law Office Management* ch. 4 (1974); Turner, The Effective Use of Lay Personnel, in American Bar Association, *Proceedings of the Third National Conference on Law Office Economics and Management* 27 (1969), abridged version in 11 *Law Office Economics and Management* 73 (1970); Turner, Effective Use of Lay Personnel Revisited, in American Bar Association, *Law Office Economics* 113 (1970); Engel, The Standardization of Lawyers' Services, *1977 American Bar Foundation Research Journal* 817, at 832–34; Israel, Systems in Law Practice: Planning for Quality and Efficiency, 26 *Wayne Law Review* 1159 (1980); and Strong and Henderson, Legal Assistants—The Systems Approach, 15 *Law Office Economics and Management* 344 (1974). Illustrative systems manuals, with forms, have been prepared for lawyers and published by the University of Utah and the Utah Law Research Institute for Utah Lawyers and include among other volumes one for *Testate Probate* (1973) and one for *Real Estate* (1974). For a bibliography of similar systems manuals, *see* Ramo, How to Find Your Way Down the Yellow Brick Road, 65 *American Bar Association Journal* 12A at 13A (March 1979).

10. *See*, for example, R. Hall, *Organizations: Structure and Process* ch. 6 (2d ed. 1977).

11. Systems are defined as follows in an American Bar Association publication:

A system is a documented logical method or way of handling transactions, procedures, or work flow in a law office so as to minimize waste, conserve professional time, and optimize productivity. . . . In our view, a "system" is not a system unless it contains these three ingredients: 1. *Information, facts or data* that are required in operating the system, and a method for efficiently obtaining them. 2. *"Forms" or documents* which are involved in the system, organized in logical sequence. 3. *Written instructions*, directions or procedures for use by those who work with the system.

Ramo, *How to Create-A-System*, *supra* note 9, at 5–6.
Further illustrative characterizations of systems are these:

Characteristics and components of legal systems include: standard letters, pleadings, forms and documents; plans which include checklists, time tables, standard time expectations, and references to authority; a division of labor based upon functional specialization among lawyers, legal assistants, and support staff and, where appropriate, clients; the use of calculated production techniques and law office technology such as dictation and word processing equipment, computer technology, and copying equipment; and written instructions, directions, protocols, and procedures. . . . Without written procedures, the office does not have a legal system, it has a custom.

Israel, *supra* note 9, at 1165–66.

Systematization reduces repetitive work to a routine, simplifying the execution of the work and minimizing the involvement of management in handling that work. Therefore, only exceptional problems are referred to the attorney, thus giving him more time to devote to the truly legal aspects of his profession from which he derives greater satisfaction and which uniquely demand his specialized skills.

Strong and Henderson, *supra* note 9, at 347.

Something comparable to internal law office systems are the formal procedures required in litigation and practice before courts and government administrative agencies. Lawyers are accustomed to these externally imposed systems and must adapt to them. Similar, although generally less complex, external systems have been developed by such private organizations as title insurers and banks for customer dealings with the organizations whether directly or through lawyers.

12. Engel, *supra* note 9, at 835–38. On computer use in law offices, also *see* Fry, The Impact of Technology on the Practice of Law, 1 *Legal Assistant Today* no. 2, at 9 (1984); Musselman, Computers and New Technology in the Law Office, *New Roles in the Law Conference Report* 220 (1982); Sherman and Kinnard, The Development, Discovery, and Use of Computer Support Systems in Achieving Efficiency in Litigation, 79 *Columbia Law Review* 267 (1979); Silverman and Keane, A Decade of Law Office Automation: 1977–1987, 68 *American Bar Association Journal* 928 (1982); Walshe, Law Office Automation: Tying Systems Together, 69 *American Bar Association Journal* 184 (1983); and symposium on computers in the legal field, 7 *National Paralegal Reporter* no. 2 (1982).

13. Paralegal use in these cases is discussed in Fairbanks, Assistants in the Personal Injury Case, 10 *Trial* no. 5, at 38 (1974); and Turner, Law Office Management: A Way to Control Litigation Costs, 14 *Forum* 1076 (1979).

14. Paralegals, also known as patent registrars, are often used in law offices that process large volumes of patent applications and foreign renewals and monitor patent termination dates. In some industrial corporations holding many patents, this is an in-house law department responsibility. For a brief elementary introduction to patent procedures, see Lieberstein, Through the Patent Maze: A Guide for the General Lawyer, 32 *The Record of the Association of the Bar of the City of New York* 339 (1977).

15. J. Ebersole and B. Burke, *Discovery Problems in Civil Cases* (1980); Brazil, Improving Judicial Controls Over the Pretrial Development of Civil Actions: Model Rules for Case Management and Sanctions, *1981 American Bar Foundation Research Journal* 873.

16. On use of computers in heavily documented litigation, *see* Emerson and Rome, Computers in Litigation Support Facilitate Many Multiple Document Cases, *National Law Journal*, Feb. 23, 1981, at 19.

17. Useful instructional materials, however, have been prepared by the Legal Services Corporation and are available to legal aid offices funded through the Corporation.

18. In California, communications between clients in relation to public social service proceedings and lay persons representing them in such proceedings, including paralegals, are privileged comparable to communication between clients and their lawyers. Welfare Rights Organization v. Crisan, 33 Cal.3d 766, 661 P.2d 1073 (1983). A similar client-lay representative privilege apparently does not exist in New York. Kent Jewelry Corp. v. Kiefer, 202 Misc. 778, at 780–82, 113 N.Y.S.2d 12, at 15–17 (1952).

19. For a more detailed description of these mortgage review operations in the early 1960s, see Q. Johnstone and D. Hopson, *Lawyers and Their Work* ch. 7 (1967). Lay reviewers were being used in-house by life insurance companies as early as 1921. *Id.*, at 251.

20. On estate planning, see Schlesinger, Post-Mortem Estate Planning: A Checklist, *National Law Journal*, Aug. 9, 1982, at 18; *id.*, Aug. 16, 1982, at 15; and *id.*, Aug. 23, 1982, at 15.

21. On paralegal work in estates, see Grove, Estate Work—A Happy Hunting Ground for the Paralegal, 19 *The Practical Lawyer* no. 3, at 73 (1973); and Mucklestone, The Legal Assistant in Estate Planning, 10 *Real Property, Probate and Trust Journal* 263 (1975).

22. On lawyer specialization and law office differentiation, see J. Heinz and E. Laumann, *Chicago Lawyers: The Social Structure of the Bar*, chs. 2 and 3 (1982); and Johnstone and Hopson, *supra* note 19, at ch. 4.

23. On big firms, see P. Hoffman, *Lions in the Street* (1973); P. Hoffman, *Lions of the Eighties* (1982); E. Smigel, *The Wall Street Lawyer* (1964); Nelson, *supra* note 1; Nelson, Practice and Privilege: Social Change and the Structure of Large Law Firms, *1981 American Bar Foundation Research Journal* 95; and Slovak, Working for Corporate Actors: Social Change and Elite Attorneys in Chicago, *1979 American Bar Foundation Research Journal* 465.

24. *National Law Journal*, September 19, 1983, at 4.

25. One authority on large law firms has classified lawyers in these organizations as finders, minders, and grinders. Finders are the entrepreneurs that attract clients; minders are an intermediate strata of partners with supervisory responsibility over other lawyers and some client responsibility but are not top policy makers within the firm; and grinders are mostly associates and young partners who do much of their work under the direction of other lawyers. Nelson, *supra* note 1, at 56–69. Paralegals constitute a lower level of grinders.

26. Partners in large firms often put their associates under great pressure to turn out quality work quickly. This can lead to associate animosity toward partners. For example, an associate in a prestigious firm who had been under such pressure told us that partners in his firm were callous about associates' feelings and ruthless in screening out associate candidates for partnership. He added that partners do the more entertaining and exciting kinds of work and expect their associates to make partners' lives more pleasant.

27. These statements are under oath and counsel for both sides are usually present, with right of cross-examination. The statements may be used for discovery or during trial and are often useful in calculating the merits of a settlement offer.

28. On small law firms, see J. Carlin, *Lawyers on Their Own* (1962); J. Handler, *The Lawyer and His Community* (1967); Landon, Lawyers and Localities: The

Interaction of Community Context and Professionalism, *1982 American Bar Foundation Research Journal* 459.

29. As of 1980, 370,000 lawyers in the United States were in private practice and 180,000 of these were solo practitioners. American Bar Foundation, *The 1984 Lawyer Statistical Report: A Profile of the Legal Profession in the United States* (1984).

30. On prepaid legal service plans and operations, *see* Business Trend Analysts, Inc., *The U.S. Market for Legal Services* 148–65 (1984); F. Marks, R. Hallauer, and R. Clifton, *The Shreveport Plan, An Experiment in the Delivery of Legal Services* (1974); W. Pfennigstorf and S. Kimball, *Legal Service Plans: Approaches to Regulation* (1977); Flaherty, Prepaid Plans: The New Look, *National Law Journal*, Dec. 6, 1982, at 1; and Murphy, Prepaid Legal Services: Development and Problems, 20 *Arizona Law Review* 485 (1978). Plans sponsored by trade unions, with costs of operation paid for by employers pursuant to union contracts, have been particularly successful. The largest plan of this sort covers 300,000 employees of General Motors and is provided for by the company's contract with the United Automobile Workers. Flaherty, *supra*. The private bar in some communities is concerned about competition from prepaid plans. Ranii, Union Legal Plan Spawns Fear Among Private Bar, *National Law Journal*, May 10, 1982, at 3.

31. Matters covered include principally divorce, evictions, small debts, bankruptcy, consumer complaints against sellers, home purchases, wills, and government benefits. The government benefits staff handles not only the usual welfare and social security problems, but also a miscellany of claims and complaints against large organizations, including veterans' benefits, crime victims' compensation, public utility cutoffs, contested credit agency ratings, and conflicts with the public schools over student suspensions. Counsel in lawsuits will be provided but with restrictions. For example, litigation services will not be provided if representation is available under an insurance policy, in matters commonly handled by private lawyers on a contingent fee basis, or for claims against the union or the employer. Administration of decedents' estates, immigration matters, tax problems, and name changes also are services not offered by the plan.

32. Most of the intake work is done by paralegals who screen all requests for service made in person or over the telephone, determine eligibility, and refer many who are ineligible to outside sources of help. At least one screener is Spanish-speaking.

33. Lawyers, not paralegals, are used in preparation of wills, even though the wills drafted usually follow simple standard forms and final copies are prepared on word processing equipment.

34. On legal clinics, *see* Business Trend Analysts, *supra* note 30, at 27–92; D. Maron, *Legal Clinics: Analysis and Survey* (2d ed. 1977); Meyers, Legal Clinics: Their Theory and How They Work, 52 *Los Angeles Bar Journal* 106 (1976); Muris and McChesney, Advertising and the Price and Quality of Legal Services: The Case for Legal Clinics, *1979 American Bar Foundation Research Journal* 179; Project, An Assessment of Alternative Strategies for Increasing Access to Legal Services, 90 *Yale Law Journal* 122 (1980); Proliferation of Legal Clinics Continues, *National Law Journal*, Dec. 31, 1979, at 5; Bodine, Legal Clinics, the Bargain Bar, *National Law Journal*, Feb. 12, 1979, at 1. On advertising by legal clinics and other

types of law offices, *see* Middleton, Ads Pay Off—In Image and Income, *National Law Journal*, March 5, 1984, at 1.

35. 433 U.S. 350 (1977).

36. This firm is Hyatt Legal Services and it has a cooperative arrangement with H & R Block, the tax return specialists, for joint use of office space in some of the Block organization's 9,000 offices. A report on Hyatt Legal Services appears in Harper, The Joel Hyatt-H & R Block Alliance, A 1000–Lawyer Firm?, *National Law Journal*, Nov. 1, 1982, at 1. In 1983, Hyatt Legal Services was the nation's fifteenth largest private law firm in terms of numbers of lawyers, up from sixtieth in 1982. *National Law Journal*, Sept. 19, 1983, at 6. By 1984, it was seventh largest. *National Law Journal*, Aug. 6, 1984, at 12.

37. On corporate law departments, *see* J. Donnell, *The Corporate Counsel, A Role Study* (1970); Johnstone and Hopson, *supra* note 19, at ch. 6; Smyser, In-House Corporate Counsel: The Erosion of Independence, in R. Nader and M. Green (eds.), *Verdicts on Lawyers* 208 (1976); Lynch, The Growth of In-House Counsel, 65 *American Bar Association Journal* 1403 (1979); McConnell and Lillis, A Comment on the Role, Structure, and Function of Corporate Legal Departments, 14 *American Business Law Journal* 227 (1976); and Slovak, *supra* note 23. For an analysis of recent declines in big-firm earnings and the possible significance of corporate law departments on income and importance of large law firms, *see* Brill, Gloom from Price Waterhouse, *The American Lawyer*, Nov. 1983, at 1; and Business Trend Analysts, *supra* note 30, at 93–97. In addition to business corporations, it is becoming fairly common for other large private sector organizations to maintain law departments, including universities, large religious bodies, and trade unions. On the legal problems of institutions of higher learning and the types of law offices used in dealing with them, *see* McCarty and Thompson, The Role of Counsel in American Colleges and Universities, 14 *American Business Law Journal* 287 (1977).

38. It is estimated that as of 1980, private industry employed over 54,000 lawyers, most presumably in law departments. This was 14.6 percent of all lawyers then working in the private sector, including private law firms. American Bar Foundation, *supra* note 29. In 1954, over 11,000 lawyers were calculated to be working in private industry, about 5.5 percent of all lawyers then working in the private sector. Cantor, Managing Legal Organizations in the 1980's, 11 *University of Toledo Law Review* 311 at 313 (1980).

39. Lynch, *supra* note 37. On techniques used by corporate general counsel to hold down legal costs, *see* Banks, Companies Struggle to Control Legal Costs, 61 *Harvard Business Review* no. 2, at 168 (1983). On efforts by corporate law departments to hold down costs of legal work referred to outside law firms, *see* Flaherty, Comparison Shopping Hits the Law, *National Law Journal*, Oct. 31, 1983, at 1.

40. The nature and causes of this prestige difference is considered in Slovak, Giving and Getting Respect: Prestige and Stratification in a Legal Elite, *1980 American Bar Foundation Research Journal* 31.

41. The structure, types of work, and use of lawyers and paralegals in a large Connecticut-based insurance and diversified financial services corporation, Aetna Life and Casualty, are described in Middlebrook and Groothuis, Managing, Evaluating the Law Department, *National Law Journal*, April 25, 1983, at 14.

42. On government law offices, *see* J. Eisenstein, *Counsel for the United States:*

U.S. Attorneys in the Political and Legal Systems (1978); R. Nader and M. Green (eds.), *Verdicts on Lawyers* pt. V (1976); S. Weaver, *Decision to Prosecute: Organization and Policy in the Antitrust Division* (1977); Flaherty, N.Y. as Client, *National Law Journal*, March 5, 1984, at 1, on the New York City Law Department and the then corporation counsel; Kuh, Careers in Prosecution Offices, 14 *Journal of Legal Education* 175 (1961).

43. On legal aid and public defender operations in the United States, *see* R. Hermann, E. Single, and J. Boston, *Counsel for the Poor, Criminal Defense in Urban America* (1977); J. Handler, E. Hollingsworth, and H. Erlanger, *Lawyers and the Pursuit of Legal Rights* (1978); E. Johnson, *Justice and Reform, The Formative Years of the American Legal Services Program* (1978); J. Katz, *Poor People's Lawyers in Transition* (1982); Legal Services Corporation, *The Delivery Systems Study, A Policy Report to the Congress and the President of the United States* (1980); National Legal Aid and Defender Association, *The Other Face of Justice: A Report of the National Defender Survey* (1973); Bellow, Legal Services to the Poor: An American Report, in M. Cappelletti (ed.), *Access to Justice and the Welfare State* 49 (1981); Brakel, Legal Services for the Poor in the Reagan Years, 68 *American Bar Association Journal* 820 (1982); Breger, Legal Aid for the Poor: A Conceptual Analysis, 60 *North Carolina Law Review* 282 (1982); Cramton, Why Legal Services for the Poor?, 68 *American Bar Association Journal* 550 (1982); Ehrlich, Save the Legal Services Corporation, 67 *American Bar Association Journal* 434 (1981).

44. Means tests determine eligibility for legal aid and public defender assistance, different offices having somewhat different tests. Income ceilings to qualify are generally similar to but somewhat higher than those for public welfare assistance. Legal aid agencies normally will not take matters covered by prepaid insurance or those that lawyers customarily take under contingent fee arrangements.

45. The New York Legal Aid Society is the oldest legal aid agency in the United States. On its earlier history, *see* H. Tweed, *The Legal Aid Society, New York City, 1876–1951* (1954).

46. The smaller organizations are Community Action for Legal Services (CALS), Bedford Stuyvesant Community Legal Services, Bronx Legal Services, Brooklyn Legal Services A, Brooklyn Legal Services B, Harlem Legal Services, Legal Services for the Elderly, Manhattan Legal Services, MFY Legal Services, and Queens Legal Services. CALS is principally an administrative body through which federal funds from the Legal Services Corporation are channeled for support of noncriminal legal aid in the city. CALS does, however, do some training of legal aid personnel and operates small units aiding handicapped persons and beneficiaries of food stamps and other food aid programs. All of the above agencies, as well as the Legal Aid Society, are recipients through CALS of federal funds, and all but the Legal Aid Society and Legal Services for the Elderly are delegates of CALS. Delegate organizations have been receiving about 98 percent of their funding from federal government sources.

Many American legal aid agencies receive some funding from sources other than the federal government, much of it coming from community chests or other private charitable giving. The amount of funding from these private sources is in most instances modest at best. With heavy demand for help coming from so many worthy causes, legal aid's share is not likely to increase much if at all from these sources, except that allocations from lawyer-controlled funds may increase if federal assistance is dropped or substantially cut back.

47. On legal aid's federal funding problems, *see* Legal Services, 70 *American Bar Association Journal* 42 (July 1984); Legal Aid for the Poor: Reagan's Longest Brawl, *New York Times*, June 8, 1984, at A16; and Brakel, Cramton, and Ehrlich, *supra* note 43.

48. The Legal Aid Society, New York, *Annual Report 1980*, at 45, showed that

Of the Society's total revenues during the year ended June 30, 1980, approximately $21,919,000 was awarded by city agencies, of which approximately $2,577,000 was awarded to such agencies by federal and state agencies; additionally approximately $11,935,000 and $2,429,000 was awarded to the Society by state and federal agencies, respectively.

49. Interviewing was in 1981.

In addition to its full-time staff of lawyers, the Society regularly draws on the services of a large cadre of volunteer lawyers, many from the big firms and corporate law departments, who donate time to serving Society clients on a part-time basis. A separate Volunteer Division has been set up by the Society to help in assigning and overseeing this pro bono work. The volunteer program is discussed in Wechsler, The Private Bar Meets the Poor, 36 *National Legal Aid and Defender Association Briefcase* 103 (1979).

50. In the smaller agencies, some modest staff attrition had occurred by this time in anticipation of federal funding cutbacks.

51. One possible explanation for New York City's sharp departure from the national paralegal to lawyer ratio is that most legal aid lawyers in New York City are engaged in criminal work as public defenders, atypical of most legal aid offices, and there appears to be less use of paralegals in public defender work than in civil legal aid operations.

52. In its 1980–81 statistical summary, the Legal Aid Society states that the Society represents over 250,000 persons a year. The New York Legal Aid Society, *Summary of Services, 1980–81.* CALS asserted at about the same time that its affiliated agencies, including the Legal Aid Society, handled 50,000 civil cases a year. Community Action for Legal Services, *What Is CALS?* 1 (1979). In fiscal 1979, the Legal Aid Society's Civil Division represented approximately 23,000 persons and its Juvenile Rights and Volunteer Division handled additional civil matters. The New York Legal Aid Society, *supra.*

53. The New York Legal Aid Society in fiscal 1979 represented in the Criminal and Supreme Courts 185,000 defendants charged with crimes. The New York Legal Aid Society, *supra* note 52. We were told that the Society represents 60 to 65 percent of all felony defendants in the city and 80 to 85 percent of all misdemeanor defendants.

54. In percentages, the major types of civil matters handled in 1981 by all legal aid agencies in the United States funded by the Legal Services Corporation were divorce/separation/annulment, 15.8 percent; landlord/tenant, 11.4 percent; AFDC/ other welfare, 4.7 percent; collection, 4.6 percent; custody/visitation, 4.5 percent. In major larger groupings of matters, the percentages were: family (divorce, custody, support, spouse abuse, etc.), 29.5 percent; income maintenance benefits (welfare, social security, unemployment compensation, etc.), 18.0 percent; housing (landlord/tenant, home ownership, public housing), 17.8 percent; consumer finance

(collection, bankruptcy, public utilities, contract warranties), 13.7 percent. Legal Services Corporation, *Annual Report 1981*, at 12.

55. We were told at one of the smaller legal aid offices in the city that if the office is forced to close for lack of funds, one of the lawyers and several of the paralegals plan to open a law office specializing in family law matters and will charge fees on a sliding scale based on ability to pay, but all clients will pay something. Those planning this venture are well-known and respected in the section of the city where they now work and believe their plan is viable if the local legal aid office is closed. Similar offices staffed by former legal aid personnel may be opened in many cities if legal aid offices are forced to close from lack of funds.

56. The Legal Services Corporation has classified different kinds of legal aid paralegals by function as these: case investigator, generalist, information and re-source specialist, intake interviewer, lawyer's assistant, litigation specialist, out-reach and community education worker, and paralegal coordinator. Legal Services Corporation, *First Year Summary Report on Paralegal Training and Career Development* 2–5 (1977).

57. The Society has a staff of criminal investigators, many of them former police officers, who are not considered paralegals. At one time, efforts were made to use paralegals as aides to these investigators but the investigators were so opposed to the aide concept that it was dropped.

58. Securing complete transcripts of trial court proceedings, for example, is a common problem as court stenographers frequently are dilatory in preparing and submitting transcripts. It may even be difficult to determine who the stenographer was in a particular case. On occasion, contempt proceedings must be brought to coerce transcript submissions.

59. The Society takes many matters on appeal that were tried by private counsel but clients cannot afford to appeal. It then must be determined if a conflict of interest exists because of Society co-defendant representation below. Conflict of interest also may arise if inadequate representation is the basis for an appeal and prior representation was by Society lawyers.

60. A 1982 survey of National Association of Legal Assistants' members sought to determine how others in the office where they worked, both lawyer and non-lawyer co-workers, perceived the role of those to whom the questionnaire was directed. A substantial majority of 207 respondents, and most of the respondents had achieved NALA certified legal assistant status, perceived that they were ac-cepted positively; but an appreciable minority, about 15 to 20 percent, thought they were merely being tolerated or not accepted by lawyers or other staff members in the office. Secretarial jealousy and insecurity on the part of young associates were seen as the main reasons for less than positive acceptance. Merzon, The Status of Legal Assistants in Law Practice, A Cameo Survey, 10 *Facts and Findings* no. 1, at 10 (1983), and supporting statistical summaries.

61. To reduce the risk of paralegal-secretary friction, some employers, we were told, will not assign a paralegal to a secretary who has been employed in the office longer than the paralegal.

2

THE PARALEGAL WORK FORCE

This chapter considers the kinds of people who become paralegals, their responses to their jobs, and employers' response to them. It is concerned with placement and career objectives as seen by paralegals and personnel policies and practices as viewed by management. The process of matching people to jobs is a complex one but certain patterns are apparent as to what persons are drawn into the occupation, how long they remain, and why. In this process, not only paralegals' skill and knowledge but their motivation, adaptability, and cost can be highly relevant. As the previous chapter shows, there are major differences among the various types of law offices in what they do and what paralegals do for them. There also are important differences among these types of offices in the kinds of paralegals employed and in the job perceptions and career lines of their paralegal employees.

PARALEGALS: WHO THEY ARE AND WHERE THEY WORK

Some basic demographic-type data about paralegals are considered below, the data coming principally from our questionnaire returns.

Age. Paralegals are relatively young, as is shown in table 8, with most of them concentrated in the 22 to 25 or 26 to 35 age brackets. This reflects the appeal of the occupation to recent college graduates as well as a high occupational dropout rate. The large private law firms, which draw heavily on bright college graduates who often treat paralegal employment as a transitory step to more permanent careers, have a particularly high concentration of paralegals in the youngest age groups. The comparatively youthful age of most paralegals is also partially attributable to the newness of the occupation as a source of large-scale employment. Many of the veterans who are making paralegal employment a permanent career are

Table 8.
Age Distribution

	Large firms	Medium-sized firms	Small firms	Corporate law de-partments	Govern-ment law offices	Legal aid	All offices
Under 22	7%	2%	3%	0%	3%	0%	3%
22–25	58	45	29	32	32	20	40
26–35	31	41	32	54	35	52	39
Over 35	4	12	35	14	30	28	17
	(N=91)	(N=113)	(N=31)	(N=37)	(N=71)	(N=46)	(N=389)[a]

[a]Twenty respondents did not indicate their ages and are excluded from the table.

still young. Our data further show that older persons, those over 35, are a minority among paralegals in every type of law office, with the greatest percentage concentration of older paralegals found in small firms and legal aid and government.

Sex. Most paralegals are women—approximately two-thirds of our total sample, as is shown by table 9. There are, however, sharp variations among different kinds of offices in the percentages of female paralegals they employ. As disclosed by table 9, medium-sized firms have the highest percentage of women and government agencies and legal aid offices the smallest. The percentage of paralegals who are women may be considerably higher in other parts of the country than table 9 implies may be the case in New York City. Sample surveys elsewhere show 85 to 95 percent of paralegals to be women.[1] There are plausible reasons for the high percentage of women paralegals. In pay and status, paralegal positions are closer to clerical than professional positions in many law offices and most clerical positions in law offices are held by women. Men are still reluctant to enter occupations characterized as women's. As a male paralegal in a corporate law department told us: "Paralegal work is largely a women's occupation and male pride discourages men from entering it. I do not intend to make paralegal work a permanent career." Another paralegal remarked: "There is a stigma attached to being a paralegal, especially for men. Paralegals are the nurses of the legal profession, and I am a bit ashamed to tell people what I am doing." Paralegal work also has a strong attraction to a great number of young women about to enter the white-collar job market but who lack the interest or qualifications to become lawyers or business executive trainees, are fitted by background and ability to become typists or secretaries, but want something more prestigious and important than a job centered on typing. The paralegal schools appeal to this group as a viable and preferred option to secretarial school. Paralegal schools have a comparable appeal to few young men.[2] There seems to be a significant correlation between recruiting sources and distribution of paralegals by sex. The type of office that apparently relies most on the paralegal schools in recruiting paralegals, the medium-sized firm, has the highest percentage of women paralegals; the type of office that relies least on the paralegal schools, the government law office, has the lowest percentage of women paralegals. (Compare tables 8 and 9.) Table 9 also shows differences in the percentages of women paralegals among different age groups, with a substantially lower percentage in the 26–35 age group compared to those in the immediately older and younger groups.

Ethnicity and religion. Table 10 reflects the ethnic identity of our questionnaire respondents.[3] It is striking that Hispanics, who constitute a sizable proportion of New York City residents, are so meagerly represented, and Blacks, who also make up a large proportion of New York City residents, show up prominently only in legal aid. Although in our interviews we heard

Table 9.
Sex by Age
(Percentages of Respondents who are Women, by Age Group[a])

Age	Large firms	Medium-sized firms	Small firms	Corporate law de-partments	Govern-ment law offices	Legal aid	All offices
Under 22	33% (N=6)	100% (N=2)	100% (N=1)	0% (N=0)	0% (N=2)	0% (N=0)	45% (N=11)
22–25	70% (N=53)	90% (N=51)	67% (N=9)	67% (N=12)	52% (N=23)	67% (N=9)	73% (N=157)
26–35	61% (N=28)	74% (N=46)	60% (N=10)	60% (N=20)	44% (N=25)	38% (N=24)	58% (N=153)
Over 35	75% (N=4)	100% (N=14)	82% (N=11)	80% (N=5)	52% (N=21)	77% (N=13)	75% (N=68)
All ages	65% (N=91)	85% (N=113)	71% (N=31)	65% (N=37)	48% (N=71)	54% (N=46)	67% (N=389)[b]

[a]Percentages are the percentage of respondents in each age category and office type who are women. The numbers in parentheses are the total number of respondents in each category.

[b]Twenty respondents did not indicate their ages and are excluded from the table. Eleven of these are women, five are men, and four did not indicate their sex.

Table 10.
Ethnicity[a]

Ethnicity	Large firms	Medium-sized firms	Small firms	Corporate law departments	Government law offices	Legal aid	All offices
Jewish	36%	34%	30%	5%	20%	9%	25%
Irish	12	16	6	29	11	19	15
Italian	10	10	12	10	14	4	10
Western European[b]	14	17	30	10	9	13	14
Eastern European[c]	2	2	3	0	1	4	2
Black	1	2	6	5	12	32	8
Hispanic	0	2	6	0	4	6	2
Asian	3	0	0	0	1	0	1
Greek	4	0	0	2	1	0	1
No response	24	24	12	41	32	23	26
	(N=92)	(N=115)	(N=33)	(N=41)	(N=81)	(N=47)	(N=409)

[a]Percentages sum to more than 100% due to multiple responses by persons of mixed ethnic background.
[b]For example, Scandinavian, English, or German.
[c]For example, Hungarian, Polish, or Czech.

nothing that would indicate that any of the offices at which we interviewed had policies of discrimination against Hispanics or Blacks in hiring paralegals, table 10 reflects a lack of affirmative action policies for paralegal hiring from these minority groups.[4] The Irish, an old and well-assimilated ethnic group in New York City, are found in all levels of society and throughout the legal system, but as paralegals they hold a particularly important place in corporate law departments. Jews are extensively represented in the American legal profession, especially in New York City, which has a large and generally well-educated Jewish population, so it is no surprise that there are so many Jewish paralegals in private New York City law firms. Another numerically prominent ethnic group in New York City is the Italians. Over the past generation, Italians in much larger numbers have been attending college and this helps explain the significant showing of Italians in almost every type of office. Ethnic makeup is no doubt one respect in which New York City paralegals differ substantially from paralegals in many other American communities. Highlights of table 11, religious preference, are that Catholics constitute a large percentage of paralegals in every type of office but are particularly prevalent in corporate law departments; Jews are most frequently represented in large and mid-sized firms; and in numbers, Protestants generally trail both Catholics and Jews but are the largest group in legal aid, partly because of the substantial incidence of Blacks among legal aid paralegals. Tables 10 and 11, however, both show a lack of numerical dominance by any ethnic or religious group within the paralegal population reporting. The polyglot character of New York City appears to carry over into this important law office support occupation.

Marital status. Overall, a substantial percentage of paralegals is married, as shown by table 12. This supports statements made to us during interviews that marriage is not a significant cause of occupational dropout for either women or men paralegals. The low percentage of married big-firm paralegals can be attributed to so many in this group being uncertain about their careers and not ready as yet to settle down. They also are somewhat younger than paralegals in other types of offices.

Higher education. Data on paralegal college attendance is presented in table 13. This table shows that the vast majority of New York City paralegals have attended college and that over three-fourths have graduated with a baccalaureate degree. We were told at a number of offices during our interviews that those offices would hire only college graduates for paralegal work. Many of the paralegals without college experience are secretaries or clerical employees who have been promoted from within the employing organization. Legal aid also has some paralegal positions, particularly some in criminal defense, for which college training is of less value than for most paralegal work. Table 14 shows that over one-third of the paralegals in our sample attended elite or prestige colleges, the concen-

Table 11.
Religious Preference

Religion	Large firms	Medium-sized firms	Small firms	Corporate law de-partments	Govern-ment law offices	Legal aid	All offices
Jewish	35%	37%	30%	5%	19%	9%	26%
Catholic	23	32	36	49	33	28	32
Protestant	21	16	21	20	16	36	20
Other	4	1	0	2	4	4	3
No preference or no response	17	15	12	24	28	23	20
	(N = 92)	(N = 115)	(N = 33)	(N = 41)	(N = 81)	(N = 47)	(N = 409)

Table 12.
Marital Status by Sex
(Percentages of respondents who are married by sex[a])

Sex	Large firms	Medium-sized firms	Small firms	Corporate law de-partments	Govern-ment law offices	Legal aid	All offices
Female	19%	32%	42%	50%	46%	42%	34%
	(N = 59)	(N = 98)	(N = 24)	(N = 26)	(N = 35)	(N = 26)	(N = 268)
Male	15%	13%	38%	58%	34%	52%	32%
	(N = 33)	(N = 16)	(N = 8)	(N = 12)	(N = 38)	(N = 21)	(N = 128)
Both sexes[b]	17%	29%	41%	53%	40%	47%	34%
	(N = 92)	(N = 114)	(N = 32)	(N = 38)	(N = 73)	(N = 47)	(N = 396)

[a]Percentages are the percentage of respondents in each sex and office type who are married. The numbers in parentheses are the total number of respondents in each category.
[b]Thirteen respondents did not indicate their marital statuses and are excluded from the table.

Table 13.
College Attendance and Degree Earned

	Large firms	Medium-sized firms	Small firms	Corporate law de-partments	Govern-ment law offices	Legal aid	All offices
Earned four-year degree	97%	80%	64%	68%	73%	60%	78%
Attended college but did not earn four-year degree	3	14	15	27	22	26	16
Did not attend college	0	6	21	5	5	15	7
	(N=92)	(N=115)	(N=33)	(N=41)	(N=81)	(N=47)	(N=409)

Table 14.
Type of Undergraduate College Attended

College type	Large firms	Medium-sized firms	Small firms	Corporate law de-partments	Govern-ment law offices	Legal aid	All offices
Elite[a]	33%	3%	18%	2%	10%	17%	14%
Prestige[b]	40	25	18	27	9	9	23
Other four-year	24	63	36	56	62	45	49
Two-year	0	1	0	2	1	9	2
Foreign	0	0	6	0	7	0	2
Attended college but college not identified	1	1	0	0	4	0	1
Attended colleges in two or more categories	2	2	0	0	1	4	2
Did not attend college	0	3	9	5	4	6	4
No response	0	3	12	7	2	11	3
	(N = 92)	(N = 115)	(N = 33)	(N = 41)	(N = 81)	(N = 47)	(N = 409)

[a]Elite colleges are the 33 four-year colleges in the United States identified as most competitive in student admissions by 1 *Barron's Profile of American Colleges* x (12th ed. 1980), e.g., Columbia, Princeton, and Yale.

[b]Prestige colleges are the four-year colleges in the United States identified by *Barron's* as highly competitive or very competitive in student admissions. *Barron's, supra* note a, at x–xii. Fifty-two colleges are listed as highly competitive, e.g., Barnard, Colgate, and Vassar; and 105 collges are listed as very competitive, e.g., Fordham, NYU, SUNY Stony Brook, and Yeshiva.

tration from such colleges being very pronounced in large firms. Substantial percentages of elite-college paralegals also were found in small firms and legal aid offices, ideological commitment to serving the poor being the apparent reason for the attraction of legal aid to those from elite colleges. Despite the advantage that persons from elite and prestige colleges seem to have in securing paralegal jobs, the paralegal occupation offers many opportunities to those from more average colleges. Overall, about half of our sample went to nonelite or nonprestige four-year colleges, and in all types of offices an appreciable percentage of the sample went to these colleges. However, medium-sized firms and government law offices seem to provide the most paralegal opportunities and most attractions to persons from colleges of lesser stature. There obviously is a large cadre of persons who have been educated in these institutions who can perform very satisfactorily as paralegals. The major field of study by paralegals while in college, reported on in table 15, discloses a remarkable concentration in the humanities or social sciences by paralegals in all types of law offices. These fields may provide excellent background training for graduate study, including law school, but generally are not aimed at direct entry into a particular vocation. Many persons with only this kind of liberal arts college training, especially if they are not graduates of elite colleges, find it impossible to enter paraprofessional employment without completing a paraprofessional training program, such as a paralegal school course of study. A college major in such subjects as history, philosophy, or political science—even with a baccalaureate degree—ordinarily does not open up very attractive job prospects without more training. The small percentage of physical and biological science majors in table 15 implies that persons with majors of this type normally take a different vocational track. These majors tend to move into such occupations as medicine, engineering, and architecture, or into a business closely related to the physical or biological sciences. At the paraprofessional level they are likely to be found in one of the paraprofessional health service occupations. Law is normally outside their sphere of vocational interest. Persons who have majored in business also are a rather small percentage of our sample, although not surprisingly their percentage is highest in corporate law departments. Business majors seem little attracted to paralegal work, probably because most of them can acquire better jobs elsewhere and because paralegal work does not fit their long-term career aspirations unless they are planning on going to law school. About one-third of our total sample of paralegals had some post-secondary school education other than college or paralegal school. This education, as appears from table 16, was either in a vocational training program, such as secretarial school, or in a university professional or graduate school. Twelve percent of the sample was currently attending law school, and 3 percent had earned a law degree. Thus a substantial minority of paralegals are in essence lawyer apprentices and their paralegal experience is tem-

Table 15.
Major Field of Study in College
(Undergraduate majors of those respondents attending college)

	Large firms	Medium-sized firms	Small firms	Corporate law departments	Government law offices	Legal aid	All offices
Social sciences	28%	28%	27%	31%	35%	42%	31%
Humanities[a]	51	34	42	18	26	16	34
Physical or biological sciences	4	5	0	3	0	5	3
Business	2	8	15	21	4	3	7
Other[b]	3	10	8	15	19	11	11
Double major in two different fields[c]	9	12	4	10	16	13	11
No response	2	3	4	3	0	11	3
	(N=92)	(N=108)	(N=26)	(N=39)	(N=77)	(N=38)	(N=380)

[a]Examples of humanities are English, history, American studies, philosophy, and fine arts.
[b]The most common other majors were education, criminal justice, and law.
[c]The most common double major in two different fields was in social sciences and humanities, 17, followed by social science and other, 17, followed by social science and other, 11. Double majors in the same field are included in that category (e.g., history and English double major is included in humanities).

Table 16.
Post-Secondary School Education Other Than College[a]

	Large firms	Medium-sized firms	Small firms	Corporate law de-partments	Govern-ment law offices	Legal aid	All offices
Attended secretarial school	4%	4%	15%	15%	7%	4%	7%
Attended other vocational school (excluding paralegal)	0	2	0	2	0	4	1
Attended or currently attending law school[b]	7	7	18	17	36	15	15
Earned law degree	0	1	3	2	10	0	11
Attended or currently attending other graduate or professional school[b]	14	14	6	15	21	13	15
Earned graduate degree[c]	7	7	6	7	15	11	9
No graduate or vocational study	80	77	64	54	53	68	64
	(N=92)	(N=115)	(N=33)	(N=41)	(N=81)	(N=47)	(N=409)

[a]Percentages sum to more than 100% due to multiple responses.
[b]Including those who earned a degree.
[c]Master's degrees, except for one Ph.D. in a corporate law department.

porary until the time comes when they are admitted to practice law or can become established as lawyers. A few of those who have law degrees are graduates of foreign law schools who have encountered difficulties in becoming qualified in the United States. In percentage terms, the apprentice group is particularly large in government law offices. Another appreciable minority of our sample, 15 percent, consists of persons with graduate or non-law professional school experience, many with master's degrees. A few in this group are using paralegal work as a temporary haven until they complete their graduate or professional programs, but most of them apparently have abandoned their prior career objectives and have taken paralegal jobs until they make more permanent plans. In a sense, these people have traded down, taking work below their previous career goals. Many of those with secretarial or other clerical backgrounds, on the other hand, have traded up, paralegal jobs being superior to their earlier career objectives.

Father's occupation. The occupation of a person's father generally is a strong indication of that person's social class background. A father's occupation usually has an important influence on family affluence and financial security and on the opportunities, aspirations, values, and status of family members. As table 17 makes evident, paralegals come from a wide range of social class backgrounds and an individual's particular background may be an important determinant of where that person is employed. Paralegals with professional or upper- or middle-level management and administration backgrounds, as disclosed by their fathers' occupations, are most extensively represented in private law firms, especially the large firms. Blue-collar backgrounds are largely absent among large-firm paralegals but heavily represented in the paralegal population of corporate law departments, government law offices, and legal aid. Overall, skilled blue-collar backgrounds are much more prevalent than semiskilled and unskilled ones, with legal aid having the greatest percentage of paralegals from unskilled blue-collar backgrounds. Assuming a social class ladder based on father's occupation of professional and upper- and middle-level management and administration at the top, semiskilled and unskilled blue collar at the bottom, and the others in between, table 17 shows large-firm paralegals to be clustered heavily at the top of the ladder, with medium-sized and small-firm paralegals following somewhat behind, and paralegals from other types of offices averaging farther down the ladder, legal aid appearing to have the lowest average class ranking.

Compensation. Paralegals almost invariably are paid less than lawyers with comparable years of experience and these pay disparities are usually very considerable.[5] Beginning lawyers in New York City are generally paid two to three times as much as beginning paralegals in the same office. In large firms, it commonly is somewhat more than triple; in most other offices it usually is about double.[6] These ratio differences are due primarily to the

Table 17.
Father's Occupation

	Large firms	Medium-sized firms	Small firms	Corporate law departments	Government law offices	Legal aid	All offices
Professional[a]	39%	13%	33%	7%	9%	13%	19%
Upper- and middle-level management and administration[b]	32	25	15	10	12	9	20
Semiprofessional and paraprofessional[c]	1	3	9	2	0	6	3
Clerical and lower-level white-collar	1	5	0	5	4	4	3
Other white-collar[d]	7	23	6	22	10	9	13
Skilled blue-collar	3	10	12	24	28	28	16
Semiskilled and unskilled blue-collar[e]	3	6	9	7	10	15	8
No response[f]	14	15	15	22	27	17	18
	(N=92)	(N=115)	(N=33)	(N=41)	(N=81)	(N=47)	(N=409)

[a]For example, lawyer, physician, university professor.
[b]For example, bank officer, hospital administrator, securities analyst, army general.
[c]For example, primary or secondary school teacher, pharmacist, library cataloguer.
[d]Mostly descriptions too vague to classify except as white-collar.
[e]For example, taxicab driver, waiter, garage attendant.
[f]Includes some responses too vague to classify.

much greater compensation that beginning lawyers receive in some types of offices than in others. Beginning paralegal salaries are more nearly the same in all kinds of offices, although we did find some corporate law departments and a few middle-sized firms that consistently paid over market for beginning paralegals, but the large firms in our sample did not. Some government law offices pay substantially below the prevailing rate.[7] A few kinds of specialist paralegals, most notably those with an accounting background assigned to estates work, frequently receive a substantial salary premium. Supervisory paralegals also receive premium pay. Paralegals frequently are paid more than secretaries with equivalent seniority, but often less than the more senior secretaries assigned to the most senior lawyers. Modest annual pay raises for paralegals are customary in most offices, based on cost of living increases, some kind of merit evaluation scheme, or a combination of the two. Some private firms pay their paralegals annual year-end bonuses, frequently varying from year to year with the financial success of the firm. In exceptional cases, paralegals may be able to double their salaries with five years or so of experience, but the more usual increases have been about 10 percent annually. In unionized offices, pay increases are usually the result of collective bargaining agreements. Pay disparities between lawyers and paralegals usually widen as the two groups become more experienced. However, in government law offices and legal aid the percentage ratio of an experienced lawyer's compensation to that of an equally experienced paralegal often remains about the same, although the dollar gap of course widens as they become more senior. In private law offices, the percentage gap may also increase considerably with experience, ratios of 5 to 1 or more being common between lawyers and paralegals of equal seniority. From what we could determine, it is unusual for any paralegal in an office to be paid more than the most junior lawyer, and in some offices we were told that there was a policy that the maximum paralegal salary must be less than the minimum salary paid a lawyer. In many private law offices there is considerable overtime work put in by both lawyers and paralegals. Table 18 indicates that overtime work for paralegals is most common in large firms, a sizable proportion of our respondents from these firms reporting very extensive amounts of overtime. By comparison, a majority of those in our sample employed by corporate law departments, government law offices, and legal aid reported that they do no overtime work. Lawyers are not paid extra for overtime; in some law offices, especially the large firms, paralegals commonly are, usually at so much per hour.[8] Overtime payment practices for different types of firms appear in table 19. Payment for paralegal overtime work is almost universal in large firms and fairly common in other types of offices except government law offices and legal aid. The Fair Labor Standards Act, a federal statute, requires that many paralegals, including those not exercising substantial discretion and independent judgment in their work, be paid overtime.[9]

Table 18.
Overtime Worked

Number overtime hours per week	Large firms	Medium-sized firms	Small firms	Corporate law departments	Government law offices	Legal aid	All offices
10 or fewer	26%	44%	27%	15%	25%	17%	29%
11–25	30	17	18	12	7	17	18
26–40	16	5	3	2	1	2	6
Over 40	16	3	3	0	1	0	5
No overtime	8	23	30	61	60	57	35
No response	3	7	18	10	5	6	7
	(N=92)	(N=115)	(N=33)	(N=41)	(N=81)	(N=47)	(N=409)

Table 19.
Percentage of Respondents Who Work Overtime Who are Paid for Overtime

Large firms	Medium-sized firms	Small firms	Corporate law departments	Government law offices	Legal aid	All offices
98%	38%	41%	42%	7%	12%	53%
(N=80)	(N=80)	(N=17)	(N=12)	(N=28)	(N=17)	(N=234)

Even though criteria in the act are ambiguous as to when paralegals are exempt from mandatory overtime payment requirements, violation by law office employers may be very prevalent. Most all paralegal compensation includes some fringe benefits of monetary value, in addition to salary.[10] These benefits are especially attractive in some of the corporate law departments and may include, in addition to the usual medical and retirement benefits, evening school tuition payments at local colleges or universities, liberal paid maternity leaves, and the option of part-time employment to mothers while their children are small.

PARALEGAL JOB PERCEPTIONS

There is a great deal of dissatisfaction by paralegals with their jobs, dissatisfaction that exceeds the normal proclivity of humans to complain about the way life is treating them. Paralegal dissatisfaction is sufficiently obvious and troublesome that it has been the subject of considerable study and commentary in the paralegal literature, along with the related subject of job satisfaction.[11] In our questionnaire we asked for the major source of job dissatisfaction; the responses are summarized in table 20. No room for advancement and boring work were the main dissatisfactions reported, with boring work showing up most prominently in answers of large-firm and corporate law department paralegals.[12] The dead-end character of paralegal work is apparent in most all law offices where paralegals are employed. To those staying in the occupation, chances to move up are limited or nonexistent and opportunities for more pay and responsibility usually are quite restricted. Dull work also characterizes the occupational life of many paralegals. Repeatedly in our interviews paralegals expressed dissatisfaction with the repetitive, boring, and uncreative tasks regularly if not exclusively assigned them. It apparently is common among many paralegals to characterize much of what they do as "idiot work," and other terms used by our informants to describe dull tasks they performed were "mindless work," "robot work," and "work that could be performed by trained apes." Offices that have an inordinate amount of dull paralegal work were referred to by some paralegals as "meat grinders," an apparent reference to the effect these offices were having on their paralegal staffs. The threat of workers becoming drones has been realized to a substantial degree by paralegals in some law offices, and the paralegal response understandably is negative. Other dissatisfactions that emerged from our questionnaire as being of some significance were that respondents' work is of little significance and their work is too hectic. In addition, during the course of interviews with paralegals we heard numerous complaints of inadequate instructions from lawyers when work was assigned, lack of feedback as to work quality when assignments were completed, and haughty and arrogant treatment of paralegals by lawyers, especially young lawyers.[13]

Table 20.
Major Source of Job Dissatisfaction

	Large firms	Medium-sized firms	Small firms	Corporate law departments	Government law offices	Legal aid	All offices
Boring work	34%	13%	9%	22%	9%	6%	17%
Work of little significance	9	2	15	5	5	6	6
Work is too hectic	2	4	3	7	9	9	5
No room for advancement	25	37	21	24	28	34	30
Work isn't socially useful	2	1	9	0	0	0	1
Too much snobbery and social ranking within the office	5	3	3	2	2	0	3
Other[a]	5	15	24	15	20	23	15
Multiple responses[b]	13	14	3	12	11	4	11
None/no response	4	11	12	12	16	17	11
	(N = 92)	(N = 115)	(N = 33)	(N = 41)	(N = 81)	(N = 47)	(N = 409)

[a]The most common other response was low salary.
[b]The question requested one choice, but 45 respondents indicated two or more choices. The most frequent choices were no room for advancement, 31, and boring work, 24, followed by work of little significance, 15; work isn't socially useful, 12; and too much snobbery, 12.

We also encountered some unhappiness among large-firm paralegals about not being invited to the occasional social affairs held for firm lawyers. This exclusion was considered a particularly objectionable affront because it could not be justified on differences in professional ability and because many of the paralegals considered themselves the social equivalents of the lawyers and their guests. There were complaints, too, from some of those who had been to paralegal school that they had not been given an opportunity to use all the skills they had learned in their school experience, particularly legal research. Rather surprisingly, we heard little objection to what paralegals were being paid. Other studies have found this to be a common complaint.[14]

Although job dissatisfaction is widely prevalent among paralegals, paralegals also consider that their work has many attractive features to it, as is shown by table 21. Working on one's own with minimal direction is by a considerable margin the most satisfying aspect of their work to our paralegal respondents, with having responsibility for important work the next most satisfying.[15] Clearly, paralegals prize autonomy and authority in the work they do. Only in legal aid is there top satisfaction disclosed from being of service to others; and the work environment, salary, and job security are major sources of job satisfaction to but few respondents.

Another way of paralegals' looking at their job settings is shown in table 22, perceptions of what makes a good paralegal. Substantive knowledge generally is not seen as a paralegal's main attribute, although one intellectual trait frequently is, the capacity to learn quickly. Ability to take on responsibility for important tasks also is very frequently seen as of primary importance, most especially in legal aid offices. The ability to keep performing dull and boring tasks appears most commonly as the principal paralegal attribute only among large-firm respondents.

There is also a widespread perception among paralegals in all types of law offices that in important respects paralegals are often superior to lawyers. As appears from table 23, a substantial proportion of our sample of paralegals expressed the opinion that in knowledge of office procedures, ability to communicate effectively with nonlawyers, considerateness of others, patience, and cooperativeness, paralegals often rank higher than lawyers. These views presumably came, for the most part, from experience in working with lawyers, and were relatively consistent among paralegals in different types of offices.

PARALEGAL CAREER LINES

There is a high degree of occupational dropout among paralegals and for many their careers as paralegals are short, a few years or less before moving on to some other career.[16] Table 24 is some substantiation of this, showing that a large percentage of paralegals in our sample, in all principal

Table 21.
Major Sources of Job Satisfaction

Single major source of job satisfaction	Large firms	Medium-sized firms	Small firms	Corporate law departments	Government law offices	Legal aid	All offices
Being part of important work	3%	7%	6%	10%	14%	6%	8%
Intellectual challenge	4	10	9	12	7	2	8
Working in a pleasant environment	7	3	0	2	1	0	3
Responsibility for important work	11	15	12	17	16	9	13
Working on own with minimal direction	26	32	33	22	15	19	25
Friendships with fellow workers	13	5	0	7	5	2	6
Being of service to others	0	3	3	0	2	32	5
A good salary	11	2	0	10	0	0	4
Job security	7	2	3	2	4	0	3
Other[a]	3	3	15	2	10	4	6
Multiple[b]	14	17	18	15	16	21	16
No response	1	1	0	0	10	4	3
	(N=92)	(N=115)	(N=33)	(N=41)	(N=81)	(N=47)	(N=409)

[a]The most frequently reported other satisfaction is learning about law and the practice of law, 8.
[b]The question asked for one choice, but 67 respondents indicated two or more choices. The most frequently reported satisfaction is working on own with minimal direction, 50 responses, followed by friendship with fellow workers, 37, and responsibility for important work, 32. Each of the remaining choices was selected by 20 to 28 respondents.

Table 22.
Most Important Paralegal Attribute

	Large firms	Medium-sized firms	Small firms	Corporate law departments	Government law offices	Legal aid	All offices
Knowledge of the law	0%	6%	3%	5%	7%	13%	5%
Willingness to follow directions	8	4	6	7	11	0	6
Ability to get on with others	1	2	0	0	4	0	1
Willingness to work long, hard hours	2	1	0	0	1	0	1
Ability to take on responsibility for important tasks	20	30	18	37	23	43	28
Capacity to learn quickly	22	36	52	24	25	15	28
Ability to keep performing dull and boring tasks	28	3	0	15	1	2	9
Other	5	6	9	2	6	4	6
Multiple responses[a]	12	10	12	10	12	15	12
No response	2	1	0	0	9	9	3
	(N=92)	(N=115)	(N=33)	(N=41)	(N=81)	(N=47)	(N=409)

[a]The question requested one choice but 48 respondents indicated two or more choices. The most frequent choices were capacity to learn quickly, 39; ability to take responsibility, 35; and willingness to follow directions, 24. Each of the remaining choices was selected by 14 to 19 respondents.

Table 23.
Important Ways in Which Paralegals Believe They Are Superior to Lawyers[a]

	Large firms	Medium-sized firms	Small firms	Corporate law departments	Government law offices	Legal aid	All offices
Ability to communicate effectively with nonlawyers	32%	43%	45%	37%	31%	51%	38%
Patience	27	28	39	20	23	30	27
Cooperativeness	26	28	33	22	22	13	24
Subservience	17	9	15	7	12	6	11
Consideration of others	35	28	36	22	22	17	27
Knowledge of office procedures	38	46	52	49	51	34	44
Ability to type or operate other office equipment	8	23	39	15	17	9	17
None	10	11	3	17	16	11	12
Other[b]	18	36	9	2	10	15	19
No response	1	2	6	7	11	6	5
	(N=92)	(N=115)	(N=33)	(N=41)	(N=81)	(N=47)	(N=409)

[a]Percentages sum to more than 100% due to multiple responses.
[b]The most common other responses were better organized, 19; more knowledge about relevant details or better at working with detail, 15; and more common sense, 8.

age groups, have less than three years of experience as paralegals; a considerable percentage have less than one year; and those with over six years are very much in the minority. Legal aid has the greatest percentage of more experienced paralegals, the large firms the smallest. Short average career spans in paralegal work are to be expected, given the high incidence of dissatisfaction among those in the occupation, the relatively young average age of paralegals, and the comparatively high educational level of most paralegals. Many find the occupation disappointing and their youth and education, supplemented perhaps by what they learned as paralegals, enable them to move into another career and to do so in a relatively short period of time.[17] Table 25 also shows the startling fact that overall only 5 percent of our respondents planned on a long-term paralegal career before becoming paralegals. The most common pre-paralegal career objective of these people was becoming a lawyer, 39 percent so reporting. In many instances, as indicated by table 26, this early objective of becoming a member of the bar was tentative, as most of our respondents planning on going to law school became paralegals to determine if they really wanted to be lawyers. This qualified outlook was most pronounced among large-firm paralegals. There are a number of other possible advantages relative to becoming lawyers that these people may gain from paralegal employment: it provides an experience base that may help them in gaining entry to the law school of their choice or in getting a job when they are admitted to practice; the experience may make them better law students and better lawyers; they want a breather before starting law school and paralegal work provides a useful and remunerative interlude; or it may help finance their way through law school.

Career plans of our respondents, as of the time they provided questionnaire responses, are considered in table 27. As of this time, 17 percent reported being satisfied with their present job and planned to stay indefinitely; the remainder expressed the intent of moving on to other jobs or activities. Eleven percent hoped to find a better paralegal job, bringing to 28 percent those that apparently expected to make paralegal work a relatively permanent career. For many of these employed paralegals, however, a lawyer career continued to have great attraction: 26 percent of the sample planned to remain in their present job only until they entered or finished law school. Going on to some other type of college or university program also remained top priority for a substantial number of respondents. Table 27 gives strong support to the proposition that for most employed paralegals, paralegal work is seen as merely a transition to some other career.

In their career plans, large-firm paralegals among our respondents are unique in several respects: the large percentage who plan on going to law school, the small percentage with some law school experience, and the small percentage planning to stay indefinitely with the current employer

Table 24.
Duration of Paralegal Employment by Age[a]

	Large firms			Medium firms			Small firms			Corporate law departments			Government law offices			Legal aid		
	Under 26	26–35	36+	Under 26	26–35	36+	Under 26	26–35	36+	Under 26	26–35	36+	Under 26	26–35	36+	Under 26	26–35	36+
Under 1 year	50%	17%	33%	33%	18%	18%	29%	22%	0%	50%	22%	0%	38%	44%	0%	22%	11%	0%
1–3 years	43	43	0	58	33	36	57	33	11	50	28	25	62	39	50	44	39	0
3–6 years	8	30	67	7	30	27	14	22	22	0	39	0	0	11	25	22	28	25
Over 6 years	0	9	0	2	20	18	0	22	67	0	11	75	0	6	25	11	22	75
	(N=40)	(N=23)	(N=3)	(N=43)	(N=40)	(N=11)	(N=7)	(N=9)	(N=9)	(N=12)	(N=18)	(N=4)	(N=21)	(N=18)	(N=16)	(N=9)	(N=18)	(N=12)

[a]Includes paralegal employment with current and previous employers. Ninety-six respondents who did not indicate age or dates of employment are excluded from the table.

Table 25.
Long-Term Occupational Objectives Before Becoming a Paralegal

	Large firms	Medium-sized firms	Small firms	Corporate law de-partments	Govern-ment law offices	Legal aid	All offices
Remain a paralegal	0%	9%	12%	5%	0%	13%	5%
Become a lawyer	46	25	55	39	42	47	39
Become a professional in an-other occupation	24	14	15	12	15	13	16
Become a law office administrator	2	3	3	2	5	0	3
Acquire an executive-level position in business or finance	8	18	0	27	6	4	11
Other[a]	3	11	3	7	10	11	8
Multiple responses[b]	7	10	12	5	9	4	8
No response/no plans	11	10	0	2	14	9	9
	(N=92)	(N=115)	(N=33)	(N=41)	(N=81)	(N=47)	(N=409)

[a]Includes two responses on the questionnaire but infrequently chosen: Become a professional assistant in another occupation, and become a secretary or other clerical worker.

[b]The question requested one choice but 32 respondents indicated two or three choices. The most frequent choice among these multiple responses was become a lawyer, 22; followed by acquire an executive-level position, 15; become a professional in another occupation, 11; and become a law office administrator, 9.

Table 26.
Reasons for Becoming a Paralegal Although Now Planning to Go to Law School

	Large firms	Medium-sized firms	Small firms	Corporate law departments	Government law offices	Legal aid	All offices
To determine if I really want to be a lawyer	28%	15%	15%	22%	11%	15%	18%
To save money to pay for law school	9	3	9	0	1	4	4
Failed to gain admission to law school of choice—to strengthen application	3	3	0	0	1	6	2
Developed interest in law school after becoming a paralegal	3	10	9	7	5	17	7
Other	3	3	15	2	5	6	5
Multiple reesponses[a]	2	1	0	0	4	0	1
Not applicable or no response	51	65	52	68	73	51	62
	(N=92)	(N=115)	(N=33)	(N=41)	(N=81)	(N=47)	(N=409)

[a]The question requested one choice, but six respondents indicated two or three choices.

Table 27.
Future Employment Plans

Percentage of respondents who intend to stay at present job until they	Large firms	Medium-sized firms	Small firms	Corporate law departments	Government law offices	Legal aid	All offices
Go to law school	30%	10%	15%	7%	10%	13%	15%
Finish law school	2	6	12	22	21	17	11
Go to a college or university program in business	2	4	0	7	1	2	3
Go to some other college program	13	4	15	2	5	6	7
Become sufficiently trained to get a better paralegal job	1	12	6	0	7	2	6
Find a better paralegal job, for which now qualified	3	6	6	2	4	9	5
Become sufficiently trained to get a better job in business or finance	9	5	0	12	2	4	6
Find a better job in business or finance, for which now qualified	8	3	0	12	4	2	5
Have a baby	3	3	0	5	1	0	2
Satisfied and plan to stay indefinitely	2	23	33	20	16	19	17
Other[a]	12	10	9	10	17	6	11
Multiple responses[b]	8	6	3	0	2	13	6
No response or no plans	7	6	0	0	9	6	6
	(N=92)	(N=115)	(N=33)	(N=41)	(N=81)	(N=47)	(N=409)

[a]The most frequent other response was complete a college or university program other than law school.
[b]The question requested one choice but 23 respondents indicated two or three choices. The most frequent choice was go to law school, 10; followed by become trained for a better job in law, 7; or business, 7; find a better job for which now qualified in law, 7; or business, 7. The remaining alternatives were each selected by 1 to 3 respondents.

or until they can acquire a better paralegal job. By comparison, several other types of law offices appear to be relying far more heavily on law student paralegals, a paralegal group with special attributes, particularly legal research abilities.

Some very able paralegals with the requisite credentials for law school have no ambition to become lawyers. Their principal interests lie elsewhere. Some of these people hope in time to move into business executive positions or another profession; others are heavily involved in the arts or the theater and are hoping for the break that will enable them to devote full time to these interests. We encountered one able paralegal who was an actress waiting for her chance. Another highly competent and experienced paralegal who could readily have gained admission to a top law school was a playwright who felt that going to law school and becoming a lawyer would take too much time from his writing and weaken his creative talents. There are, of course, some paralegals who are incompetent, are dismissed, or drop out of the occupation because they cannot find another paralegal job. We heard of few such people. Employer demands usually are not very stringent and once in the occupation it is usually possible to stay in if the paralegal so desires.

There is considerable shifting of experienced paralegals among employers, the usual objective being to find a better job. Some upward mobility also may be possible with the same employer, other than salary increases or informal shifts to more important work assignments. An occasional office has two or more formal paralegal classifications and paralegals can be promoted from one class to a higher one.[18] Law students working as paralegals have the possibility in some offices of being hired as lawyers upon admission to practice, although many firms will not make such promotions. There also are instances of experienced paralegals being elevated to office administrator positions. In addition, it is possible for experienced paralegals in many corporate law departments to be moved up to better paying non-paralegal positions outside the law department, with more promising futures in the company if they receive such promotions. These latter opportunities are sufficiently realistic possibilities that they often influence paralegals in seeking and retaining employment in corporate law departments.

It is common for paralegals to have held other kinds of full-time jobs before becoming paralegals. Table 28 shows how frequent such employment has been and the types of jobs previously held by those responding to our questionnaire. The frequency of prior employment is due partly to the recent rapid expansion in numbers of paralegal jobs, with the result that to fill them many persons are pulled away from other and generally less desirable kinds of employment. The prior employment pattern indicates further that some kinds of jobs, especially law office secretarial positions, are considered in some settings to be good preparation for paralegal

Table 28.
Full-Time Job Just Prior to Paralegal Employment

	Large firms	Medium-sized firms	Small firms	Corporate law departments	Government law offices	Legal aid	All offices
White-collar management and administration[a]	21%	21%	15%	22%	21%	11%	19%
Semiprofessional or paraprofessional other than paralegal[b]	9	2	0	5	7	4	5
Lower-level social service workers[c]	9	2	0	2	6	23	7
Law office secretarial and clerical	8	13	24	17	11	15	13
Other secretarial and clerical	4	9	12	12	6	11	8
Skilled blue-collar	1	1	0	2	0	0	1
Semiskilled and unskilled blue-collar	2	3	0	0	1	0	1
Professional[d]	0	1	0	0	4	0	1
Response too vague to classify	3	3	0	2	4	2	3
No prior nonparalegal employment	34	38	30	29	30	26	33
No response	10	8	18	7	10	9	10
	(N=92)	(N=115)	(N=33)	(N=41)	(N=81)	(N=47)	(N=409)

[a]These are mostly lower-level positions, such as trust company marketing assistant, corporate executive trainee, real estate management agent in small firm, and administrative assistant.

[b]Examples are social worker, primary and secondary school teacher, and librarian.

[c]Examples ae community organizer, social work aide, and probation intern.

[d]Most of these are foreign lawyers who held lawyer positions before coming to the United States but are not admitted to practice law in New York.

work, with the result that there is a regular flow of experienced workers from these jobs to paralegal positions.[19] Secretaries and other law office support staff also are often well situated to know what the attractions are of paralegal employment and to be aware of paralegal job openings where they work. There also are many paralegals who move laterally into paralegal work from white-collar jobs of roughly comparable status and salary that turn out to be of unstable duration or otherwise unsatisfactory. This is apparent from table 28. That table also shows that movement into paralegal work from blue-collar jobs is rare. The few persons among our respondents who held professional jobs prior to their paralegal employment are mostly foreign lawyers not as yet qualified to practice law in New York and some may never become qualified. They are doing what they know best but in lower-echelon positions.

Special reference should be made to a type of paralegal often employed in legal aid agencies and generally having somewhat different qualifications and career lines from other paralegals. These are the so-called community paralegals, persons from poverty communities with close ties to and deep understanding of those communities. In many instances the formal education of community paralegals did not extend beyond high school and most of them are non-White. They are particularly helpful in dealing with minority clients, witnesses, and others from minority neighborhoods. In some instances, the language facility they may possess is very useful, especially if they are of Hispanic background and are employed in an office serving Hispanic neighborhoods. Community paralegals are often older than the average in the occupation, as they frequently become paralegals somewhat later in life and tend to remain longer in the occupation. To them paralegal work has considerable prestige and there may be little opportunity to acquire jobs that are more attractive. From our interviews with some of these people, it appeared that they were generally more satisfied with their jobs than most paralegals, but we did talk to several with a decade or more of legal aid employment who were frustrated and provoked by lack of upward job mobility and the constant repetitiveness of their work. Some of the earliest community paralegals were products of a special new careers training program in New York City that had as one of its principal goals providing new careers through affirmative action to persons from low-income minority neighborhoods.[20] The original new careers movement faded away, but community paralegals have become important to the operations of many legal aid offices and no doubt reliance on persons of this type will continue.

LAW OFFICE PERSONNEL POLICIES AND PRACTICES

In staffing law offices with paralegals, difficult problems can arise as to recruitment, job design, compensation, and promotion. What recruitment sources to rely on can be a matter of concern to law offices both as to dependability and cost. Whom to hire from the many diverse types looking for paralegal employment when the relevance of credentials may be uncertain can prove troublesome. How to fit paralegals into the office job hierarchy and how much to pay them can be serious problems, too, especially as paralegal work so often falls in the vague area between professionals and clericals, and paralegal work assignments in this area may engender considerable interoccupational friction and jealousy. The high incidence of dissatisfaction among working paralegals and the high job turnover and dropout rate in the occupation also can be cause for concern. Should the employer take dissatisfaction and job-shifting risks into consideration when selecting among applicants, and can paralegal jobs be designed to reduce materially these risks? Or can risks of this sort be largely ignored by an employer because they have little or no effect on the amount and quality of work that the particular office turns out? These are worrisome questions for law offices and answers may not be the same for all employers.

Law offices usually resolve their personnel problems concerning paralegals and other support staff without elaborate study, complex procedures, or resort to such scientific expertise as is available. Law office staffs seldom are big enough or part of big enough enterprises to justify having personnel officers and the kinds of detailed testing, job descriptions, and job performance appraisals so often found in very large industrial and service organizations.[21] What impressionistically seems needed and effective, what is acceptable within the office, and what comparable offices are doing tend to determine most law office personnel planning and practice.

The major law office recruitment sources for paralegals are paralegal school placement services, in-house employees interested in advancement, and unsolicited applications responding to leads provided by applicants' friends or family members. Many offices also receive unsolicited resumes from applicants without specific job leads or sponsorship but who apply on the chance that there are or soon will be openings. Employment agencies are also resorted to by some law offices, particularly in hiring experienced or temporary paralegals. Table 29 highlights the extent to which these various sources are utilized and by what kinds of offices. It shows particularly heavy reliance by medium-sized firms on paralegal school placement services, with considerable resort to this source by small firms and corporate law departments as well. Advancement of secretarial and clerical personnel to paralegal positions appears fairly common in all types of offices except large firms. As recruitment sources, large firms are heavily dependent on leads provided applicants by applicants' friends or family members and on resumes sent to the firms by those seeking paralegal employment.

The data in table 29 was supported further by comments made by those we interviewed, with explanations in some instances as to why particular

Table 29.
How First Paralegal Job Was Obtained[a]

	Large firms	Medium-sized firms	Small firms	Corporate law departments	Government law offices	Legal aid	All offices
Paralegal school placement service	5%	40%	21%	27%	0%	13%	18%
Friend or family member	40	11	12	5	10	19	18
Advancement from secretarial or clerical job with same employer	3	17	15	37	12	19	15
Contacts from previous job	5	1	6	5	1	11	4
Employment agency	8	8	15	5	10	6	8
Newspaper advertisement	1	3	3	0	5	4	3
Distributing resumes	24	8	3	0	4	6	9
College or law school placement service	4	2	18	10	7	9	6
Civil Service publicity and testing	0	1	0	0	22	0	5
Other[b]	7	8	0	10	17	13	10
No response	2	3	6	2	11	0	4
	(N=92)	(N=115)	(N=33)	(N=41)	(N=81)	(N=47)	(N=409)

[a]Responses are listed under the category of office in which respondents were employed when they filled out the questionnaire. In a few instances first jobs were in a different category of law office.
[b]The most frequent other responses were through the CETA program, 8, and as a volunteer, 4.

sources were used. The big firms have a strong preference for recent graduates of elite colleges. As one big-firm partner told us: "We hire the best and the brightest paralegals just as we hire the best and the brightest associates." A large-firm paralegal supervisor who participated in paralegal recruitment remarked that the firm preferred Ivy League types and added: "I would rather have someone from Princeton over say an applicant from Florida State." When queried about selecting persons from more modest local educational backgrounds her response was: "Have you talked with any community college students recently?"

Because few Ivy League types go to paralegal school, other sources are resorted to for hiring paralegals with elite college backgrounds. What has evolved is a steady flow of applicants from top colleges or with top records from lesser colleges who, largely through peer group and family contacts, become aware of big-firm paralegal employment opportunities well-suited to those looking for short-term jobs in respectable surroundings with no obligation to make long-term commitments. It was reported to us that the pool of good prospects of this sort always is greater than the firms' needs, especially for the mundane tasks usually required in heavily documented litigation. In paralegal selections among well-qualified candidates, an applicant with good connections is likely to get the job over others, and strong recommendations from a client or a partner can make the difference in who gets hired. In one firm, selections on the basis of such personal backing were referred to as "political appointments." A big-firm partner in discussing these appointments noted emphatically that of course whom an applicant knows is never a consideration in hiring associates at his firm. This kind of personal favoritism, he clearly implied, is acceptable in selecting paralegals but not in selecting lawyers.

The fact that the turnover rate among those in the "best and the brightest" paralegal category is abnormally high does not seem particularly troublesome to the big firms provided that the tasks these paralegals perform can be quickly learned by those that succeed them. As a lawyer in one big firm told us: "We are not sorry when these paralegals leave," the intimation being that high turnover saves money, as fewer pay raises through seniority then must be granted. However, we did hear expressions of concern about paralegal turnover in large firms when the work involved takes some months to learn, with substantial loss in time and money when replacements must be brought in and trained. Estate planning and administration of decedents' estates were mentioned as fields in which loss of experienced big-firm paralegals can be disruptive and costly. If need be, to attract paralegals to these jobs in which longer tenure is highly desirable, the big firms will seek out candidates from other than their usual elite student sources. They also commonly seek temporary paralegals from other sources, including employment agencies, when work loads are exceptionally heavy.

Offices that rely heavily on the paralegal schools in recruitment do so because this procedure is quick, convenient, and economical. It also results in beginner candidates that by going through a paralegal training course have exhibited serious interest in the occupation and start work being familiar with legal terminology and with some of the procedures and concepts common in law offices. For most paralegal work, those who have completed paralegal school programs generally need less on-the-job training when they start work than do beginners without such training, and the paralegal school people usually become fully productive more quickly.

Offices that recruit many of their paralegals by promotion of secretarial and clerical personnel from within the organization usually impose less stringent educational requirements on those being promoted than on other paralegals they hire. For example, insiders at some offices, unlike outsiders, may not be required to have had either college or paralegal school educations. It is felt that the morale boosting benefits of in-house promotion policies and the advantages of selecting persons whose attitudes and capabilities have been carefully observed on the job make up for any educational deficiencies insiders may have compared to outsiders. Some offices also are finding that those secretaries and clericals promoted from within the organization to paralegal positions are less likely to be dissatisfied with their jobs than the frequently better-educated persons hired from outside.[22]

From what those in law offices who hire paralegals told us, criteria that recruiters of paralegals also frequently look for are initiative and the ability to operate with some degree of independence. One recruiter told us, "I am looking for self-starters." Another said: "I want people who respond well to supervision but can be trusted to make minor judgment calls intelligently themselves." Despite the dead-end character of most paralegal work, employers obviously want their paralegals to exhibit enterprise and creativity, provided they do what they are told and are not chronic complainers. This behavioral blend can be difficult for paralegals to develop or sustain.

We encountered in government offices covered by civil service what appears to be a widespread reaction: approval that the system bars patronage but objection to the red tape and staffing mediocrity that civil service so often brings. In attempts to acquire more able paralegals, some government offices have circumvented or manipulated the system by hiring short-term or provisional paralegal employees.

Some law offices have overcome the dead-end nature of paralegal work by providing promotion opportunities to their paralegals. So, as discussed previously, some offices have established formal grades of paralegals, with promotion possible from grade to grade, and some employers will promote, when qualified, paralegals to attorney or other positions within the organization. These promotion-from-within policies are seen not only as helpful to employee morale but as strengthening the organization by attracting and better utilizing employees of proven worth, the same ends as are served by insider promotions to paralegal jobs. Large corporate and government organizations with many staff positions outside their law departments have obvious advantages in implementing in-house promotion policies for paralegals.

A law office characteristic that can have a major effect on staff morale, including the morale of paralegals, is the degree of equality within the office. Some offices are rigorously stratified, not only in work assignments, but in authority and status. In others, the staff is less rigidly differentiated and ranked. Some people have difficulty adjusting to highly stratified work environments; others find such environments quite acceptable whatever their position in the hierarchy. The negative features to many of highly stratified work situations usually become less objectionable if there is a strong sense of community within the work force resulting from friendly personal interactions carried over to off-work contacts. This is especially so if the off-work interactions are among persons from different levels in the office hierarchy. Table 30 shows considerable after-work socializing by paralegals with other paralegals from the same office, substantially less with lawyers from the same office, especially partners or other senior lawyers. Large-firm and corporate law department paralegals are least likely to socialize after work with office personnel other than paralegals; legal aid paralegals are most likely to do so. Middle-sized firm paralegals in our sample, in addition to those from legal aid, engage in the most after-work fraternization with office junior lawyers and with secretarial and clerical employees of the office. As table 31 shows, patterns of paralegal companionship or lack of same with office personnel after work are similar to those of companionship at lunch, except that associations at lunch appear to be more frequent and to involve more persons from within the office than those after work.

Paralegal staffing has been particularly troublesome for offices hiring their first paralegals and uncertain as to how paralegals will be received and how useful they will be. However, even some offices experienced in the use of paralegals have encountered staffing problems with their paralegals and are reconsidering their personnel policies for this occupational group. Paralegal discontent and turnover have raised doubts as to what personnel management practices are best. Overqualification of many paralegals for the work assigned them has suggested to some lawyers that more important and responsible work should be assigned to paralegals. Emergence of paralegal schools as major placement sources has resulted in new approaches to recruitment by many paralegal employers. Increasingly reliable and expanded employment agency services for those recruiting paralegals has become a further recruitment factor of significance. These are illustrative of what is to be expected, adaptation of law offices in staffing, as well as in so many other respects, to a maturing paralegal occupation with its own increasingly visible and effective organizations.

Table 30.
Regular Social Companions After Work[a]

	Large firms	Medium-sized firms	Small firms	Corporate law departments	Government law offices	Legal aid	All offices
Other paralegals, same office	45%	24%	0%	20%	10%	34%	25%
Associate or junior lawyers, same office	9	16	12	5	6	28	12
Partners or senior lawyers, same office	2	7	21	2	1	17	7
Secretaries or clerical personnel, same office	4	18	6	2	11	19	11
Paralegals, other offices	5	7	9	7	5	17	8
None/no response	54	55	64	66	75	49	60
	(N = 92)	(N = 115)	(N = 33)	(N = 41)	(N = 81)	(N = 47)	(N = 409)

[a]Percentages sum to more than 100% due to multiple responses.

Table 31.
Usual Lunch Companions[a]

	Large firms	Medium-sized firms	Small firms	Corporate law departments	Government law offices	Legal aid	All offices
Other paralegals, same office	87%	58%	18%	59%	35%	60%	57%
Associate or junior lawyers, same office	22	29	21	15	27	45	27
Partners or senior lawyers, same office	3	14	36	10	16	26	15
Secretaries or clerical personnel, same office	13	43	45	17	26	43	31
Paralegals, other offices	8	21	12	5	4	23	12
Others from outside the office	38	53	45	37	43	51	45
Alone	42	50	58	27	54	40	46
No response	0	3	3	7	6	2	3
	(N=92)	(N=115)	(N=33)	(N=41)	(N=81)	(N=47)	(N=409)

[a]Percentages sum to more than 100% due to multiple responses.

NOTES

1. Ninety-five percent of those responding to a 1979 sample survey of paralegals in twelve areas nationwide were women. S. Cramer, Study of Preferences in Continuing Legal Education Programs for Paralegals, at a5 (1979) (unpublished study by the Director of the Illinois Paralegal Association). A 1978 survey of paralegals in San Francisco showed 85 percent were female. San Francisco Association of Legal Assistants, *1978 Survey* 10 (1978), cited hereafter as San Francisco Survey. A survey in 1977 of a paralegal sample in the State of Washington reported that 86 percent of those responding were women. Washington Legal Assistants Association, 1977 Survey Results, in Kansas City Bar Association and University of Missouri-Kansas City Law Center, in cooperation with the Kansas City Association of Legal Assistants, *Systems for Legal Assistants, Resource Manual* 209, at 211 (1980). All of these surveys were made under the auspices of paralegal associations and a high proportion of those surveyed were paralegal association members. It is possible that women are disproportionately represented in paralegal associations compared to the paralegal population as a whole and hence that the percentage of women paralegals in the geographical areas surveyed is somewhat lower than the survey percentages.

2. Other reasons for the high percentage of women paralegals were suggested by some of the lawyers and paralegals we interviewed: many paralegals are women who would have gone into primary and secondary school teaching but that occupation has lost status and there are fewer teaching job openings than formerly; women are more accepting than men of dead-end jobs as fewer women than men view working careers in terms of upward mobility; women are more willing than men to take low-paid jobs, such as paralegal work, especially women who are second earners in a family; paralegal work has a particular appeal to women coming back into the job market after divorce or after their children are grown or of school age; many secretaries are willing to take paralegal jobs if offered because these jobs are seen as a step up in status; many families provide more working career push and encouragement to boys than to girls, which means that boys are more likely to become lawyers and girls paralegals.

3. The ethnicity question was a sensitive one to some respondents, with the result that some refused to answer the question or gave an ambiguous or incomplete response, such as "American."

4. A Black lawyer in a corporate law department told us that he believes the small number of Black paralegals in New York City is partly because the occupation is new and there is little awareness of its existence in the Black community. Compare this, he said, with nursing and other paramedical occupations, well-known to Blacks and in which Blacks are well-represented.

5. Our questionnaire included no request for salary information, except for an innocuous question on overtime compensation. This omission was conscious, as questionnaires were submitted to paralegals through their employers, we knew many employers were sensitive about the salaries they paid, and we were concerned that employers would not cooperate if salary information was asked for in the questionnaire. We were, however, able to secure considerable data on paralegal salaries from interviews. Some data on paralegal compensation in New York City,

as of 1977, also appears in Guinan and Ferguson, The Changing Role of Paralegals, 40 *Unauthorized Practice News* 280 (1977). Other survey data on paralegal salaries appear in Pener, Results of a Survey of Legal Assistants Programs, *Journal of the American Association for Paralegal Education, Retrospective 1983*, at 9 (1983), data as of 1983 on starting and average paralegal salaries in a number of communities; Kaiser, Salary Surveys of University of California Los Angeles Extension Attorney Assistant Training Program, *Journal of the American Association for Paralegal Education, supra*, at 219, salary data 1979–83 for graduates of the U.C.L.A. paralegal program; Robon, Survey of University of Toledo Legal Assisting Technology Graduates, *Journal of AAfPE, supra*, at 277, salary data as of 1981 for graduates of the University of Toledo paralegal program; Childers and Jennings, Paralegal Salary and Job Function Survey, 21 *Law Office Economics and Management* 506 (1981), paralegal salary data for Arizona; and Law Poll, 69 *American Bar Association Journal* 1626, at 1627 (1983), data from a national sampling. A review of paralegal salary data from a number of surveys appears in Weisberg, Compensation of Paralegals, *Legal Assistants Update '81*, at 49 (1981).

6. In the early 1980s, the annual salary for a beginning paralegal in New York City was generally between $10,000 and $14,000 per year. An employment agency official, specializing in experienced paralegal placements, told us that in 1980, the usual salary for beginning New York City paralegals was $10,000 to $12,000; with two to three years experience, $12,000 to $15,000; and with over three years experience, $15,000 and up, top salary being $35,000 a year for fiduciary accountants doing estates work.

A 1981 survey of paralegals who attended Adelphi University's paralegal program between May 1975 and December 1976 shows average starting paralegal salaries of respondents working in the Greater New York City area as $9,838 and average 1981 salaries of these paralegals as $21,346. Adelphi-trained paralegals responding to the survey not working in the New York City area had starting salaries averaging $9,229 and 1981 salaries averaging $17,676. A 1982 study of Adelphi graduates who attended the school during 1980 and 1981 and had one to two years of paralegal experience in New York City disclosed average starting salaries of $12,851 and current salaries of $17,255 after one or two years of paralegal work. Data on Adelphi-trained paralegals were obtained from the National Center for Paralegal Training, a paralegal school consultant organization.

A January 1983 survey of graduates of the University of California at Los Angeles extension program for paralegals shows an annual median salary of $16,800 for those with less than six months experience in paralegal employment and a median of $30,000 with six years or more experience in such employment. These figures are for 228 respondents working in the Los Angeles area and do not include bonuses. Kaiser, *supra* note 5, at 245.

Many law firms bill clients for paralegal time at an hourly rate, as they also frequently do for partners and associates. A recent study sampling firms nationwide found the average rate for paralegal billings to be $34 an hour. Law Poll, *supra* note 5.

A rule of thumb in computing annual compensation for law firm paralegals, as well as associates, is to pay the employee one-third of what that employee is expected to bring in during the year from total chargeable hours of work. The hourly rate should then be the average amount that the employee would be expected to produce in fees per chargeable hour. Under this guideline, another third of what the employee produces goes for overhead and the remaining third is profit. On the so-called rule of thirds, *see* Ulrich, Legal Assistants Can Increase Your Profits, 69 *American Bar Association Journal* 1634, at 1636 (1983).

7. One major government law office in New York City pays its paralegals at such a low rate that an important paralegal school in the area reportedly will not recommend that office to its students for employment.

8. Some offices pay time and a half for evening overtime, double time for weekends. One office reported that because paralegals complained so about being asked to come in weekends for what turned out to be very short assignments, the firm now guarantees at least five hours pay for any weekend work.

9. Fair Labor Standards Act, 29 U.S.C.A. §§207 and 213 (1984 supp.). Also *see* Langer, The Wage and Hour Issue: Exempt vs. Non-Exempt, 6 *National Paralegal Reporter* no. 3, at 2 (1982).

10. For law office fringe benefits and their incidence, *see* Childers and Jennings, *supra* note 5, at 509.

11. On paralegal job satisfaction and dissatisfaction, *see* particularly Larson and Templeton, Job Satisfaction of Legal Assistants, in *Legal Assistants Update '80*, at 55 (1980); Templeton, Legal Assistant Job Satisfaction: A Further Analysis, in *Legal Assistants Update '81*, at 37 (1981); San Francisco Survey, *supra* note 1, at 51–83; and Childers and Jennings, *supra* note 5, at 511–12. In a 1979 survey of paralegals in different parts of the country, 72 percent reported that they were dissatisfied with their present position. Cramer, *supra* note 1, at a-11. In the study reported on by Larson and Templeton, *supra* at 59, paralegals ranked sixth among nine somewhat comparable occupations in their overall job satisfaction based on a long list of criteria. The other occupations with which paralegals were compared are accountants, engineers, managers, nurses, nursing supervisors, social workers, teachers, and secretaries. Only accountants, nurses, and nursing supervisors had general job satisfaction scores lower than paralegals. *Id.*, at 60. There are findings, however, that job dissatisfaction is high in most lower white-collar occupations, and major grounds for this dissatisfaction are diminishing opportunities to be one's own boss and undue emphasis on work efficiency that results in an oppressive and dehumanizing work environment, particularly objectionable to younger and better-educated members of the work force. *Work in America, Report of a Special Task Force to the United States Secretary of Health, Education and Welfare* 13–23 (1973).

12. The Larson and Templeton study shows paralegals least satisfied with the way co-workers get along with one another and the chance for advancement on the job, followed by the chance to do things for other people, the way company (firm) policies are put into practice, and the chance to do something that makes use of the paralegal's abilities. Larson and Templeton, *supra* note 11, at 59. All the paralegals included in this study were members of one or the other of the two major national paralegal associations. *Id.*, at 57.

13. A paralegal supervisor told us that a memorandum on how to treat paralegals and directed at new associates was needed in her firm. She felt that junior associates too often were discourteous and disrespectful in their dealings with paralegals and that paralegal resentment of this treatment was accentuated when the associates and paralegals came from similar social and educational backgrounds, as often was the case. Junior associates, in her view, do not like to feel that they are at the

bottom of the lawyer ladder in the office and seek to make up for their lowly status by emphasizing their dominance over paralegals with whom they work.

A Yale law student, following a summer clerkship in a large Wall Street law firm, had this to say about the firm's attitude toward paralegals: "They are regarded rather like office furniture. People tend to have conversations in front of them."

14. For example, see Larson and Templeton, supra note 11, at 59; and Childers and Jennings, supra note 5, at 512.

15. This corresponds rather closely to the findings of Larson and Templeton, supra note 11, at 59, in which the chance to work alone on the job was most satisfying, followed by the chance to try the paralegal's own methods of doing the job, freedom to use the paralegal's own judgment, and working conditions.

16. Some indication of relatively early dropout is the length of employment as paralegals of those still employed in the occupation. Other studies show that large percentages of paralegals have been in the occupation for three years or less: 82 percent in the San Francisco Survey, supra note 1, at 11; and 51 percent in the Cramer study, supra note 1, at a-9. The existence of a high occupational dropout rate for paralegals also was frequently mentioned by those we interviewed. No statistical study we are aware of has been made of the duration in the occupation of those who have dropped out.

17. Other kinds of career opportunities for those with paralegal experience are discussed in Farren, Legal Assisting: A Stepping Stone to Other Careers, in Legal Assistants Update '80, at 81 (1980).

18. For example, a major New York City firm has created a career path for its paralegal staff: senior paralegals, paralegals, and paralegal clerks. Senior paralegals have supervision and training responsibilities. The American Lawyer, May 1983, at 29. A leading San Francisco-based law firm has a somewhat similar three-tier classification: case clerk, legal assistant, and senior legal assistant. Case clerks apparently are assigned mostly to elementary and repetitious tasks in complex litigated matters involving a large volume of documents. Canillo, The Legal Assistant Career Ladder in a Private Law Firm, in Legal Assistants Update '81, at 3 (1981).

19. This is supported by the San Francisco Survey, supra note 1, at 11, which shows 11 percent of the respondents obtained their present paralegal jobs by promotion from secretary.

20. On the new careers movement involving paralegals and others, see A. Pearl and F. Riessman, New Careers for the Poor (1965); and S. Robin and M. Wagenfeld (eds.), Paraprofessionals in the Human Services (1981).

21. The personnel knowledge base utilized by personnel experts in large organizations is illustrated by the coverage in these texts: W. French, The Personnel Management Process (5th ed. 1982); S. Huneryager and I. Heckmann, Human Relations in Management (2d ed. 1967); and B. Schneider, Staffing Organizations (1976).

22. In one of the offices at which we interviewed, with a relatively large staff of paralegals, paralegals were overqualified, dissatisfied, and pressuring management for more training and responsibility. As those in charge of the office had decided that paralegal responsibilities would not be increased, added paralegal training by the office or paid for by it was refused. Management's feeling was that upgrading paralegal skill and knowledge under these circumstances would merely increase

dissatisfaction. This office has also altered its recruitment policies and is hiring more of its paralegals from its clerical ranks, as these people are more content with the kind of paralegal work the office offers and less prone to demand that the work be upgraded.

3

PARALEGAL ORGANIZATIONS

This chapter considers the various kinds of paralegal organizations that have emerged, with emphasis on paralegal associations and paralegal schools. Occupations characteristically develop organizations transcending the workplace. These organizations aim at furtherance of occupational interests in many different ways, as by enhancement of knowledge about the occupation, occupational education and training, help in placement of the occupation's personnel, improved rewards for occupational work, enunciation and enforcement of occupational standards of behavior, generation of support for occupational positions on economic and political issues, and increased occupational cohesiveness for the social enjoyment as well as power potential this can bring. Some occupational organizations are concerned with benefiting the occupation at large, others with benefiting only an occupational subgroup. Also, occupational organizations may concentrate their activities in a very limited geographic area or they may focus their attentions on a much larger area, even nationwide. The success of an occupation and perpetuation of its influence obviously can depend heavily on the effectiveness of its organizations.

As paralegals came to be recognized as a separate occupation and numbers of persons working in the occupation rapidly increased, paralegal organizations quickly emerged. These organizations are all marked by strong identification with the interests of paralegals and they commonly are modeled after lawyers' organizations.

All types of paralegal organizations have been going through an evolutionary stage of change and uncertainty, which is to be expected given their brief histories, and it may be some time yet before they reach a more fixed and stable existence. Progress by the paralegal associations and schools has been particularly impressive, but both associations and schools suffer from underfunding and overfragmentation. Unlike organizations of many other occupations, especially the established professions, paralegal organizations so far have generated little research or writing about their occupation or the disciplines in which paralegals work. Teaching materials directed principally at those preparing to enter the occupation are an exception to this. The massive preemption by lawyers and their organizations of published professional writing about law and the legal profession is an obvious deterrent to similar writing efforts by paralegals. In volume and quality the legal publication field is already well-covered. Another significant observation about paralegal organizations, discussed more fully in the next chapter, is that they are politically weak and not as effective as they are likely to become in identifying and taking stands on major issues important to the occupation.

ASSOCIATIONS

A common type of occupational organization is the trade, professional, or paraprofessional association formed to further occupational interests. Lawyers have many such organizations, including a network of general-purpose local and state bar associations and the mammoth American Bar Association with over a quarter of a million members, a large full-time staff, and an annual income of about $50 million.[1] It was to be expected that with the rapid growth in the number of paralegals and of their recognition as a separate occupation, paralegals would form their own associations. In the mid-1970s the present two major national paralegal organizations were founded, the National Association of Legal Assistants (NALA) and the National Federation of Paralegal Associations (NFPA).[2] There also are many local, regional, and state paralegal associations, most of them members or affiliates of either NALA or NFPA.[3]

NALA has approximately 1,500 individual members, including some student members and a small number of lawyer sustaining members. It also has twenty-nine state and local paralegal association affiliates,[4] and through individual and affiliate memberships represents approximately 3,500 paralegals.[5] NALA's home office is in Tulsa, Oklahoma, where it has a very small administrative staff, its officers and directors being working paralegals from all over the United States. NFPA, based in Washington, D.C., is essentially a federation of local and state paralegal associations, although it does have some individual sustaining members. The thirty-two association members of NFPA have a combined membership of about 6,000 paralegals.[6] NFPA has a paid executive director. NALA and NFPA each functions as do most national occupational associations: an annual members' conference and business meeting several days to a week in duration; volunteer officers and directors elected by the membership; a committee structure to assist in programming and administration; educational and informational publications pertaining to the occupation, including a newsletter distributed quarterly or more often;[7] development of an ethical code for its members and the occupation generally;[8] and programs that push for the occupation's best interests with outside groups based on the association's perceptions of those best interests.

Despite the two organizations being competitive as well as duplicative in much of what they do, differences between them exist. NFPA, as a federation, is more concerned with performing coordination and information exchange functions for its constituent associations. It has, however, sought to reach more working paralegals by a regional structure, with each region responsible for periodic conferences.[9] NALA's activities are aimed more directly at the individual paralegal and the association has placed considerable emphasis on continuing and basic education of paralegals. Its annual meetings include a series of workshops on legal subjects, it publishes and distributes text and cassette materials for self-study or use in paralegal school courses,[10] and since 1976 it has administered a voluntary certification program for paralegals.

Organized along lines of the American Bar Association's sections, NALA also has sections in each of five specialty fields of particular importance to paralegals: litigation, probate and taxation, real estate, corporate, and law office management. Only NALA members may join a section and there are added annual dues for section membership. Each section has its own officers, its own newsletter, and holds seminars in its specialty sphere.[11] NFPA also recently set up specialty sections, with separate sections for independent contractors, litigation, probate, public interest and advocacy, and real estate.[12]

NALA text and cassette materials include coverage of doctrinal fields of law frequently encountered by paralegals, suggestions for performing common paralegal work tasks, and checklists and forms particularly relevant to paralegal work. Some of these materials are designed as study aids for NALA's certification examination. The two-day certification examination, covering substantive law and law office management and skills, is given annually at regional testing centers. Educational and experience prerequisites are required to take the examination, and those who pass are recognized by NALA as being certified and are entitled to use the designation C.L.A. (Certified Legal Assistant) after their names.[13] Membership in NALA is not a requirement for certification and about one-third of those who take the examination are not NALA members. By 1984, 820 paralegals had been certified under the NALA program.[14] Participation in prescribed continuing legal education (CLE) programs and activities is required to retain certification.[15] In no state is NALA certification a legal requirement to working as a paralegal, but obviously those certified hope that certification will increase their status and salary.

The two associations have also taken somewhat different positions on intervention by bar associations in the affairs of paralegals, NFPA being more negative on such intervention than NALA. Thus NFPA questions the appropriateness of bar regulation of an "allied profession" and is critical of bar association guidelines directed at lawyers and prescribing proper utilization of paralegals by lawyers.[16] NALA considers as acceptable reasonable guidelines and procedures formalizing attorney responsibilities for paralegals.[17] NFPA also has opposed, at least until recently, the process by which the American Bar Association approves paralegal schools;[18] NALA apparently accepts it.[19] On state bar association inclusion of paralegals in divisions within the bar association structure, NFPA is opposed[20] and NALA favorable.[21] NFPA is concerned that such divisions will inhibit development by paralegals of their own state and local associations and reduce the membership and autonomy of the paralegal associations.[22] A similar NFPA-NALA split has existed as to proposals that the ABA set up an associate membership category for paralegals.[23]

One of the NFPA member associations is the New York City Paralegal Association (NYCPA). Founded in 1974, this local association of approximately 400 members has no paid staff and is operated by a dedicated group of volunteer officers, directors, and committee members. The association regularly publishes a newsletter for its members,[24] holds an annual business meeting, offers continuing legal education seminars for its members and others,[25] and maintains a placement service for members looking for jobs or hoping to switch jobs.[26]

Much of the membership in NYCPA consists of paralegals working in medium-sized private law firms, an indication that occupational commitment and push for professionalization are perhaps strongest among paralegals in this type of office. About 15 percent of the members are men, we were told. Despite the large concentration of paralegals in New York City and periodic membership drives by NYCPA, the association has had difficulties in building its membership. Many paralegals are unaware of NYCPA's existence, and others do not consider the association worth the time or required dues money. As table 32 shows, only 9 percent of the paralegals in our questionnaire sample reported that they currently were NYCPA members; an even smaller percentage reported being national association members. NYCPA membership among big-firm paralegals in the sample was almost nonexistent, and it was only 5 percent among our respondents in corporate law departments and government law offices.

The geographical size of the New York City area deters local paralegal association membership because of inconvenience in getting to seminars and other meetings. Many paralegals live in outlying suburban communities and are reluctant to stay in the city for evening meetings. Travel time from offices in other sections of the city makes it difficult for many even to get to luncheon meetings. Occupational turnover, with such a high percentage of paralegals remaining in the occupation less than three years, also is a factor that tends to hold down association membership, as is NYCPA's emphasis on the interests and concerns of private law firm paralegals, with

Table 32.
Organizational Membership[a]

Percentage of respondents belong-ing to	Large firms	Medium-sized firms	Small firms	Corporate law de-partments	Govern-ment law offices	Legal aid	All offices
New York City Paralegal Association	1%	17%	12%	5%	5%	11%	9%
National Association of Legal Assistants	1	3	3	0	0	6	2
National Federation of Paral-egal Associations	0	1	0	0	1	0	0
A paralegal trade union	0	5	0	0	27	55	13
Other association	0	8	0	2	4	4	4
None/no response	98	75	88	93	65	36	77
	(N=92)	(N=115)	(N=33)	(N=41)	(N=81)	(N=47)	(N=409)

[a]Percentages sum to more than 100% due to multiple responses.

little attention to the special needs and problems of paralegals working in the public sector or legal aid offices.[27] Paralegal associations in some cities apparently are doing much better than NYCPA in attracting and keeping members, but nationwide only a modest percentage of paralegals are members of local or state paralegal associations. NALA and NFPA can claim to represent only a minority of paralegals, partly because of the limited memberships of their local affiliates.[28] But, of course, paralegal associations are all quite new; and in their early years, most bar associations, too, grew rather slowly. As is true of many volunteer organizations, NYCPA also has had some difficulty in securing membership help for needed administrative and committee work and some of its seminars have been poorly attended.[29] Maintaining the association as a viable organization has been a struggle.

What do paralegals believe should be the main priority of paralegal organizations? As table 33 reveals, the most frequent response to this question was upgrading the status and influence of the paralegal occupation. By a wide margin, occupational upgrading was preferred as an organizational priority over other organizational activities. Even paralegals working in settings that have been organized by labor unions were generally most favorable to occupational upgrading as the main priority of paralegal organizations. The next paralegal organization priorities that received strongest support from our respondents were continuing education and pushing for improved paralegal salaries and working conditions. Providing an employment service, something a number of paralegal associations offer, was considered a prime priority by but few of those stating a preference.

In addition to participation in their own associations, there has been some very limited paralegal participation in the work of bar associations. Paralegals have attended and taken part as speakers and panel members in bar association seminars on paralegals. The American Bar Association Standing Committee on Legal Assistants has an advisory commission, with paralegal members, that may attend meetings of the committee. In 1981, the State Bar of Texas established a Legal Assistants Division, an organization of paralegals to be governed by paralegals but affiliated with the State Bar. The State Bar, an association of lawyers throughout the state, exercises considerable control over the division, and to become members, paralegals must be sponsored by the attorneys responsible for their work.[30] Some paralegal associations view the Texas Bar's paralegal division with suspicion and as a threat to the independence of paralegals and their organizations.[31] The American Bar Association has considered establishing a similar paralegal division but recently rejected a proposal to create a class of paralegal associate members.[32]

PARALEGAL SCHOOLS

As paralegals have increased in number, so have the schools that offer formal training to paralegals. Constituting both a response to and contrib-

Table 33.
Preferred Major Priority of Paralegal Organizations

The main priority of paralegal organizations should be	Large firms	Medium-sized firms	Small firms	Corporate law de-partments	Govern-ment law offices	Legal aid	All offices
Continuing education	11%	17%	15%	34%	15%	21%	17%
Employment service	4	0	0	2	9	2	3
Pushing for improved paralegal salaries and working conditions	21	15	3	12	20	17	16
Upgrading status and influence of the profession	48	47	52	41	27	36	42
Multiple responses[a]	9	10	9	7	10	19	11
No response	8	10	21	2	20	4	11
	(N=92)	(N=115)	(N=33)	(N=41)	(N=81)	(N=47)	(N=409)

[a]The question requested one choice, but 43 respondents indicated two or more choices. The most frequent choices were upgrading status of the profession, 35; pushing for improved salaries, 32; and continuing education, 29. Chosen less frequently were employment service, 14; and developing social contacts, 6.

uting cause of growing law office interest in hiring paralegals, paralegal educational programs have emerged in schools throughout the country.[33] The over 300 schools now offering paralegal education have become highly influential in creating and strengthening a sense of occupational identity and common occupational interest among those entering this field of employment. Their efforts to recruit and place students, including their rather aggressive advertising for students, have also enhanced awareness of the occupation by the public at large and lawyers in particular. Whether proprietary or nonproprietary, and both kinds exist, the schools are persistent and highly self-interested proponents of paralegals as a separate, respected, and influential occupational group.

The paralegal schools, however, are faced with serious and difficult problems. One of these problems is how to deal with the diverse types of persons being attracted to the occupation. In age, academic background, work experience, career ambitions, financial resources, and overall competence, there are great differences among those interested in obtaining a paralegal education. Which groups should the schools reject, and how can educational programs be adapted to accommodate the varied body of students that will be accepted? Funding and resource allocation are also major problems. Is paralegal education something that can be adequately financed solely from student tuition, or will it be necessary for the colleges and universities to provide substantial subsidies if satisfactory paralegal programs are to be offered? How much of the cost of paralegal education will employers pick up by paying placement fees to the schools, paying tuition of their employees enrolled in paralegal courses, or making gifts to the schools? How important are paralegal programs perceived to be by colleges and universities offering such programs; and what staffing, classroom space, and library books and facilities should the programs be assigned? The paralegal schools are at best modestly funded, and attracting and justifying more and better resources and the money to pay for them are among the schools most crucial concerns.

The nature and scope of education that the paralegal schools should offer is another of their basic problems. Given the wide range of paralegal work in law offices, how should training be tailored to the realities of the workplace? How much emphasis should be given to background understanding of the legal process; how much to training in such skills as writing, drafting, legal analysis, and data assembly; and how much to developing how-to-do-it competence in a particular specialty? Should the principal aim of the schools be to turn out persons capable of immediately filling narrow specialty slots in law offices, with minimal on-the-job orientation, or should it be to provide such persons with more broad-based grounding and skills so that they can take on a wide range of law office tasks but will need considerable on-the-job training effectively to handle most of them? Should the schools devote their attention exclusively to students with no prior paralegal experience, or should they also seek to provide experienced paralegals with continuing legal education? If the schools become involved in continuing legal education, should they offer programs jointly to lawyers and paralegals, with special attention to effective cooperation and division of responsibility between lawyers and paralegals? In their curriculums, teaching materials, and teaching techniques, should the paralegal schools be merely watered-down versions of law schools, or in what and how they teach should they depart in major respects from the law schools? If major departures from the law schools are needed, what should they be? Furthermore, to what extent should paralegal school instruction have liberal arts, non-trade school objectives: for instance, generating intellectual curiosity and broadening student understanding of subject matter being studied irrespective of what direct on-the-job benefits may thereby accrue to the students? Should paralegal schools offer both full- and part-time programs, how long should programs take to complete, and should there be degree-level and certificate-level programs? The paralegal schools are committed to attracting and training able paralegal candidates. But can they perform these functions effectively without overselling the occupation and creating expectations about opportunities that misrepresent what most paralegals can expect from available jobs? This, too, is a problem and one the schools are reluctant to admit even exists. Such, then, are issues about the nature and scope of their educational offerings that the paralegal schools are struggling with and trying to sort out.

Teacher staffing also poses a problem to the paralegal schools. Given their budgetary restrictions, what kinds of teachers should they be trying to attract: lawyers and paralegals or persons with other academic or occupational qualifications; those interested in teaching as a principal and permanent career or part-time adjuncts willing to take on classroom responsibilities as occasional diversions from practice or business; persons interested in scholarly writing and research as a major component of their academic work or those whose academic concerns are only teaching, with perhaps some supplementary administrative duties? Related to teacher recruitment problems is the problem of developing sufficient paralegal school reputation and status to attract outstanding teacher prospects, especially those willing to teach full-time. In most all respects, the law schools so overshadow the paralegal schools that enticing experienced lawyer academics into paralegal education rarely can be successful as conditions presently stand. However, in education as with other aspects of their occupation, should paralegals be seeking to model their institutions after those of lawyers or should they be moving in different and more independent directions?

The problems of the paralegal schools are similar to those of most other educational institutions offering vocational training,[34] but in paralegal education the problems are generally more pressing and unresolved because paralegal school programs are so new and their patterns of operation less fixed than in most fields of formal vocational training. Paralegal school programs go back only to the late 1960s, the first paralegal training program offered by an institution specializing in education apparently being given at the University of Denver College of Law in 1968 to a group of housing specialists.[35] Other programs followed soon after, offered by established educational institutions or by new schools concentrating on paralegal instruction. Among the earliest was a joint undertaking of Columbia Law School, the College for Human Services, and Community Action Legal Services to train minority legal aid generalists for neighborhood legal aid offices in New York City.[36] This pilot program had a new careers objective, too, and sought to provide paraprofessional career opportunities for persons from low-income minority neighborhoods.[37] Other early programs, more significant to paralegal education as it evolved, were offered by the Institute for Paralegal Training, a school in Philadelphia started in 1970 by several practicing attorneys solely to educate paralegals and still a major force in paralegal education. The Institute has been widely viewed as the leading quality paralegal training school in the United States and its organization and training formats have been models for a number of other schools.[38] In 1983 it opened a second training center, this one in Houston. The Institute also has a Continuing Education Division that offers short one- or two-day seminars in various big cities on topics of concern to experienced paralegals.[39] Originated as a proprietary school, the Institute is now owned by the Center for Legal Studies, Inc., a Washington-based consulting and educational organization. For a time it was owned by Bell & Howell, a large corporation principally engaged in manufacture and development of communications equipment and systems, including audiovisual and learning systems.

The number of new paralegal schools increased rapidly in the 1970s. An ABA study published in 1977 describes the paralegal programs of 125 colleges, universities, and institutes in the United States then offering such programs, excluding programs basically devoted to legal secretarial or criminal justice training or principally concerned with continuing legal education.[40] By 1981 the number of schools offering such programs had increased to 340[41] and to 380 in 1983.[42] California has the largest number of paralegal schools, with almost fifty of them, and there are schools in all but four states.[43] Enrollment in all paralegal programs is estimated to be about 32,000,[44] an average of fewer than 100 paralegal students per school.[45]

Most of the schools offering paralegal education programs are two- or four-year colleges, many of them community colleges and many of them serving local commuting students. There also is a considerable number of universities and private specialty training schools offering paralegal programs, the specialty schools restricting their training entirely or principally to paralegals and many of them proprietary institutions. Some of the university programs are offered by extension, continuing education, or general studies divisions of the universities. A substantial number of programs are offered by business schools or business departments.[46] Only a few law schools are assuming any responsibility for paralegal education.[47] The top-rank universities in scholarly prestige terms, with rare exceptions, have shown no interest in paralegal education, consistent with their lack of interest in most paraprofessional training.

There are about twenty-five paralegal schools in New York City or within reasonable commuting range of the City.[48] Most of these schools concentrate exclusively or principally in training persons with no prior paralegal experience, although some also have continuing legal education programs for experienced paralegals. It is possible that as the number of paralegals increases, more schools in New York City and elsewhere will offer continuing legal education programs for paralegals or expand the number of such programs that they now offer. Many of these CLE programs are likely to be very short-term, only a day or a few evenings in duration. CLE has an appeal to those paralegals interested in upgrading their competence, informing themselves about new legal or office procedure developments, or learning a new legal specialty. Short-term CLE programs, in particular, can be attractive to the schools because they can be financially quite profitable and can enhance the reputations of the schools offering them.

Paralegal programs most frequently referred to by law office personnel during our interviews were the ones at Adelphi University, New York University, and the Paralegal Institute (New York),[49] as well as one outside the area, the Institute for Paralegal Training in Philadelphia. From our questionnaire returns, as shown in table 34, Adelphi, the first paralegal school in the area to have received American Bar Association approval, appears to have trained about half of all paralegals working in New York City law offices who have attended paralegal school.[50] Given the number of schools in the area, this degree of dominance by one of them is remarkable. As table 35 shows, paralegals trained by paralegal schools are concentrated most heavily in medium-sized firms, 64 percent of all our questionnaire respondents from such firms reporting that they had attended a paralegal school. Quite substantial percentages of paralegal school attendance were also reported by paralegals working in corporate law departments, small firms, and legal aid. Attendance at paralegal schools is a major determinant of the setting in which new entrants into the occupation will work. Which school one attends in a large metropolitan area such as New York City also affects chances of getting a paralegal job. However, as yet, academic rank among those completing paralegal training programs is not, unlike law school rank for lawyers, a significant factor in the nature and quality of initial job placements.

It should be underscored that in the New York City area, as elsewhere, having attended a paralegal school is not a legal prerequisite for becoming

Table 34.
Paralegal Schools Attended
(By those attending paralegal school)

Most frequently attended paralegal schools	Large firms	Medium-sized firms	Small firms	Corporate law departments	Government law offices	Legal aid	All offices
Adelphi	53%	58%	25%	79%	18%	25%	51%
New York Paralegal Institute	24	9	17	5	27	6	12
New York University	12	7	17	0	0	13	7
Philadelphia Institute of Paralegal Studies	6	11	0	11	0	0	7
Long Island University	0	3	0	0	27	19	5
Other	6	12	50	5	27	44	18
	(N=17)	(N=74)	(N=12)[a]	(N=19)	(N=11)	(N=16)[a]	(N=149)

[a]Percentages sum to more than 100% because one respondent each in the small-firm and legal aid categories attended two schools.

Table 35.
Paralegal School Attendance

	Large firms	Medium-sized firms	Small firms	Corporate law departments	Government law offices	Legal aid	All offices
Percentage of total sample that attended paralegal school	18% (N=92)	64% (N=115)	36% (N=33)	46% (N=41)	14% (N=81)	34% (N=47)	36% (N=409)

or remaining a paralegal and that many successful paralegals have never been enrolled in paralegal school programs. Table 35 indicates that the percentage of all paralegals working in New York City who have attended paralegal school is probably under 50 percent, as it was only 36 percent in our sample.[51]

In our interviews, we encountered different employer attitudes toward paralegal school education as a factor in recruitment of new paralegal staff. In many offices, such training is considered irrelevant; in some offices it is something of a plus, especially for nonlitigation specialty positions; and in some places, having completed a paralegal school program is a prerequisite or near prerequisite to serious consideration of candidates. We found no instances of employer insistence on post-employment paralegal attendance at paralegal school, although some employers encourage such attendance, especially by their less experienced paralegals, and may even pay expenses of attending. Whatever criteria employers apply in hiring paralegals, most of those responding to our questionnaire who had attended paralegal school were of the opinion that their paralegal school attendance had helped substantially in securing employment. This is manifest from table 36. This table also shows a fairly widespread feeling that the paralegal school experience made those attending more competent paralegals but reflects less positive feelings about the helpfulness of paralegal school attendance in obtaining salary raises or job promotions.

Most paralegal school students are young women with college degrees or some college experience, with no prior work experience in a law office, who wish to be employed in a white-collar occupation, and are attracted by the prestige of law offices and the perceived interesting nature of law office work. Many consider becoming paralegals as preferable to becoming secretaries, one of their other viable options. An official from one of the major paralegal schools in the New York City area, fairly typical of many American paralegal schools, described to us its student body as 75 percent women, mostly younger women but about 20 percent women over forty who wish to reenter the job market or switch jobs; almost all are college graduates, a college degree being a school requirement for entry unless an applicant is sponsored by a law office; few are graduates of Ivy League or other top-prestige colleges; most live in the suburbs; under 10 percent drop out or fail the program; and only a few go on directly to law school from paralegal school, but 5 to 10 percent go on to law school after working in law offices for a year or so.

Although most paralegals included in our survey who had attended paralegal school seemed generally satisfied with the experience, some experienced paralegals who enrolled in general or specialty paralegal school programs after extensive law office work complained that they learned little or nothing of value from the programs. Quite obviously, training of experienced paralegals, even in specialties with which they are not familiar,

Table 36.
Usefulness of Paralegal School Training[a]

Percentage attending paralegal school that	Large firms	Medium-sized firms	Small firms	Corporate law departments	Government law offices	Legal aid	All offices
Believes it helped substantially in securing a paralegal job	59%	84%	58%	68%	91%	81%	77%
Believes it helped substantially in securing a job promotion	6	4	25	21	9	0	8
Believes it helped substantially in increasing salary	0	12	58	21	9	19	16
Believes it helped substantially in becoming a more competent paralegal	6	47	67	37	27	50	42
Does not report that paralegal school helped substantially in any of the above ways	29	1	0	11	0	6	6
	(N=17)	(N=74)	(N=12)	(N=19)	(N=11)	(N=16)	(N=149)

[a]Percentages sum to more than 100% due to multiple responses.

should involve some differences in approach from the training of those with no prior paralegal experience.

Law offices differ markedly in their willingness to pay the tuition or fees of their paralegals who wish to attend outside paralegal training programs. Some categorically refuse under any circumstances, some will do so if benefits to the office are obvious, and others are more generous and consider helping their employees in self-improvement education good for morale whether otherwise useful to the office or not.[52] Some offices will also permit paralegals release time from work to attend training programs and may even pay travel expenses if programs are given out of town. Employers are more likely to pay for short one- or two-day seminars than for semester or longer courses, and they are more likely to pay for outside training if in-house training is considered inadequate.

Paralegal schools exhibit wide variations in admission requirements. The most common requirements are a high school diploma, often with added screening through interviews with admissions personnel, testing, or proof of relevant work experience. A minority of schools for admission insist on successful completion of college work; some require only one or two years of college credits, others a baccalaureate degree.[53] Most schools accept a majority of applicants that apply to them.[54] Schools offering continuing legal education programs to paralegals usually have quite different requirements for these programs, relevant law office experience often being the only prerequisite, if any, to admission.

Most paralegal school curriculums bear a resemblance to core offerings in law schools, except that the courses are less intensive and less demanding than comparable law school courses. Typically, paralegal schools offer some kind of introduction to law and the legal process course and then a series of courses in specialty fields of law.[55] If the introduction to law course does not cover legal research, a separate legal research course is usually offered; and as table 37 shows, legal research was the most frequently taken paralegal school subject by our questionnaire respondents. The specialty courses are mostly in such basic fields of law practice as corporations, estates and trusts, real estate transactions, contracts, matrimonial law, and criminal law. Litigation is a widely offered and popular course and usually includes an introduction to pleading, evidence, and trial practice. The larger schools often give a wider range of specialty courses. It is also becoming increasingly common for law office internships to be provided as part of the instructional program, each student being assigned to a law office, usually part-time for several months, working on problems of actual clients under supervision of office lawyers or paralegals. Faculty from the school monitor the intern arrangements and may provide supplemental group instruction drawing on the experiences of the students as interns.[56] At most paralegal schools, students do some supervised writing, including instrument drafting; and a few schools are experimenting with other kinds

Table 37.
Paralegal Courses Taken at Paralegal School
(Percentages reporting that they took particular courses[a])

	Large firms	Medium-sized firms	Small firms	Corporate law de-partments	Government law offices	Legal aid	All offices
Introduction to law	24%	53%	67%	37%	27%	63%	48%
Introduction to the paralegal profession	12	23	33	32	36	75	30
Legal research	88	91	75	74	73	81	85
Corporations	35	41	58	63	64	44	46
Employee benefits	0	5	17	0	9	13	6
Estates and trusts	53	38	67	32	55	50	44
Litigation	59	64	92	53	73	69	65
Real estate[b]	29	31	67	42	45	50	38
Matrimonial law	35	20	67	26	45	69	34
Criminal law	24	20	33	32	27	31	25
Contracts	29	31	58	21	45	38	34
Securities regulation	18	23	17	11	36	25	21
Other courses taken[c]	35	24	25	11	9	63	27
	(N=17)	(N=74)	(N=12)	(N=19)	(N=11)	(N=16)	(N=149)

[a]Percentages sum to more than 100% due to multiple responses.
[b]Includes landlord and tenant.
[c]Other courses listed more than once: torts, 6; substantive law, 6; tax, 4; welfare law, 4; procedure or jurisdiction, 3; administrative law, 2; antitrust, 2; writing or drafting, 2.

of basic skills training, including interviewing and fact investigation.[57] Instruction in using Lexis or Westlaw as a legal research tool is being provided at an increasing number of schools.[58]

To our question as to how those who attended paralegal school believe their paralegal school program could have been improved, the most common responses were more how-to-do-it emphasis and more coverage of law office management. Other recommendations for improvement with considerable support were more instruction on electronic data retrieval systems, better teachers, and what are probably inconsistent proposals—coverage of more fields of law and more intense coverage of fewer fields of law. These responses appear in table 38. The diversity and even inconsistency of responses indicate the difficulty in trying to enhance the appeal of paralegal educational programs to that crucial constituency, the students.

Paralegal training at relatively few schools is part of a four-year baccalaureate degree program. Many schools offer a two-year associate degree program. In the two- and four-year degree-granting schools, paralegal work is usually treated as a major supplemented by required and elective liberal arts courses and frequently by business school courses as well. Some of the other schools award a diploma or certificate for successful completion of their paralegal program.[59]

With so many paralegal schools and large enrollment nationally of paralegal students, there has been an outpouring of published textbooks for paralegal school courses.[60] As with law school casebooks and other law student texts, the paralegal texts generally are broad enough to be usable in any American jurisdiction. However, they differ from law school casebooks, so heavily relied on for law school instruction, in that the paralegal books contain few if any judicial opinions or statutory excerpts; they are concerned less with formal legal doctrine and more with how-to-do-it procedures; the level of presentation tends to be more elementary; and many of the paralegal books contain considerable factual information about paralegal roles, institutions, and career opportunities. Most of the books focus heavily either on legal or other source materials and legal research techniques[61] or on a major field of practice, such as litigation, real estate law, or domestic relations.[62] Some have broader coverage, however, concentrating on a number of skills and functions[63] or on a series of legal doctrinal fields.[64] Most of the paralegal books were prepared as teaching materials for paralegal school courses, but nearly all of them can be useful aids to self-study by paralegals and a few are intended also for lawyers[65] or law students.[66] The authors of paralegal textbooks are either lawyers or paralegals, with lawyers predominating. Most of the authors are practitioners, but the person who has been most active in writing and compiling published paralegal teaching materials, William P. Statsky, was a full-time law professor when most of his texts were published.

A majority of paralegal school teachers apparently are practicing lawyers

Table 38.
Major Way in which Paralegal School Could be Improved

	Large firms	Medium-sized firms	Small firms	Corporate law de-partments	Govern-ment law offices	Legal aid	All offices
More how-to-do-it emphasis	24%	23%	0%	0%	27%	13%	17%
Broader background on the nature of law and the legal system	0	1	0	0	9	0	1
More on helping the poor and disadvantaged	0	1	0	0	0	0	1
Coverage of more fields of law	6	1	17	5	9	6	5
More intense coverage of fewer fields of law	6	7	8	26	0	6	9
More coverage of law office management	6	5	8	21	0	0	7
More on electronic data re-trieval systems	6	1	8	5	0	0	3
Better teachers	12	3	8	0	9	0	4
Other[a]	18	11	0	5	9	6	9
Multiple responses[b]	24	35	42	26	27	69	36
None/no response	0	11	8	11	9	0	8
	(N=17)	(N=74)	(N=12)	(N=19)	(N=11)	(N=16)	(N=149)

[a]The most common other response was more emphasis on legal research, 4.
[b]The question requested one choice, but 54 respondents indicated two or more choices. The most frequent choices were more how-to-do-it emphasis, 27, and more coverage of law office management, 25. The remaining answers were each selected by 15 to 18 respondents, except for helping the poor and disadvantaged, which was selected by 8 respondents.

who teach part-time, commonly a course in their specialty field of practice, but some schools also employ practicing paralegals as teachers, and there occasionally are persons from other disciplines and backgrounds who teach paralegal courses, accountants and librarians, for instance.[67] Comparatively few teachers are employed full-time at paralegal schools and those teachers who are so employed are likely to have substantial administrative or placement duties in addition to their teaching assignments.[68]

Law book collections of paralegal school libraries are generally meager, but commonly schools have made arrangements for their students to use nearby law school, government, or public law libraries. An advantage of a paralegal studies program being offered by a major university or college is that such institutions often have good working law libraries whether or not they have law schools. Classrooms and administrative offices also can pose difficulties. Some schools, especially for evening classes, rent for a few hours each day classroom space that is used principally by other organizations. This can mean that the school administrative offices and library may be remote from classrooms, causing inconvenience to students and staff and weakening their sense of institutional identity. Even when paralegal programs are being offered by colleges or universities, as campus newcomers they often are assigned dingy, noisy, or cramped quarters.

Job placement is an important service offered by the paralegal schools and a major inducement to student enrollment. As the schools attract mostly persons with no prior paralegal experience, their placement efforts are directed primarily at finding jobs for beginners, not with finding better jobs for experienced paralegals. A high percentage of those completing paralegal programs at New York City area schools find employment through school placement services. However, school placements, according to table 29, are heavily concentrated in middle-sized law firms, with a considerable volume of such placements in corporate law departments and small firms as well.[69] Schools in the New York City area provide job placement assistance to their students at no charge to the students or to employers hiring through the schools. The Institute for Paralegal Training in Philadelphia and Houston, which does considerable placement in New York City, charges substantial fees to employers with whom the Institute places paralegals who have completed its resident training programs. Rather than stressing local placement as do most paralegal schools, the Philadelphia Institute maintains a nationwide employment service and devotes more staff resources to placement than do most other schools. There are those who see the Institute as a combined school and employment agency that specializes in high-quality paralegal prospects.[70] The Institute's fees to employers deter many New York City law offices from hiring paralegals through the Institute, even some employers who can readily afford the fees but believe that they can obtain quite satisfactory paralegals in the massive New York City paralegal market without paying placement fees.

The paralegal schools have recently established their own association, the American Association for Paralegal Education (AAfPE). Founded in 1981 at a meeting of paralegal educators held at the American Bar Association headquarters in Chicago, the principal concern leading to creation of the association was the approval process for paralegal schools and a desire to maintain ABA involvement in that process.[71] Shortly after the first paralegal school programs were offered, the ABA established a paralegal school approval procedure under which those schools meeting standards set by the ABA were designated as ABA approved. This designation has had and was intended to have considerable value in increasing the reputation and student drawing power of approved schools. Standards and procedures for ABA paralegal school approval have been modeled after those for ABA approval of law schools that have long been in effect, although the paralegal school standards are generally less demanding and much less expensive to meet than those for law schools.[72] The paralegal school standards require, for approval, that a paralegal program be at the post-secondary level, include the equivalent of at least two full-time academic years of credit, and consist of both general education and law-related courses.[73] Programs of four-year colleges and universities, two-year colleges, law schools, comprehensive technical institutes, and vocational schools may be approved.[74] An approved school may be a proprietary institution, one operated for profit.[75] Among other standards are those requiring that the program director be a full-time member of the faculty or the administration of the institution;[76] instructors must possess education, knowledge, and experience in the paralegal field;[77] admission criteria must reflect a rational selection process so that success as paralegals can be reasonably predicted;[78] student services must provide for counseling and advising students and assisting graduates in securing suitable employment;[79] and an adequate library[80] and suitable physical space and equipment[81] must be available. Approval ultimately is by the ABA House of Delegates following an on-site visit by an evaluation team, a report by the team, and recommendations by the ABA Special Committee on Legal Assistants.[82] The ABA Special Committee on Legal Assistants has lawyer members only, but for some years has been aided by an advisory commission that includes paralegals. Schools must request ABA approval and by mid-1982, sixty-eight schools had been approved, only 20 percent of those then in existence. Presumably, the advantages of approval are sufficiently great so that any school with good prospects of being approved will apply. The ABA paralegal school approval program has been held not to violate federal antitrust laws.[83]

In 1981, the ABA decided to withdraw from the process of approving paralegal schools.[84] Important factions among paralegal educators believed that total withdrawal of the ABA from granting approvals was undesirable, and they worked out with the ABA modifications that would include a continued but lessened role for the ABA and an enhanced role for paralegals and representatives of paralegal organizations. Under the new arrangement, the advisory commission to the ABA Standing Committee on Legal Assistants has been restructured and given primary responsibility for approving and reapproving paralegal school programs. The commission will review approval applications, have site visits conducted, and prepare reports and recommendations on approval, with final approval continuing to be by the ABA House of Delegates upon recommendation of the Standing Committee on Legal Assistants.[85] To retain its approved status, a school must seek reapproval every five years.[86] The commission is to have eleven members: three paralegal educators, another educator, two paralegals, three lawyers, a legal administrator, and an "ad hoc" member.[87] The ABA's financial contribution to the approval process, which has been substantial,[88] will be phased down until in a few years its contribution apparently will be little more than sending a committee representative to commission meetings.[89] Eventually, it is expected that approved schools and those applying for approval and reapproval will carry the major financial burden of maintaining the approval process. Leadership of the AAfPE and a liaison committee of that association were influential in persuading the ABA to remain active in the approval process and helped work out details of the new arrangement.[90]

AAfPE has also assumed responsibility for a conference each year on paralegal education. For five years such conferences were sponsored by the ABA Standing Committee on Legal Assistants, after which the ABA dropped its sponsorship. In 1981 and 1982 similar annual conferences were organized by conference planning committees of paralegal educators. Publications on paralegal education can also be expected from AAfPE, quite possibly taking over from the ABA as the major source of published monographs on the status and needs of paralegal education.[91] Voting membership in AAfPE is restricted to paralegal schools approved by the ABA or in substantial compliance with ABA approval standards and institutionally accredited by a national accrediting agency.[92] Nonvoting membership is open to all individuals, firms, and organizations interested in promoting AAfPE's purposes.[93] The association is primarily dependent on its membership for financial support, which will substantially limit its activities. What AAfPE can accomplish will depend largely on how much time and energy representatives of its school membership are willing to volunteer.

In addition to some of the paralegal schools, there are other educational organizations that provide continuing legal education programs for experienced paralegals.[94] Many of the programs offered by such organizations are short, often taking only a day or two or but part of a day. As has been seen, the paralegal associations commonly present programs of this sort. On occasion some bar associations also do so, usually opening them to lawyers as well as paralegals. The Practicing Law Institute regularly offers two-day paralegal workshops in New York City and Los Angeles on specialty subjects in such fields as real estate transactions, estate planning, corporations, and litigation.[95] An organization in Washington, the National Public Law Training Center, provides two-day to two-week training programs for paralegals, lay advocates, and others working in legal aid and a variety of social service agencies.[96] Many of the Center's programs deal with legal fields of concern to those who serve the poor, the handicapped, and consumers. Some employers have set up their own formal in-house training sessions for their experienced paralegal personnel. If useful CLE programs are available locally, however, employers interested in more staff training often find it cheaper and easier to send their paralegals to outside programs and pay the attendance fees.

Overall, the extent of formal paralegal post-employment training is quite limited. The principal means of training is not through formal programs but rather by on-the-job learning by doing, with help from office supervisors when needed. During the learning stage, a supervisor may closely monitor a new paralegal's work or the new paralegal may observe an experienced paralegal at work and gradually take over task assignments as understanding and mastery develop. During our interviews, at one office this latter approach was referred to as "shadowing," at another as the "buddy system." Table 39 does, however, show some significant exceptions to the usual pattern of little or no formal in-house training of employed paralegals. The legal aid agencies provide considerable training of this sort, prompted and aided by the Legal Services Corporation that has long emphasized staff training.[97] Also, to a lesser extent, corporate law departments stress inside formal training.

Not only have most paralegals in our sample not had formal in-house training following their employment but, as table 40 discloses, few of them have attended any short seminars or workshops put on by such organizations as bar associations, paralegal associations, or the Practicing Law Institute. Continuing formal education of paralegals, conducted either inside or outside employers' offices, appears to be a field with great potential, little of which has yet been realized.

In most metropolitan areas, there is keen competition for legal education students in the paralegal field, especially for beginners. In the New York City area and other big-city communities, this competition is likely to drive out some of the financially marginal paralegal training programs as the more successful schools and other training organizations take over larger shares of the available student market through better advertising, better programs, and better reputations. In New York City, the dominant position of Adelphi makes it particularly difficult for some of the other schools to establish a viable position in paralegal education. Continuing education offers additional opportunities for paralegal schools provided they can

Table 39.
In-House Training (Training received in first full-time paralegal job, other than learning by doing[a])

Percentage of respondents attending	Large firms	Medium-sized firms	Small firms	Corporate law de-partments	Govern-ment law offices	Legal aid	All offices
Orientation program of one day or less	38%	8%	9%	15%	10%	15%	17%
Orientation program of one week or less	4	6	6	5	2	19	6
Orientation program of more than one week	0	3	3	22	0	21	6
Short seminars or workshops	5	5	0	15	1	43	9
Occasional post-orientation lectures	22	10	6	12	7	38	15
Other	1	0	0	2	1	0	1
None or no response	47	75	82	37	78	34	61
	(N = 92)	(N = 115)	(N = 33)	(N = 41)	(N = 81)	(N = 47)	(N = 409)

[a]Percentages sum to more than 100% due to multiple responses.

Table 40.
Attendance at Short Seminars or Workshops Not Organized by Employer[a]

Percentage of respondents attending short seminars or workshops organized by	Large firms	Medium-sized firms	Small firms	Corporate law departments	Government law offices	Legal aid	All offices
A bar association	0%	10%	6%	2%	4%	6%	5%
Practicing Law Institute	4	17	9	2	4	13	9
A paralegal association	0	3	3	0	2	0	2
Some other organization	7	17	6	10	6	9	10
Did not attend seminars	92	67	79	93	89	77	82
	(N=92)	(N=115)	(N=33)	(N=41)	(N=81)	(N=47)	(N=409)

[a]Percentages sum to more than 100% due to multiple responses.

develop programs that experienced paralegals think sufficiently useful to merit the required time and cost and consider superior to what PLI and other organizations make available.

OTHER PARALEGAL ORGANIZATIONS

There are other paralegal organizations of significance, including trade unions to the extent that paralegals have been organized by trade unions. Law offices generally have not been organized but there are important exceptions,[98] and some trade union officials consider paralegals a particularly promising occupation for union membership in the future. Union organization efforts and union affiliation involving paralegals usually result in enhanced integration of paralegals as an occupational group, for the unionization process encourages each occupation to coalesce in pushing its interests against management and sometimes against other employee occupations as well.

In New York City and many other parts of the country, both lawyers and support staffs are extensively unionized in legal aid offices and local and state government law offices. As to paralegals, this is substantiated by table 32, although not all paralegals in unionized offices have joined the union. Support staffs in a small scattering of private law firms about the country have been organized but private firms and corporate law departments are everywhere almost all nonunion.[99] Lack of trade union affiliation in private law firms and corporate law departments is reflected in table 32, union membership among our respondents in these types of offices being reported only by paralegals working for a union-operated medium-sized law office serving clients under an employer-paid plan. In recent years serious attempts were made to organize support staffs in several major private law firms in New York City but efforts were dropped when it appeared they would be unsuccessful. As of 1981, 65 of the 232 legal aid programs receiving federal funding through the Legal Services Corporation were organized;[100] and in New York City, except for one small nonunion office, Legal Services for the Elderly, both lawyers and support staff in all legal aid offices, big and small, operate under union contracts. At the New York Legal Aid Society, the lawyers are in one union and the paralegals and other support staff are in another.[101] At the remaining unionized legal aid offices in New York City, lawyers, paralegals, and other support staff are members of the same union, with a single contract covering all offices and with substantially the same salaries and benefits in all offices for each particular type of employee.[102] Staff employees, lawyers and paralegals included, are unionized in such important New York City public law offices as the Attorney General's Office and the Law Department of the City. However, under New York's Taylor Law, these and other government employees do not have the legal right to strike; but the Taylor Law does not apply to legal aid employees, even though funded from government sources.

Widespread dissatisfaction of paralegals with their jobs and the dead-end character of most paralegal positions make paralegals prime targets for unionization.[103] But the high turnover rate of paralegals and the tendency of many paralegals in private law firms to identify with the interests of lawyers, often because they intend to become lawyers and private firm lawyers generally have no interest in becoming union members, militate against paralegal unionization.

Since 1977, private law firms have been considered subject to the federal government's National Labor Relations Act[104] and this could eventually be an important aid to unionization of difficult to organize law offices. Employees subject to the act have the right to bargain collectively and the right to seek remedies from the National Labor Relations Board when their employer commits an unfair labor practice. The board is a powerful force in asserting and protecting union rights as prescribed by the act. Legal aid organizations also are subject to the National Labor Relations Act and the jurisdiction of the National Labor Relations Board,[105] but government offices are exempt from these controls. In determining what is a proper unit for collective bargaining purposes, the board recently held that law firm paralegals could not be forced into a bargaining unit with clerical employees but should be in a separate unit.[106] Paralegals may, however, be included in a unit with other employee groups if the parties agree.

Of the unionized segments of the New York City legal profession, trade unions have had the most impact in legal aid. To be sure, management personnel in unionized government law departments is sensitive to how the unions react to departmental policies and problems, and certainly the negotiation and enforcement of collective bargaining agreements involving government law department employees are taken very seriously by both management and the unions. But in legal aid, the unions have had even more influence. One reason for this is the willingness of legal aid unions to strike. They have the right to strike and have taken advantage of this right frequently enough that their bargaining position has increased substantially, although the strikes have seriously disrupted services provided legal aid clients. There have been several strikes of Legal Aid Society employees in recent years, including one of paralegals and other support staff in 1981 lasting six weeks[107] and a ten-week strike of lawyers in late 1982, the latter resulting in a tremendous increase in case backlogs at the city's criminal courts. During the 1982 strike, serious consideration was given by city officials to dropping the city's agreement with the Legal Aid Society for providing legal representation to indigents charged with crimes and substituting a public defender system under which attorneys would be city employees prohibited by law from striking.[108] Two years before the

ten-week strike by lawyers at the New York Legal Aid Society, employees
of the other legal aid agencies in New York City were out for eleven weeks
in a bitter strike.

In our interviews with legal aid paralegals, the interests they expressed
a desire to have furthered by their unions, in addition to better salaries
and other financial benefits, were layoff priority in case of funding cutbacks,
greater range of work tasks and responsibilities assigned them, and filling
of job vacancies by promotion of existing staff. Several minority paralegals
we interviewed also indicated that they viewed the union as a forum for
resisting moves to raise educational and other standards for paralegal employment that could result in exclusion of many minority individuals from
the occupation. One legal aid management official, who had engaged in
labor negotiations with both lawyers and paralegals, told us that the collective bargaining posture of the two employee groups varies considerably,
with the lawyers raising all kinds of issues and mixing in ideology, but the
paralegals and other support staff restricting themselves mostly to realistic
self-interest, making negotiations with them easier to carry on.[109]

Although the evidence is tenuous, paralegal unionization seems to result
in decreased paralegal dissatisfaction and quite possibly, as a result, reduction in job turnover among paralegals belonging to unions. It was obvious that some of the legal aid paralegals we talked with felt their union
had helped them financially and also provided a mechanism that assured
serious consideration being given to other aspects of their jobs that they
found objectionable or threatening.

Another type of paralegal organization is the commercial employment
or placement agency that on a fee basis finds law office jobs for paralegals.
The fee is usually paid by the employer when the paralegal is placed and
commonly is a percentage of the annual salary rate at which the employee
is hired. There are about ten agencies in New York City that do a substantial
volume of paralegal placements. Some are small offices staffed by but one
or two persons that specialize in placing paralegals and usually other law
office personnel as well; some agencies are much larger and provide office
personnel to a variety of businesses in addition to law offices. Placement
staff in some of the agencies includes former paralegals and it can be
expected that more persons with paralegal experience will in the future
move into this kind of work. The commercial placement agencies concentrate on experienced paralegals, especially those with considerable competence in a legal specialty. Employers usually will not resort to the
commercial agencies for new entrants into the paralegal market, as from
the paralegal schools and other sources there is a sufficient supply of in-
experienced persons on a no-fee basis. Paralegals with just the right experience background, however, can be much more difficult to find without
agency help, and there is the added advantage that applicant screening and
reference checking by the employer may be largely eliminated if a good

agency is used. An agency may also act as headhunter, approaching highly qualified paralegals and interesting them in moving to another employer even though they had been content where they were with no thoughts of looking elsewhere. Most agency placements are for permanent jobs but it is relatively common for law offices to use the agencies when looking for temporary paralegal help. Some agencies will provide temporary paralegals on a per day charge basis, eliminating recruitment costs to the law office and frequently reducing its personnel record keeping as the temps may remain agency employees. Temporary paralegals from agencies have proven to be particularly useful to law offices in handling a surge of document review work in complex litigated matters. Some offices also use temporary paralegals from agencies as trial hirings for possible permanent employment. It can be easier to terminate a temporary placement than someone taken on for what ostensibly was a permanent job.

Private law firms most frequently use agencies for paralegal placements but corporate law departments are increasingly calling on the agencies for help in obtaining needed paralegals. Government law offices and legal aid rarely if ever resort to placement agencies for staffing, as these employers generally will not pay placement fees.

Many placement agencies are strong advocates of paralegals as money-saving additions to law office staffs, and in their promotional efforts and other contacts with employers often stress the value of using qualified paralegals. This has been one of the contributing factors to the rapid expansion that has occurred in law office hiring of paralegals. Placement agencies that also sell management systems and advice to law offices have been particularly effective in promoting paralegal use.[110]

In June 1981, an important four-day national conference on the topic "New Roles in the Law" was held in Washington at Georgetown University and dealt principally with the development, problems, and needs of paralegals. The great majority of the approximately 300 persons in attendance were paralegals, but also present were lawyers, paralegal educators, lay office administrators, placement agency personnel, and lay advocates. Most prominent paralegal organizations were represented as well as a broad cross-section of working paralegals and those involved with paralegals. What was most significant about the conference was the exposure it provided to many present and prospective occupational leaders on a wide range of paralegal functions, institutions, and problems, as well as varying views as to how problems should be approached.[111] Common concerns emerged not previously recognized; but, equally important, group differences in interest and outlook also emerged. Some of these differences may prove irreconcilable. The conference was billed as the first national meeting of its kind, which no doubt it was, and there was talk of future conferences of the same sort, with formation perhaps of a national commission of allied legal services. The 1981 conference was a remarkable organizational endeavor and reflected the vitality of a young, growing, and not fully formed paralegal occupation, but one with internal frictions that are beginning to surface and uneasy relations with other occupational groups in the legal services field. Common interests and concerns may not be sufficient to overcome differences and enable an equally broad-based conference to be staged in the future or enable the formation of a viable national commission or consortium of allied legal services truly representative of all relevant groups. But there clearly are those who would like to see some kind of permanent umbrella organization established that would bring together for exchange of views and for collective action all segments of the paralegal occupation and other occupations in the legal services field.

NOTES

1. On ABA membership and financing, *see* Annual Report of the Association, 1982–83, 70 *American Bar Association Journal* 17 and 19 (Jan. 1984).

2. For a comparison of NFPA and NALA, *see* NFPA/NALA Focus: Two Perspectives, *Legal Assistants Update* vol. 3, at 81 (1983).

In 1982 another national paralegal association was formed, the National Paralegal Association, headquartered in Doylestown, Pennsylvania. Membership is open to paralegals, lawyers, and others "supportive of the paralegal concept." The principal activity of the association apparently is publication of *The Paralegal*, a magazine about paralegals and legal matters of concern to paralegals. The association also operates an employment exchange.

3. For a listing of forty-one local and state paralegal associations compiled by the American Bar Association, *see* R. Berkey, *New Career Opportunities in the Paralegal Profession*, Appendix 2 (1983). A list of ninety-six local and state associations has been compiled by staff at the University of San Diego. Conference Papers, Eighth Annual Conference for Legal Assistant Program Directors and Educators, San Diego, California, October 5–8, 1983.

4. 10 *Facts and Findings* no. 4, at 22 (1983).

5. NFPA/NALA Focus, *supra* note 2, at 86. NALA has declared its goals to be promulgation of a code of professional responsibility for legal assistants; establishment of a national voluntary certification program; cooperation with local, state, and national bar associations in setting standards for legal assistants; promotion of the profession of legal assistants, educating the public for the advancement and improvement of the profession and broadening public understanding of the function of legal assistants; and informing its members through continuing legal education and providing a forum of exchange where members share experiences, opinions, and knowledge with peers. National Association of Legal Assistants, Goals, Purposes and Benefits of Membership, 10 *Facts and Findings* pp. A-C (1984). Following the above goal declaration are examples of how NALA has implemented its goals. *Id.*

6. *Id.*, at 84. For a listing of local and state association members of NFPA as of 1983, *see* 8 *National Paralegal Reporter* no. 3, at 20 (1983).

7. NFPA's newsletter is the *National Paralegal Reporter*, published quarterly; NALA's newsletter is *Facts and Findings*, published six times each year. Each issue

now approaches magazine length and most issues contain news about the associ- ation, plus a few articles about the paralegal occupation, the legal profession, and the law. *Facts and Findings* in its initial years of publication was the official pub- lication of the Legal Assistant Section of the National Association of Legal Secretaries.

8. These codes are the "Code of Ethics and Professional Responsibility of the National Association of Legal Assistants" and "Affirmation of Responsibility of the National Federation of Paralegal Associations." Each is a brief statement of standards of conduct that should be followed by paralegals. The codes are reprinted in W. Statsky, *Introduction to Paralegalism* 212–14 (2d ed. 1982); and in Ulrich and Mucklestone (eds.), *Working with Legal Assistants*, vol. 2, at 291–94 (1981). Canon by canon commentary on the NALA code appears in W. Park (ed.), *Manual for Legal Assistants* ch. 2 (1979). *See also* NFPA's Affirmation of Professional Responsibility, *Legal Assistants Update '81*, at 137–39 (1981); and Brookes, Do Independent Contractors Have Special Ethical Considerations?, 9 *Facts and Find- ings* no. 3, at 7 (1982). NALA has also adopted guidelines relating to standards of performance and professional responsibility that are intended as aids to para- legals and lawyers. National Association of Legal Assistants, Model Standards and Guidelines for Utilization of Legal Assistants. The guidelines, adopted in 1984, appear in 11 *Facts and Findings*, no. 1, at 6 (1984).

In referring to Canon 12 of NALA's Code of Ethics and Professional Respon- sibility, NALA's Ethics Chairman has said: "As members of NALA, we have agreed to be 'governed' by the Code [the ABA Code of Professional Responsibility] and perhaps the best interpretation of NALA's Canon 12 is that we read the American Bar Association Code and substitute the words 'legal assistant' for 'law- yer.' " Weathersby, Ethical Conduct and the Unauthorized Practice of Law, 10 *Facts and Findings* no. 3, at 5 (1983).

9. There are four NFPA regions, and New York is in a region with ten other northeastern and midwestern states. Volunteer regional directors monitor paralegal activities in their area and encourage the formation of new local and state associations.

10. The most ambitious of these publications are *NALA Manual for Legal Assistants* (1979), 544 pages in length; and *NALA Form Book and Procedures Manual for Legal Assistants* (1979), 200 pages in length.

11. The sections were established in 1980 and a minimum enrollment of 100 members was required before a section could be formed. 7 *Facts and Findings*, no. 1, at 1 (1980).

12. 8 *National Paralegal Reporter* no. 3, at 18 (1983).

13. Subjects covered by the examination are communications (mostly writing skills), ethics and human relations, interviewing techniques, judgment and analyt- ical ability, law office management, legal research, legal terminology, the American legal system, and four sets of questions that the applicant selects from the fields of real estate, estate planning and probate, litigation, bankruptcy, contracts, tax law, and corporate law. Eligibility requirements to take the examination are set forth in National Association of Legal Assistants, Model Standards and Guidelines, *supra* note 8, at Exhibit A. Those eligible, among others, are persons with a bachelor's degree and one year's experience as a paralegal and also graduates of an ABA-approved paralegal training course. On NALA certification, *see* Sanders- West, Voluntary Certification for Legal Assistants, 45 *Texas Bar Journal* 968 (1982);

Terhune, The Case for Certification, in *Legal Assistants Update '80*, at 6 (1980); Judd, Certification: Join a Growing Number in Your Profession, 10 *Facts and Findings* no. 3, at 19 (1983); and Farrell, President Farrell Meets with ABA Standing Committee on Legal Assistants, 9 *Facts and Findings* no. 3, at 11 (1982). On the NALA test, *see also* Terhune, Who Needs a CLA?, 19 *Law Office Economics and Management* 456 (1979).

14. 10 *Facts and Findings* no. 6, at 21 (1984). The pass rate is slightly over 50 percent. Sanders-West, *supra* note 13, at 969. The certifying board consists of five paralegals, two attorneys, and two paralegal educators. *Id.* NALA also has a specialty certification program for those who have completed the CLA examination. Judd, *supra* note 13.

15. Five units of NALA-granted continuing legal education credit are required every five years for maintaining certification. NALA allocates credit for passing specialty examinations, taking courses, participating in conferences and workshops, and publication or other approved activities of high occupational merit. NALA, *Requirements for Maintaining Certified Legal Assistant Credit* (1977).

16. NFPA/NALA Focus, *supra* note 2, at 93.

17. *Id.*, at 92.

18. *Id.*, at 91–92; and Gregson, An Explanation of the Federation's Position on Accreditation, 7 *National Paralegal Reporter* no. 3, at 2 (1983).

19. NFPA/NALA Focus, *supra* note 2, at 91.

20. *Id.*, at 94–95.

21. *Id.*, at 94.

22. *Id.*, at 94–95.

23. On arguments favorable to an ABA associate membership category, *see* Ulrich and Tempero, American Bar Association Associate Membership for Legal Assistants—the Reasons Why, 10 *Facts and Findings*, no. 4, at 5 (1984).

24. The NYCPA newsletter, *Venue*, is published bimonthly and distributed to members. It includes news items about the association and other paralegal associations, including NFPA, and short articles on legal topics, most of them written by NYCPA members.

25. Many of the continuing legal education seminars are lunch or dinner sessions with a guest speaker; but in 1981, NYCPA held a national seminar, with a number of participants from outside New York City. Topics considered at this two-day seminar were how the paralegal can teach the attorney most effectively to use paralegal skills; ethics and professional responsibility of the paralegal in the law firm; professional development, including how the attorney can expand the professional development of the paralegal; public relations and paralegal practice; communications, including body language; post-mortem estate planning; litigation, including case management; real estate, including title abstracts and real estate financing; and securities registration. The seminar faculty was almost equally divided between lawyers and paralegals, plus some specialists in office administration. On the seminar, *see* 7 *Venue* no. 4, at 1–3 (1981).

26. The operation of this so-called job bank is described in 4 *Venue* no. 9, at 7 (1979).

27. Focus of attention on private-firm interests has also had a limiting effect on membership in some voluntary bar associations. Johnstone, The Future of the Legal Profession in Connecticut, 55 *Connecticut Bar Journal* 256, at 281–82 (1981).

28. By contrast, the national association of another rapidly growing law office occupation, law office administrators, is having more success attracting members. The Association of Law Office Administrators, with a much smaller occupational group to draw from, is increasing its membership at a rate of 10 percent per year, and in 1982 had 3,200 members, up from 100 in just over a decade. Ranii, New Roles for Firm Managers, *National Law Journal*, Oct. 25, 1982, at 1. Law office administrators may become associate members of the American Bar Association and in 1982 there were 900 such administrator associate members. Ulrich, Legal Assistants and the Organized Bar—Where Do We Go From Here?, 10 *Facts and Findings* no. 2, 14, at 17 (n. 5) (1983). The ABA By-Laws provide as follows:

§21.12. Associates. Persons who are ineligible to be members of the Association may qualify for election by the Board of Governors as associates if they are in one of the following classifications and satisfy such further eligibility requirements as may be approved by the Board: . . . Law Office Administrative Associates. Persons who, although not members of the legal profession, (1) hold degrees in law office administration, accounting, or business administration and are employed full-time in helping lawyers deliver legal services or (2) are employed full-time in law offices as managers or administrators.

American Bar Association, *Constitution and By-Laws* (1982–83).

29. For expressions of frustration on membership response to association needs and activities, *see* an article by NYCPA's then President, Bandel, The Role of the Professional Organization, 6 *Venue* 6 (March 1981).

30. On the State Bar of Texas Legal Assistants' Division, *see* Keaton, Recognition and Opportunity: The Genesis for a Growing Profession, 10 *Facts and Findings* no. 6, at 13 (1984), includes criteria for membership; State Bar Approves Legal Assistants Division, 45 *Texas Bar Journal* 50 (1982); Legal Assistants Division By-Laws, *id.*, at 53; Legal Assistants Division Committees, *id.*, at 757; and Legal Assistants Division Annual Membership Meeting, *id.*, at 1125. By 1984, the Legal Assistants Division of the State Bar of Texas had over 1,400 members. Keaton, *supra*, at 16.

31. Nicolas and Bandel, An Opinionated View, *Venue* 4 (Aug. 1982); Mc-Millian, Comments on the Texas State Bar, *id.*, at 8; Polsinelli, Bar Association Involvement in the Paralegal Profession: Helpful or Harmful?, 6 *National Paralegal Reporter* no. 2, at 4 (1982); and Locke, The State Bar of Texas Legal Assistant Division: Will It Work?, *id.*, at 3. *See also* Hussey, Paralegals and the Bar, 1 *Legal Assistant Today* no. 1, at 12 (1983), discussing arguments for and against bar association paralegal divisions.

32. American Bar Association, *Summary of Action of the House of Delegates, 1982 Annual Meeting* 2. However, the ABA has been reconsidering the matter, with support for associate membership status for paralegals coming particularly from within the Standing Committee on Legal Assistants and the Economics of Law Practice Section Council. Ulrich and Tempero, *supra* note 23. *See also* Schumann, Status Report, ABA Associate Membership, 8 *National Paralegal Reporter* no. 2, at 15 (1983). On associate ABA membership for law office administrators, *see supra* note 28.

33. For a survey of 101 paralegal school programs and resources, *see* Pener, Results of Survey of Legal Assistant Programs, *Journal of the American Association for Paralegal Education, Retrospective 1983*, at 11 (1983). Survey questionnaires

were sent to 350 schools and responses were received from 101. Forty-eight of the 101 schools were approved by the American Bar Association at the time of the survey. *Id.*, at 13. On a 1983 survey conducted by NALA's Student/Liaison Committee, *see* Hill, Results of School Survey Announced, 10 *Facts and Findings* no. 2, at 8 (1983). Unfortunately, the report on this study fails to provide figures on the number of schools from which data was sought or received.

34. *See*, for example, Glazer, The Schools of the Minor Professions, 12 *Minerva* 346 (1974). The law schools, too, are currently perceived as having serious problems. *See*, for instance, American Bar Association, Special Committee for the Study of Legal Education, *Report and Recommendations* (1980); American Bar Association Section of Legal Education and Admission to the Bar, *Report and Recommendations of the Task Force on Lawyer Competency: The Role of the Law Schools* (1979); Cramton, The Current State of the Law Curriculum, 32 *Journal of Legal Education, 321 (1982);* Gee and Jackson, Current Studies of Legal Education: Findings and Recommendations, *id.*, at 471; Klare, The Law School Curriculum in the 1980s: What's Left?, *id.*, at 336; and MacDonald, Curricular Development in the 1980s: A Perspective, *id.*, at 569. For an excellent history of American legal education, *see* R. Stevens, *Law School: Legal Education in America from the 1850s to the 1980s* (1983).

35. The early history of paralegal education is discussed in Statsky, The Education of Legal Paraprofessionals: Myths, Realities, and Opportunities, 24 *Vanderbilt Law Review* 1083, at 1106–22 (1971); Brickman, Expansion of the Lawyering Process Through a New Delivery System: The Emergence and State of Legal Paraprofessionalism, 71 *Columbia Law Review* 1153, at 1219–48 (1971); and Haemmel, Paralegals/Legal Assistants—A Report of the Advances of the New Paraprofessional, 11 *American Business Law Journal* 103 (1973).

36. Statsky, *supra* note 35, at 1108–09. Another early program, one offered by the University of Minnesota General College, is discussed in Larson, Legal Paraprofessionals: Cultivation of a New Field, 59 *American Bar Association Journal* 631 (1973).

37. On the new careers movement, *see* A. Pearl and F. Riessman, *New Careers for the Poor* (1965); and S. Robin and M. Wagenfeld (eds.), *Paraprofessionals in the Human Services* (1981).

38. On the Institute for Paralegal Training, *see* Statsky, *supra* note 35, at 1120–21; Sapadin, Institute for Paralegal Training (Philadelphia), *New Roles in the Law Conference Report 134* (1982); and R. Cole, Paraprofessionalism and the Institute for Paralegal Training (1974), unpublished paper in the Yale Law Library collection.

39. On these seminars, *see infra* note 70.

40. ABA, Standing Committee on Legal Assistants, *Legal Assistant Education: A Compilation of Program Descriptions* (1977). Additional paralegal programs offered in the mid-seventies by schools and other organizations are described in ABA, Standing Committee on Legal Assistants, *Survey of Non-Degree Legal Assistant Training in the United States* (1976).

41. These schools are listed in American Bar Association, *Institutions Offering Legal Assistant Education Programs* (Feb. 1981).

42. 1 *The Paralegal* no. 4, at 22 (1983). However, some of these schools have dropped their paralegal programs. A 1983 questionnaire survey sent to 350 schools received responses from 16 schools reporting that they no longer offered paralegal

programs and five questionnaires were returned as nondeliverable. Pener, *supra* note 33, at 11.

43. ABA, *supra* note 41.

44. The ABA Standing Committee on Legal Assistants, in a widely circulated memorandum dated May 18, 1982, and directed to persons interested in legal assistant program approval, stated that there then were 10,550 paralegal students enrolled in the 80 programs approved or being considered for approval by the ABA and a "safe underestimate" of 20,000 students in the other 260 programs offered by paralegal schools. In 1983, Paul Ulrich estimated that there were then about 32,000 students enrolled in 350 paralegal training programs nationally. Ulrich, Legal Assistants Can Increase Your Profits, 69 *American Bar Association Journal* 1634 (1983).

45. In the 1983 Pener survey, thirty-seven of eighty-nine responding schools reported current enrollments of over 100 students; four schools reported current enrollments in excess of 300, and one in excess of 400. Pener, *supra* note 33, at 12.

46. In the Pener survey, 35 of the 101 schools responding to the question reported that their paralegal programs were located in business departments, divisions, or schools. Pener, *supra* note 33, at 14.

47. These include Antioch School of Law, the University of Bridgeport School of Law, the University of Denver College of Law, Memphis State University School of Law, and the University of Southern California Law Center.

48. *See* list in ABA, *supra* note 41.

49. All three of these schools hold paralegal classes in New York City, and Adelphi and NYU also have classes at suburban locations. In addition to its Paralegal Diploma Program, designed for newcomers to the field, NYU's Institute of Paralegal Studies also offers separate courses as part of its Practicing Paralegal Program for experienced paralegals interested in acquiring additional skills.

50. The Adelphi paralegal program was established in 1973, in cooperation with the National Center for Paralegal Training, a New York City-based organization that has continued to act as consultant and to provide administrative services to the Adelphi program and to similar programs in Chicago and San Diego. The Center also operates a paralegal school in Atlanta.

51. A 1978 survey of all known paralegals in San Francisco shows that 53 percent of respondents had received some type of formal paralegal or legal training and 27 percent had completed a legal assisting educational program. Three of the 255 respondents held J.D. degrees. San Francisco Association of Legal Assistants, *1978 Survey* 1, at 10 (1978). A 1979 questionnaire study by the Illinois Paralegal Association of paralegals in different parts of the nation shows that 24 percent of the 502 persons responding had participated in courses at a paralegal "college," and 19 percent had participated in programs of institutes for paralegal training. S. Cramer, Study of Preferences in Continuing Legal Education and Programs for Paralegals, tables 17 and 19 (1979), unpublished study by the Illinois Paralegal Association. This questionnaire was distributed to members of twelve of the fifteen associations then belonging to the National Federation of Paralegal Associations. A major figure in paralegal education estimated to us that 50 percent of paralegals nationally have had paralegal school training. This estimate may be unduly high.

52. Surveys have shown that most employers will reimburse paralegals for at

least some costs of outside training. Cramer, *supra* note 51, at 10; and San Francisco Association of Legal Assistants, *supra* note 51, at 6.

53. For the range of admission criteria, *see* American Bar Association, *Legal Assistant Education*, *supra* note 40. The Pener survey lists the following admission requirements by numbers of schools, some schools having multiple admission standards: high school diploma or equivalent, seventy-six; proficiency tests, twenty-two; fifteen or more college credits, fifteen; four-year college degree, twelve; law-related experience, twelve; two-year college certificate, twelve. Pener, *supra* note 33, at 23.

The prestigious Institute for Paralegal Training in Philadelphia generally requires for its longer-term programs not only a college degree but a strong academic record in college plus an entrance examination and personal interview. Georgetown University's program has had a special interest in older persons with foreign language competence or fairly high-level occupational experience who are looking to paralegal employment as an opening wedge into a second career. Some of these older people are political refugees or other recent migrants to the United States, some are women coming back into the employment market later in life.

54. The ratio of applicants to students accepted was over 50 percent for forty-four of sixty-eight paralegal schools responding to this ratio question in the Pener study. Thirty-one of these schools reported accepting 91 to 100 percent of applicants. Ten schools stated that they accepted 25 percent or less of those applying. Pener, *supra* note 33, at 23.

55. Sample curriculums appear in Berkey, *supra* note 3, at 20–39.

Courses most commonly offered by paralegal schools, as disclosed by the Pener survey in order of number of schools offering the courses, are family law/domestic relations, probate/estate planning, legal research/writing, business organizations/corporate law, introductory paralegal courses, litigation, real estate/property law, criminal law, law office management, income taxation, insurance/torts, contracts, administrative law, and commercial law. Twenty-nine additional courses were reported as offered by one or more schools. Pener, *supra* note 33, at 18.

Each student at the Institute for Paralegal Training (Philadelphia and Houston) concentrates mostly on one of these legal fields: tax and financial planning, corporate finance and business law, employee benefit plans, estates and trusts, litigation management, or real estate law. There presumably is considerable demand for well-trained paralegals in each of these fields.

56. At Antioch and the University of San Diego, paralegals work with law students in law school clinics.

57. For an innovative and thoughtful approach to teaching litigation advocacy to paralegals, *see* Statsky, Paralegal Advocacy Before Administrative Agencies: A Training Format, 4 *University of Toledo Law Review* 439 (1973).

58. Lexis and Westlaw are computerized legal research systems that aid in finding legal authorities on particular points of law.

59. For example, New York University awards a diploma for completion of a two-semester part-time paralegal program consisting of a Basic Concepts in Paralegal Education course and one of its advanced legal concept courses. Long Island University grants a certificate to those completing 212 classroom contact hours of paralegal instruction. At the time of our interviews Adelphi University did not award a degree, certificate or diploma for completion of any grouping of paralegal

courses, although offering a range of semester-length courses in day and evening programs. Adelphi also offers a twenty-six–week evening generalist program designed to prepare students as paralegals in small law offices engaged in general practice and covers more briefly than in its semester-length specialty courses the following subjects: legal research; introduction to law; corporations; estates, trusts and wills; litigation, real estate and mortgages; matrimonial law; and criminal law. There are other schools that offer similar comprehensive generalist courses in addition to specialty ones.

60. West Publishing Company alone has fifteen books in its Paralegal Series.

61. For example, G. Finnigan and M. Kennedy, *Effective Factual Research for Paralegals: A Guide to the Location and Use of Information Sources* (1983). *See also* M. Cohen and R. Berring, *How to Find the Law* (8th ed. 1983); and M. Rombauer, *Legal Problem Solving: Analysis, Research and Writing* (3d ed. 1978).

62. For example, R. Blanchard, *Litigation and Trial Practice for the Legal Paraprofessional* (2d ed. 1982); C. Bruno, *Paralegal's Litigation Handbook* (1980); Institute for Paralegal Training, *Introduction to Real Estate Law* (1978); Institute for Paralegal Training, *Introduction to Corporate Law* (1978); W. Statsky, *Family Law* (1984); W. Statsky, *Torts: Personal Injury Litigation* (1982).

63. For example, T. Brunner, J. Hamre, and J. McCaffrey, *The Legal Assistant's Handbook* (1982); T. Eimermann, *Fundamentals of Paralegalism* (1980); W. Park (ed.), *Manual for Legal Assistants* (1979), prepared under the auspices of the National Association of Legal Assistants; and W. Statsky, *Introduction to Paralegalism: Perspectives, Problems, and Skills* (2d ed. 1982), widely used, thorough, and with many helpful problem assignments. There also are books that principally are paralegal career guides, for example, Berkey, *supra* note 3; and N. Shayne, *The Paralegal Profession* (1977).

64. For example, D. Larbalestrier, *Paralegal Practice and Procedure: A Practical Guide for the Legal Assistant* (1977); and P. Ulrich and R. Mucklestone (eds.), *Working with Legal Assistants* (2 vols. 1980), published by the American Bar Association's Section of Economics of Law Practice and its Standing Committee on Legal Assistants.

65. For example, Ulrich and Mucklestone, *supra* note 64. R. Kurzman and R. Gilbert, *Paralegals and Successful Law Practice* (1981) is aimed principally at lawyers and suggests how paralegals may effectively be utilized in law offices.

66. For example, Cohen and Berring, and Rombauer, *supra* note 61, apparently prepared principally for law school students.

67. For example, a recent catalog of Adelphi University's paralegal courses lists twenty teachers, all of them lawyers except a legal placement consultant who gives preemployment orientation lectures. All teachers are part-time and most are in private law practice, although one is a judge and another is a law professor at a nearby law school. Other examples in the New York City area are paralegal programs at New York University's Institute of Paralegal Studies and the Paralegal Institute (New York), all of whose teachers apparently are lawyers except for one accountant at NYU who teaches an advanced business organizations course; Mercy College, White Plains, that lists fourteen faculty members, twelve of them lawyers and two of them paralegals; and Long Island University's Paralegal Studies Program with a teaching faculty of nineteen lawyers and two paralegals. The Pener survey gives the occupational background in reporting schools of full-time faculty, other

than program directors, as 149 attorneys, 15 paralegals, and 1 judge. Pener, *supra* note 33, at 21. Occupational background of part-time faculty is listed as 806 attorneys, 69 paralegals, and 20 other. *Id.*, at 22. Average salaries were $25,385 for program directors and $22,825 for full-time teachers. Part-time faculty were paid an average of $243.50 per credit hour, $1,008 per course, or $51.75 per contact hour, depending on which form of compensation was adopted. *Id.*, at 21.

68. Of fifty-six schools responding to a question on number of full-time faculty in their paralegal programs, thirty-two schools reported only one full-time faculty member and ten reported having two full-time faculty members. Pener, *supra* note 33, at 20.

69. We were informed by an Adelphi University consultant that Adelphi students, upon completion of the paralegal program, recently have been finding jobs with the following kinds of employers: 70 percent with independent private law firms, 10 percent with corporate law departments, 10 percent with insurance companies, 4 percent with banks, 3 percent with government agencies, and 3 percent with other public sector employers. The school assists in making most of these placements. The vast preponderance of placements are as paralegals, but a small percentage are taking business jobs, such as pension work, in which some legal training is considered helpful.

70. The Institute has trained 5,000 paralegals at its Philadelphia residential center. It recently has also been offering specialist courses on an independent study basis in such fields as employee benefit plans, estates and trusts, and civil litigation. Students study on their own in their home area using workbooks, textbooks, and cassettes. In addition, the Institute gives a series of one- or two-day seminars in major cities throughout the United States. These seminars are offered to paralegals and other law-related professionals on such topics as discovery skills, trial preparation and evidence, techniques of fact investigation and legal interviewing, effective legal drafting, computers and litigation support, pension plans, legal malpractice and the legal assistant, and post-mortem estate planning. On the Institute, *see supra* note 38.

71. On the history of AAfPE, *see* Kaiser, American Association for Paralegal Education—A History, *Journal of the American Association for Paralegal Education, Retrospective 1983*, at 3 (1983). AAfPE, however, has additional purposes to fostering an approval process for paralegal schools. Its by-laws, *id.*, at 5, state that the association's purposes are to:

(a) Promote high standards for paralegal education.

(b) Provide a forum and opportunities for professional improvement for paralegal educators.

(c) Further develop a vehicle for the accreditation of paralegal education programs in cooperation with the American Bar Association and other institutions and associations.

(d) Hold an annual conference for the Association.

(e) Provide technical assistance and consultation services to institutions, educators, employers, and others.

(f) Promote worthwhile research endeavors and to collect, develop, and disseminate information related to paralegal education and the profession.

(g) Promote the goals and interest of the Association through cooperation with other national, regional, and local groups and organizations.

72. *See* American Bar Association, *Guidelines and Procedures for Obtaining ABA Approval of Legal Assistant Education Programs*, as amended (1983); and McCord, Should the ABA or Anyone Else Be Involved in Approving Or Accrediting Paralegal Training Programs?, 1 *Legal Assistant Today* no. 3, at 14 (1984), discussing the ABA approval process and guidelines. Of help to paralegal schools seeking ABA approval is American Bar Association, Standing Committee on Legal Assistants, *Legal Assistant Programs: A Guide to Effective Program Implementation and Maintenance* (1978).

73. American Bar Association, *Guidelines*, *supra* note 72, at §G-303.

74. *Id.*, at §G-206.

75. *Id.*, at commentary to §G-206.

76. *Id.*, at §G-402.

77. *Id.*, at §G-401.

78. *Id.*, at §G-501(c).

79. *Id.*, at §G-502.

80. *Id.*, at §G-601.

81. *Id.*, at §§G-701 to G-703.

82. *Id.*, at 21–25.

83. Paralegal Institute, Inc. v. American Bar Assn., 475 F. Supp. 1123 (1979).

84. American Bar Association, Standing Committee on Legal Assistants, Update on Legal Assistant Education Approval Program, *Legal Assistants Update*, vol. 3, at 103 (1983). For a brief history of the ABA Special and then Standing Committee on Legal Assistants, *see* Ulrich, *supra* note 28, at 14–15.

85. American Bar Association, *supra* note 84, at 105.

86. *See* American Bar Association, *Guidelines*, *supra* note 72, at 25.

87. On membership requirements, *see* American Bar Association, *supra* note 84, at 106.

88. In 1982, the ABA contribution to the paralegal approval process was $90,000. ABA Standing Committee on Legal Assistants, Memorandum of May 18, 1982, at 5.

89. *Id.*

90. NFPA originally was opposed to the ABA approval process and NALA apparently believed that an alternative means of approval should be sought. *See* NFPA/NALA Focus, *supra* note 2, at 91–92. At its 1983 annual meeting, however, NFPA agreed to participate for one year in the ABA advisory commission to approve paralegal training programs, participation to be evaluated at the end of the year. Policy Resolutions, 8 *National Paralegal Reporter* no. 1, at 7 (1983). For diversity of views within NFPA on this issue, *see* Moon, President's Column, 7 *National Paralegal Reporter* no. 3, at 1 (1983); Sheehy, ABA Approval—Another Viewpoint, *id.*, at 2; and Gregson, An Explanation of the Federation's Position on Accreditation, *id.*, at 3. Doubts about the ABA paralegal school approval process were also expressed at the 1981 Georgetown conference, *New Roles in the Law Conference Report* 166–67, 238 (1982).

91. The AAfPE already is publishing a semi-annual journal, the first number of which, *Retrospective 1983*, is book-length.

The ABA Committee on Legal Assistants has published a number of useful monographs on paralegal education. Among these are *Proposed Curriculum for Training of Law Office Personnel*, preliminary draft (1971); *Training for Legal*

Assistants, San Francisco Pilot Project Report (1971); *Legal Assistant Education* (1974); *Survey of Non-Degree Legal Assistant Training in the United States* (1976); and *Legal Assistant Programs: A Guide to Effective Program Implementation and Maintenance* (1978). It has also published several volumes of *Legal Assistants Update*, containing articles of interest to paralegals.

92. AAfPE By-Laws, arts. 2.1 and 2.2.

93. *Id.*, at art. 2.3.

94. Some of these programs are discussed in American Bar Association, Standing Committee on Legal Assistants, *Survey of Non-Degree Legal Assistant Training in the United States* (1976).

To aid in planning continuing legal education seminars, the Illinois Paralegal Association conducted a nationwide survey of paralegal CLE participation and preferences. On results of this survey, *see* Cramer, *supra* note 51.

95. For examples of the lengthy sets of reading materials distributed to students in these courses, *see* Practicing Law Institute, *Commercial Law and Practice, Course Handbook Series nos. 238 and 239, Legal Assistants 1980* (2 vols. 1980).

96. On the work of the Center, *see* Powers, Legal Advocacy: An Expanding Field, *New Roles in the Law Conference Report* 147 (1982). The Center has recently included training in use of computers so as to assist legal aid and human services agencies in automating some of their work.

97. On Legal Services Corporation in-house training, *see* Legal Services Corporation, Community Legal Education and Paralegal Unit, *Training and Career Development Status Report for the Client* (1979); and Legal Services Corporation, *Community Legal Education Conference Workbook* (June 1978).

98. On unionization of law offices, *see* Bureau of National Affairs, *Unionization in the Legal Profession*, a BNA Special Report (Aug. 18, 1981); Lewis, Unionization of Law Firms and How to Avoid It, 50 *New York State Bar Journal* 471 (1978); Schorr, Unionization in Legal Services: Beginning the Discussion, 14 *Clearinghouse Review* 836, at 841 (1980); Stavitsky, Lawyer Unionization in Quasi-Governmental Public and Private Sectors, 17 *California Western Law Review* 55 (1980); Comment, Unionization of Law Firm Associates?, 32 *Southwestern Law Journal* 987 (1978); Note, The Unionization of Law Firms, 46 *Fordham Law Review* 1008 (1978); and Flaherty, Attorneys: Look for the Union Label, *National Law Journal*, Aug. 15, 1983, at 1.

99. An important private law office that is unionized is the one providing prepaid legal services to New York City municipal employees. These services are provided by District Council 37, American Federation of State, County, and Municipal Employees, pursuant to a collective bargaining agreement with the city, and the office is commonly referred to as MELS (Municipal Employees Legal Services). Staff lawyers, paralegals, and social workers are in one union, other support staff in another union. Some private firms that represent labor unions also are unionized and so are some public interest law firms.

100. Nationwide, the National Organization of Legal Services Workers represents over half of the legal aid employees covered by collective bargaining agreements. Bureau of National Affairs, *supra* note 98, at 18.

101. The lawyers are affiliated with District Council 65 of the United Automobile Workers; the support staff union is Local 1199 of the Drug and Hospital Workers Union.

102. This union is the Legal Services Staff Association, a charter member of the National Organization of Legal Services Workers. For an example of organizational literature of LSSA summarizing terms of its labor contract, *see* Bureau of National Affairs, *supra* note 98, at 43.

Schorr, in his excellent article about legal aid unionization, has this to say about bargaining-unit structure generally in American legal aid offices:

Looking at the contract recognition clauses to find a pattern of units is not enlightening. Some programs have unionized lawyers but not clericals, while others have unionized clericals but not lawyers. Many programs have all categories of employees unionized, some in one unit, some in two units. Some programs include a half dozen administrative personnel and all managing attorneys; some programs exclude only three or four managerial employees altogether. There is no apparent pattern.

Schorr, *supra* note 98, at 841.

103. Bureau of National Affairs, *supra* note 98, at 16.

104. This was decided in Foley, Hoag & Elliot, 229 NLRB No. 80, 95 LRRM 1041 (1977), in which the National Labor Relations Board asserted jurisdiction over private law firms for the first time.

105. Wayne County Neighborhood Legal Services, Inc., 229 NLRB No. 171, 95 LRRM 1209 (1977).

106. Stroock & Stroock & Lavan, 253 NLRB no. 52, 105 LRRM 1609 (1980).

107. In this strike, largely over salaries, 400 support staff employees were on strike. *New York Law Journal*, Oct. 8, 1981, at 1; and *id.*, Nov. 17, 1981, at 1.

108. On what were then perceived as possible consequences of the Legal Aid Society attorneys' strike, *see* an editorial, "Suicide for Legal Aid?," *New York Times*, Dec. 26, 1982; a news review in the same newspaper on the same day, with the headline, "Is There a Better Way Than Legal Aid?," *id.*, at E7; *New York Law Journal*, Oct. 26, 1982, at 1; and *id.*, Dec. 20, 1982, at 1. Salaries were the main issue in the strike, but high attorney caseloads and arbitration procedures for settling the strike also were points of difference between the union and management. The contract finally signed included a provision for mediation of future disputes but retained the union's right to strike. Wage increases under the agreement were only slightly better than what management initially offered. *New York Law Journal*, Dec. 30, 1982, at 1; *New York Times*, Jan. 2, 1983, at E6.

109. The unionization process in legal aid organizations has on occasion moved into issues of control over policy decisions and sharing of these decisions by management with the union. Whether the unionization process is a workable vehicle for collective policy control is questioned in Schorr, *supra* note 98, at 842.

110. Articles by Hal Cornelius, vice-president of Career Blazers Law Services, a New York and Washington support and placement agency for law offices, illustrate agency promotional arguments for paralegal use. *See*, for example, Cornelius and Luberda, Suggestions Offered on Recruitment, Training, Use of Paralegal Staffs, *New York Law Journal*, March 23, 1981, at 23; Cornelius, Paralegals, Outside Special Services Aids to Cost Efficiency, *New York Law Journal*, Oct. 18, 1977, at 4; Cornelius, Organization of the Modern Paralegal Department, *New York Law Journal*, June 5, 1979, at 4.

111. The scope of representation in the National Advisory Commission that planned the conference is indicative of the broad and diverse outlook the conference

sought to provide. The National Advisory Commission included a person from each of these organizations: United States Department of Justice, National Paralegal Institute, Institute for Paralegal Training (Philadelphia), American Bar Association Standing Committee on Legal Assistants, National Capital Area Paralegal Association, National Association of Legal Assistants, National Federation of Paralegal Associations, Legal Services Corporation, Georgetown University Legal Assistant Program, George Washington University Legal Assistant Program, Antioch School of Law, National Lawyers Guild, National Clients Council, National Public Law Training Center, Legal Counsel for the Elderly, National Resource Center for Consumers of Legal Services, and National Citizens' Coalition for Nursing Home Reform.

Among topics that the conference considered were these: new concepts of paralegal work; new concepts in delivery of legal services; changing patterns in education and training of paralegals and lay advocates; some new ways of looking at the unauthorized practice of law; present and future needs of paralegals, public sector advocates, educators, and employers; and the future of paralegal work. On the conference, *see New Roles in the Law Conference Report* (1982).

4

SOCIAL CONTROL OF PARALEGALS

As is true of all occupational groups, paralegals are subjected to a diversity of social controls and also seek to impose such controls for their own benefit.[1] Social controls can exert influence on all important characteristics of an occupation, including entry criteria, career lines, types of work performed, acceptable work performance standards, remuneration, status, and the nature and power of the occupation's organizations. The controls can expand as well as restrict an occupation's functions and the benefits accruing to its members.

The process of generating and imposing social controls often involves efforts to achieve or protect an occupation's preferential position relative to other occupations. It is also common for one segment of an occupation to seek controls that will benefit it at the expense of other segments of the same occupation. Furthermore, occupational controls may be sought by other groups, including consumers and those who purportedly represent a broader public interest. Occupational control efforts may seek to strengthen the competitive position of one occupation or occupational segment, provide it with monopoly advantages, or create or maintain its benefits from the dependency of another occupation or occupational segment. Opponents often resist these efforts but may accept an agreement or accede to an accommodation if they thereby receive at least some of what they want.

Law is a frequently utilized form of occupational social control, the authority of government being brought to bear through formal rules and regulations promulgated by legislatures, courts, and administrative bodies. For law to be effective, however, may require enforcement activities initiated by public authorities or private persons. Mere promulgation of legal requirements does not necessarily assure compliance. It is common, particularly in a democratic society, for those on whom legal controls are being imposed to be heard and often to exert some influence on the nature of the legal controls to which they are being subjected. How effective they will be in shaping or resisting these controls will turn on such factors as the intensity with which they push the positions they are advocating, their political power, and the perceived legitimacy of their positions by government decision makers and the public at large.

This chapter discusses the major forms of paralegal social control. Relevant laws and the legal process, rather than being treated under a separate heading, are considered as they affect the other forms of control. Law frequently acts as a social control mechanism by regulating other social control mechanisms. At the end of the chapter, some of the currently controversial issues involving paralegals are examined. These not only provide examples of how social controls over paralegals operate but also give indications of possible changes that may occur in control patterns.

An important aspect of paralegal control is the relatively limited influence that paralegals and paralegal organizations have so far exerted over external control of the occupation and their modest efforts to impose internal control. These features of paralegal control are due in part to the occupation being undeveloped and its members until recently lacking even a sense of occupational identity. They are also partially due to the dominance that lawyers have exerted and continue to exert over the paralegal occupation, this dominance being another very important aspect of paralegal control. As the paralegal occupation matures and develops stronger organizations, it can be expected to increase its influence over processes controlling it, whatever outer limits may exist to this influence. Paralegals are a satellite occupation, but satellites can exert substantial power over their own well-being as they perceive it.

CONTROL BY THE MARKET

The market for legal services exerts tremendous control over paralegals and is a major determinant of how many paralegals are employed, the work they do, and the pay they receive. On the supply side there are more than enough lawyers available to fill most legal service demands and lawyers are generally better trained than paralegals to perform most legal service tasks. As has been seen, the principal appeals of paralegals are that they are cheaper than lawyers and that they will perform dull routine tasks that lawyers would rather not do. Increased specialization and systematization of law office work have enhanced opportunities for effective use of paralegals, and increased competitive and cost pressures on law offices have enhanced the economic attractiveness of paralegals. On the demand side, most clients currently seem to prefer having the more skilled aspects of their legal work performed by lawyers but, when aware of paralegal input, generally consider it acceptable for simple routine tasks, especially if the result is lower fee charges.

So far as paralegals are concerned, however, the market for legal services is tightly regulated by the law. Even if clients are or might become willing to have a broader range of their legal work performed by paralegals, there are drastic legal restrictions on access to this market by paralegals and other lay persons unless supervised by lawyers. Lawyers have long had extensive monopoly privileges in supplying the legal services market. Unauthorized practice laws are an important source of these privileges and sharply limit the right of nonlawyers to provide legal services to others except when supervised by lawyers. These laws also prohibit nonlawyers from making court appearances for clients whether employed or directed by lawyers or not. Lawyers' standards of ethical practice, as promulgated by bar associations and courts, are additional sources of restriction on lay persons practicing law. These standards are directed at lawyers but regulate how lawyers may utilize or cooperate with lay persons in providing client services. As applied to paralegals, they have effectively deterred paralegals from competing with lawyers by independently representing clients. They also have limited what paralegals may do and how much autonomy they have in doing it even when working for lawyers. Paralegals, however, may form their own firms and as freelance independent contractors provide paralegal services to law offices, and some firms of this sort do exist,[2] but paralegals may not set up their own firms to represent clients independently.

Typical of American laws proscribing unauthorized practice of law is this broad New York statutory provision:

> It shall be unlawful for any natural person to practice or appear as an attorney-at-law . . . for a person other than himself in a court of record in this state . . . or to furnish attorneys or counsel . . . to render legal services, or to hold himself out to the public as being entitled to practice law as aforesaid . . . or to assume, use, or advertise the title of lawyer, or attorney and counselor-at-law, . . . in such a manner as to convey the impression that he is a legal practitioner of law . . . without having first been duly and regularly licensed and admitted to practice law in the courts of record of this state. . . .[3]

A similar statutory provision prohibits corporations and voluntary associations from practicing law.[4] Violation of these provisions is a crime[5] and violators may also be enjoined by the courts from committing further infractions.[6] Comparable prohibitions on the unauthorized practice of law by nonlawyers exist in all American states.

The American Bar Association, a national organization of lawyers to which a majority of American lawyers belong, is a major source of guidance to American lawyers on professional standards of behavior. Its Model Rules of Professional Conduct, adopted by the Association's House of Delegates in 1983 following many revisions and much discussion and debate within the profession, is intended by the ABA to replace its Code of Professional Responsibility, adopted by the ABA House of Delegates in 1969. The Code subsequently was adopted by state bar associations throughout the United States and as rules of court in most states, this latter giving it the force of binding government-declared law. Whether or not the Model Rules will be as widely adopted as the Code remains to be seen, but in any states not adopting the new Rules, the Code presumably will remain in effect.

Interpretations of the Code by bar association ethics committees have been helpful in clarifying ambiguities in the Code and frequently have influenced judicial decisions dealing with the propriety of lawyer conduct. The American Bar Association and state and major local bar associations have ethics committees that issue Code interpretations in response to lawyer requests and will similarly interpret the Model Rules where adopted.

Rule 5.5 of the ABA Model Rules provides: "A lawyer shall not: . . . (b) assist a person who is not a member of the bar in the performance of activity that constitutes the unauthorized practice of law."[7]

Official written comment following each of the Model Rules is intended as a guide to interpretation, and the comment following Rule 5.5 states in part:

Paragraph (b) does not prohibit a lawyer from employing the services of paraprofessionals and delegating functions to them, so long as the lawyer supervises the delegated work and retains responsibility for their work. See Rule 5.3. Likewise, it does not prohibit lawyers from providing professional advice and instruction to nonlawyers whose employment requires knowledge of law; for example, claims adjusters, employees of financial or commercial institutions, social workers, accountants and persons employed in government agencies.

Rule 5.3 of the Model Rules is as follows:

With respect to a nonlawyer employed or retained by or associated with a lawyer:
(a) A partner in a law firm shall make reasonable efforts to ensure that the firm has in effect measures giving reasonable assurance that the person's conduct is compatible with the professional obligations of the lawyer;
(b) A lawyer having direct supervisory authority over the nonlawyer shall make reasonable efforts to ensure that the person's conduct is compatible with the professional obligations of the lawyer; and
(c) A lawyer shall be responsible for conduct of such a person that would be a violation of the rules of professional conduct if engaged in by a lawyer if:

(1) the lawyer orders or, with the knowledge of the specific conduct, ratifies the conduct involved; or
(2) the lawyer is a partner in the law firm in which the person is employed, or has direct supervisory authority over the person, and knows of the conduct at a time when its consequences can be avoided or mitigated but fails to take reasonable remedial action.

EC 3-6 of the Code also contains language of great importance to paralegals:

A lawyer often delegates tasks to clerks, secretaries, and other lay persons. Such delegation is proper if the lawyer maintains a direct relationship with his client, supervises the delegated work, and has complete professional responsibility for the work product. This delegation enables a lawyer to render legal service more economically and efficiently.[8]

No doubt, problems of interpretation as to proper work and role recognition of paralegals will arise under the Model Rules as they have under the earlier Code. Bar association committee opinions have sought to answer some of the questions concerning paralegals not clearly answered by the Code and some of these opinions will probably be relevant in efforts by bar association committees and others to interpret the Model Rules. Examples of ABA or New York bar association committee opinions interpreting the Code on matters pertaining to paralegals are that a paralegal should not independently advise a client concerning the client's legal rights or duties; a paralegal may prepare a deed, provided his lawyer-employer assumes responsibility for it; a paralegal may attend mortgage closings, with limited responsibilities; a paralegal's status should be disclosed at the outset of his contact with his employer's client, any attorney, or member of the public; a paralegal's name may not be listed on a lawyer's letterhead; a paralegal may answer court calendar calls where no argument is necessary, investigate questions of law, interview prospective witnesses, and assist in the preparation of briefs, affidavits, subpoenas, and pleadings; but a paralegal may not engage in conduct involving the exercise of a lawyer's professional judgment.[9] Some of these opinions raise additional questions, and there still are grey areas between what clearly is and is not proper lawyer and paralegal conduct. Particularly troublesome and often interrelated problems are how closely must lawyers supervise paralegals, when must the professional judgment of a lawyer be brought to bear on the work of paralegals,[10] what constitutes independent legal advice by a paralegal to a client, and are there special professional conduct risks when a lawyer hires paralegals as independent contractors rather than employees?[11]

Although the supply of legal services in the United States has long been heavily preempted by lawyers, and unauthorized practice laws and codes of professional conduct have aided in providing lawyers with a monopoly over the market for legal work, this monopoly is not complete. There are situations in which nonlawyers may validly provide legal services. Individuals, for instance, may perform legal work for themselves, including representing themselves in court, so-called pro se representation; and organizations also are entitled to do their own legal work, hiring lay employees for the purpose, although court representation by these lay employees is generally not permitted.[12] In addition, some well-established lay occupational groups, including, among others, real estate brokers, bank trust officers, title insurers, and accountants, are legally authorized to provide limited legal services to others. Rationales for authorizing these groups to perform certain legal tasks for their customers or clients are that the permitted work is so simple and the law involved so certain that nonlawyers can be trusted with it; that the legal work is incidental to the principal function of the occupational group; or that, as with insurers, the organizations employing the lay actors are in effect representing themselves and hence the pro se exception applies. Some government administrative agencies with adjudicative responsibilities have also been authorized by federal or state government to permit nonlawyers to represent clients in hearings before agency officials, even though the nonlawyers are not working for or supervised by lawyers. Examples of administrative bodies before whose hearing officers nonlawyers may have rights of audience are state welfare agencies, the United States Patent Office, and the United States Treasury Department.

Since the 1960s, the bar associations have been less vigilant and aggressive than formerly in their attempts to restrict major businesses and professions, such as the banks and accountants, from providing legal services, especially legal services that these groups had a well-established pattern of providing. The era of major unauthorized practice test case litigation pushed by the organized bar against established practices of other major occupational groups seems largely to have passed.[13] This has resulted from the high cost to the bar of major lawsuits, loss of some important unauthorized practice cases by the bar,[14] concern that the bar's unauthorized practice activities might be held antitrust law violations,[15] and popular and even some lawyer antipathy to imposing the lawyer's monopoly where there appears to be little or no risk of harm to the public.[16] Although the bar associations now seem reluctant to challenge lawyers' major competitors as unauthorized practitioners, especially as to those competitors' established practices, new and innovative types of lay activities that arguably constitute unauthorized practice of law are likely to be met with enforcement action from bar associations, including injunction and other judicial proceedings to close down any new incursions into legal services.[17] Extensions beyond the status quo of well-entrenched practices no doubt will be resisted.

CONTROL BY CONCEPTS OF LEGITIMATION

Concepts of legitimation are an important means of achieving social control over paralegals as well as over lawyers and other occupations. These concepts, when advanced in relation to an occupation, are justifications or rationalizations for the occupation, its activities, and its policies.[18] They are arguments that seek to create credibility and acceptance, and they frequently are attempts to convince those inside or outside the occupation of the merits or morality of the occupation and the privileges or obligations it aspires to, has assumed, or has been granted. The process of legitimation may seek to achieve such objectives as drawing clients or recruits to an occupation, developing occupational self-esteem, encouraging adherence to standards of occupational conduct, or generating popular or political support for legal or market occupational advantages. If legitimation efforts are successful, target groups are persuaded that what is being advocated is valid and justified, hence has legitimacy.[19]

The process of legitimation may involve negative as well as positive arguments about an occupation and can include unfavorable comparison of one occupation with another. Occupations often compete with other occupations and may seek to do so by trying to justify their views or discredit those of their opponents. Efforts may be made to achieve legitimation for the views of an entire occupation or for groups and organizations within it, groups and organizations whose interests may conflict.

Legitimacy on occupational issues is often achieved through the speeches or writings of respected individuals. Laws and other authoritative pronouncements on occupational rights and duties also can have great influence in creating the acceptance and justification that legitimation seeks to attain. Statutes, judicial opinions, and canons or codes of occupational conduct are illustrative of authoritative declarations that can contribute to legitimacy on occupational issues, especially when reasons for the rules they set forth are convincingly included. Occupational journals, scholarly writing on occupations, and occupational teaching materials often advance legitimation arguments; and the mass media, of course, in reporting on a host of events—legislative proposals, occupational conventions, and labor-management conflicts, for instance, as well as the advertising the media carries—are an important means for furthering legitimation efforts. Legitimacy on occupational issues is usually the result of many forces, often cumulatively brought to bear, but once achieved exerts a controlling influence of its own.

Since the late 1960s there has been a strong push to legitimate paralegals as providers of legal services, but as subordinates and dependents of lawyers. Legitimacy of this position, with little dissent, has now been achieved. Its principal advocates have been lawyers, including authoritative bar association figures, but paralegals have also spoken out in support of this view. Typical of justifications given for paralegals as valued lawyer assistants and adjuncts are these statements appearing in the legal literature:

The rationale of the paralegal concept is simple—by use of a less expensive human resource, the firm can produce a higher volume of legal services to clients at lower costs, with the same or better profit margin than firms producing the same service with the use of either partners or associates. In turn, the partner or associate is freed for performance of more sophisticated legal tasks, which can be billed at higher rates.[20]

With paralegal assistants, lawyers are free to spend more time doing substantive legal work and can greatly increase their client load. As a lawyer, I can highly recommend paralegal help as a solution to the challenges of law office economy.[21]

The paralegal is not in competition with the attorney for a limited market. Rather, the paralegal is a valuable ally through which the attorney can reach a vast untapped market. Increased utilization of paralegal assistants by the legal profession is the vehicle to more complete public service and greater prestige and profits for the attorney.[22]

Generally, an attorney should use paralegals because he can make more money by employing them than he can by not employing them. . . . The use of paralegals can also result in substantial cost savings to the attorney who has the opportunity, if not the responsibility, to pass it on to his clients.[23]

Cost savings to lawyers and clients is the major justification advanced for paralegals as lawyer assistants but occasional added arguments have been that paralegals may perform some legal representation tasks more competently than do lawyers;[24] through the use of paralegals, lawyers' time can be freed for more challenging tasks;[25] and paralegals can help provide for the unmet legal service needs of low- and moderate-income persons.[26]

The legitimacy of paralegals as lawyers' assistants quite arguably is consistent with the legitimacy of an extensive lawyers' monopoly in providing legal services. Paralegals, because lawyers supervise them and are responsible for their work, cannot threaten client and public benefits from a lawyers' monopoly, so the argument runs.

Lawyers have long sought, and in considerable measure obtained, legitimacy as possessors of monopoly privileges, despite recent inroads on this monopoly. Traditional justifications for the lawyers' monopoly, although appearing in many sources,[27] are well set forth in the ABA's Code of Professional Responsibility:

EC 3–1. The prohibition against the practice of law by a layman is grounded in the need of the public for integrity and competence of those who undertake to render legal services. Because of the fiduciary and personal character of the lawyer-client relationship and the inherently complex nature of our legal system, the public can better be assured of the requisite responsibility and competence if the practice of law is confined to those who are subject to the requirements and regulations imposed upon members of the legal profession.

EC 3–3. A non-lawyer who undertakes to handle legal matters is not governed as to integrity or legal competence by the same rules that govern the conduct of a lawyer. A lawyer is not only subject to that regulation but also is committed to high standards of ethical conduct. The public interest is best served in legal matters by a regulated profession committed to such standards. The Disciplinary Rules protect the public in that they prohibit a lawyer from seeking employment by improper overtures, from acting in cases of divided loyalties, and from submitting to the control of others in the exercise of his judgment. Moreover, a person who entrusts legal matters to a lawyer is protected by the attorney-client privilege and by the duty of the lawyer to hold inviolate the confidences and secrets of his client.

EC 3–4. A layman who seeks legal services often is not in a position to judge whether he will receive proper professional attention. The entrustment of a legal matter may well involve the confidences, the reputation, the property, the freedom, or even the life of the client. Proper protection of members of the public demands that no person be permitted to act in the confidential and demanding capacity of a lawyer unless he is subject to the regulations of the legal profession.

Some have placed more stress on lawyer training and competence in arguing for legitimacy of the lawyer's monopoly:

When a person holds himself out to the public as competent to exercise legal judgment, he implicitly represents that he has the technical competence to analyze legal problems and the requisite character qualifications to act in a representative capacity. When such representations are made by persons not adequately trained or regulated, the dangers to the public are manifest. . . . [28]

The legitimacy of paralegals as lawyers' assistants has become well-established, but there are some persons who believe that justifications exist for relaxing unauthorized practice laws and permitting paralegals to practice law and represent clients independently of lawyers. There has been relatively little effort to promote such an expanded view of the paralegal role, but support for it does exist, particularly among independent lay advocates and those who provide training programs for them. Justifications for expanding the paralegal role are that lay principals might be more available and work more cheaply than lawyers, particularly for lower-income persons in need of legal services;[29] lawyers are overselected and overtrained for much of what they do and it would be better for them and the public if more mechanical legal tasks were turned over to independent paralegals;[30] and, with appropriate safeguards, independent paralegals should be able to serve clients in some specialty fields as effectively as do lawyers and at the same time preserve consumers' freedom of choice to select whomever they prefer as their suppliers of legal services.[31] There seems no doubt, however, that efforts by paralegals to move out on their own and represent clients independently in matters from which as independent practitioners paralegals are now excluded would be met by vigorous opposition from powerful forces within the bar and presumably from the courts as well.[32] Without major shifts among lawyers and judges in their preceptions of how paralegals should be permitted to operate, such an expanded role for paralegals will be extremely difficult to achieve.

The concepts of legitimation discussed above are of major significance in determining the service niches now filled by paralegals and lawyers in contemporary American society as well as the relationship of these two occupational groups with one another. Concepts of legitimation pertaining to paralegals and paralegal organizations are considered in the context of particular control issues at the close of this chapter.

CONTROL THROUGH OCCUPATIONAL EDUCATION

Another significant source of control over paralegals is paralegal education, especially those programs provided by the paralegal schools. The impact of the schools is felt not only in the knowledge, training, and attitudes they impart to students but also in their influence on occupational recruitment and placement. In generating and screening new candidates for the occupation and then helping to channel into paralegal jobs those who successfully complete the schools' programs, these educational bodies are a potent control force. Their occupational gatekeeper role, however, is not as important as that of the law schools and medical schools to the occupations they train for, as half or less of all paralegals enter the occupation through the schools whereas all or substantially all new lawyers and physicians receive pre-entry professional school training. Nor do most paralegal schools screen out as high a percentage of applicants nor require as extended exposure to occupational education as do these other educational institutions.

Paralegal education and training, whether through formal programs or on-the-job work experience, exert considerable control over student and trainee attitudes about their occupation, which control in turn influences career expectations and choices. Views about the paralegal occupation presented by educators and trainers generally present paralegals as useful aides in providing legal services but as subordinates of lawyers. Admonitions are common that paralegals should not engage in unauthorized practice of law, and efforts are often made to provide guidance on what constitutes unauthorized practice. But in picturing the work of paralegals, the paralegal schools tend to overstate the prominence of paralegals in the practice of law and exaggerate the extent to which individual paralegals are relied on by law offices. Paralegals are often portrayed by classroom instructors as only slightly reduced versions of lawyers, and the impression is given that paralegals can and do perform most all tasks performed by lawyers except representation of clients in court.[33] These views, which have some literal accuracy, are readily subject to misconstruction by students and have caused discontent among neophyte paralegals when they start to work and discover how restricted and relatively trivial are their tasks compared to those of lawyers in the office. This discontent among paralegals can lead to resentment toward their employers and dissatisfaction with their jobs. The paralegal schools, nevertheless, do see paralegals as being engaged in a separate occupation from lawyers offering a permanent career of its own, not just providing an apprentice or testing stage to becoming a lawyer. They may even turn down or discourage entry of applicants who plan on later going to law school, thereby underscoring the separate character of the paralegal occupation and their role in preparing people for it.

Clearly, the paralegal schools are in something of a dilemma in their depiction of the paralegal occupation, a dilemma common to vocational education. On the one hand, the schools must turn out a product that employers, in this instance lawyer-run offices, will find acceptable; and, on the other, they feel obliged to put the occupation they are training for in a most favorable light so that they will continue to draw students. This dilemma causes problems.

CONTROL BY THE WORKPLACE

The workplace is an important focal point for controls determinative of paralegal work tasks and roles. Influence of such forces as the market for legal services, concepts of legitimation, and the paralegal educational process all converge to help shape the employment relationship, that crucial relationship of all working paralegals. In this relationship, paralegals are employees, not employers or proprietors; and in the workplace setting they are supervised and directed by one or more lawyers. Very experienced paralegals may be granted considerable work autonomy and may even supervise other paralegals, but ultimate responsibility for and formal authority over their work is in lawyers. In a sense, freelance paralegals may be an exception to this, as legally they may be independent contractors and not employees; but in the work they perform, lawyer authority over them is substantially the same as with paralegal employees.

The dominant role of lawyers in paralegal employment relationships keeps within bounds that are usually quite favorable to lawyers the competitive threat of paralegals to lawyers. As has been seen, this dominanace is supported by unauthorized practice laws and lawyers' rules of professional conduct, standards enforceable by the power of the state through the courts. To be sure, in the employment relationship there may be considerable room for paralegals to bargain on wages and the work they will perform, and employed paralegals can always quit if their jobs become unsatisfactory. However, if they remain as paralegals, the upward mobility of most of them is severely circumscribed. They may move from workplace to workplace and conceivably improve their lot, but unless they become lawyers, an impenetrable attainment ceiling soon is reached.

In addition to unauthorized practice laws and laws pertaining to lawyers' professional conduct, malpractice liability is another body of law significant to restricting the workplace activities of paralegals and the responsibilities delegated to them.[34] Lawyers in recent years have become increasingly vulnerable to malpractice claims for alleged improper handling of client matters. Under well-established concepts of agency and employment law, lawyers' malpractice liability extends to conduct of paralegals and others working for lawyers. Liability may be vicarious under the doctrine of *respondeat superior* or lawyers may be responsible for delegating work to paralegals unqualified to perform the work or for inadequate supervision of paralegals.[35] Also, paralegals may be personally liable to clients of the office where they are working if the paralegals' work performance is improper and causes client damage.[36] However, as the paralegals' employers are usually liable as well and more capable of paying, claims for such losses normally are made against the employers rather than the paralegals.

Most malpractice claims are for money damages that clients assert they suffered from improprieties of lawyers or those employed or supervised by lawyers, and most malpractice liability results from negligence by lawyers or their aides in dealing with client problems. In some circumstances lawyer malpractice liability can extend not only to clients but to certain third parties as well.[37] Malpractice claims paid can be substantial, in some instances over six figures, but one report states that most claims are being settled for $6,000 to $10,000 each.[38] Malpractice risks make many lawyers extremely cautious about the tasks they delegate to paralegals, particularly if careful lawyer review of those tasks is not considered feasible or if the lawyers are dubious of paralegals' competence to peform without error the tasks in question.

Many lawyers insure against malpractice liability, one authority estimating that 75 percent of lawyers carry this form of insurance,[39] and it has been asserted that one of every twenty lawyers is being sued for malpractice each year, with recoveries in one out of four of these suits.[40] Malpractice coverage can and often is carried for all law firm employees, including paralegals;[41] but an added premium is required for employee coverage,[42] increasing the expense of this costly form of insurance. A substantial percentage of malpractice claims results from law office administrative-type errors, such as failure to meet statutes of limitations and other procedural deadlines and failure to file required papers.[43] Risk of these types of errors usually can be reduced considerably by effective docket control and checklist systems, systems that many paralegals can competently administer.[44] Other common types of malpractice claims are faulty research or abstracting, errors in preparation of documents, and inadequate or incorrect advice.[45] Malpractice risks of these kinds many lawyers consider too great to merit delegating the tasks involved to paralegals. There can be particularly serious malpractice risks if lawyers assign to paralegals tasks requiring considerable legal skill and knowledge, unless the work is carefully monitored; and yet the requisite monitoring may be uneconomic or require a restructuring of office procedures unacceptable to the lawyers involved. Quite clearly, the malpractice threat acts as a deterrent to many American law offices hiring paralegals and to many others expanding the work and responsibilities of those they have hired. It is a significant control force.

CONTROVERSIAL CONTROL ISSUES

Examination of a few quite different but controversial social control issues involving paralegals can help highlight how the social control process operates. These issues, observed in the context of events surrounding them, can illustrate such common features of the control process as the interplay of different forms of social control, the attention given to developing and promoting concepts of legitimation in seeking to resolve conflicts, the maneuvering of competing interest groups to achieve ascendancy by the stands they take or refuse to take on troublesome issues, and the indefinite stalemate in resolving many issues. They also may show instances in which proponents of control in a particular situation consider law an inappropriate or less favored form of control. Law, despite all its advantages, often is not the best solution to problems, something of which lawyers and legal scholars need frequent reminding.

One issue that has been controversial since paralegals came to the fore as a recognized occupation is whether or not paralegals should be formally credentialed, more particularly, should they be certified and/or licensed. Lawyers everywhere in the United States are licensed and in some states have the opportunity of becoming certified.[46] Should paralegals be similarly controlled? Occupational certification is the official public recognition by a government or private body that certain persons have specified qualifications to engage in a designated occupation. Uncertified persons normally can engage in the occupation, so the control exerted by certification is principally the information it provides consumers and others as to the qualifications of those certified, and inferentially perhaps, the lack of qualifications of those not certified. Competence and trustworthiness for certification may be established by testing or other means of candidate evaluation. Occupational licensing, on the other hand, is a process by which government authorizes by law certain persons to engage in a designated occupation, often after competence and trustworthiness have been evidenced by testing and other evaluative means. Unlicensed persons usually are prohibited by law from engaging in the occupation.

The only paralegal certification program now operating in the United States is the one administered by a private organization, the National Association of Legal Assistants (NALA), offered to paralegals nationally, and with a relatively small number of paralegals certified.[47] For a few years, the Oregon State Bar Association conducted a certification program for Oregon paralegals but discontinued it in 1980 apparently because so few paralegals sought qualification under the program.[48] Bar associations or legislatures in at least eight states have seriously considered instituting certification programs for paralegals but have dropped the idea.[49] In 1971, the ABA's Special Committee on Legal Assistants recommended certification for paralegals, but in 1975, following a series of open hearings on the question, the committee concluded that paralegal certification was premature although in the future it might be an appropriate means of identifying qualified paralegals.[50]

The case for and against paralegal certification has been thoroughly presented, often from a partisan point of view.[51] The major arguments advanced for certification are that it provides recognition and perhaps added compensation to those certified; upgrades the occupation by setting high standards of performance and supplying an expanding number of working paralegals who have demonstrated their capacity to meet those standards; gives definition and status to an occupation that has lacked both; creates a focus for paralegal educational programs; and facilitates law office recruitment when the search is for quality workers likely to have long-term occupational commitments. Proponents of certification argue further that the above benefits can be achieved by a voluntary credentialing system that does not exclude from the employment market those who by choice, lack of experience, or limited competence are uncertified. There also are those favoring paralegal certification who believe the best system would be paralegal specialist certification, an arguably more useful and acceptable form of credentialing.[52]

Principal arguments advanced against paralegal certification are that it is premature and could, if widespread, unduly restrict development of an occupation still in an early evolutionary stage; discourage needed experimentation and innovation in paralegal education and turn the paralegal schools into cram courses for the certification examinations; discourage and unfairly stigmatize those who are uncertified; and could be a first step to breaking down the legal restrictions on practice of law by paralegals and could also be a first step to licensing. Some of those who see paralegal work as a particularly promising field for lower-income minority entry into law office employment are concerned that extensive paralegal certification could become a serious deterrent to such entry. The National Federation of Paralegal Associations (NFPA) has also expressed opposition to NALA's certification on the grounds that eligibility criteria to take the examination are not objective, some examination questions are irrelevant to practicing paralegals, and the examination is not "an effective measure of a person's ability to work successfully as a paralegal."[53]

Paralegal certification remains a lively and contentious issue. NALA continues to push vigorously its certification program and the numbers it certifies continue to grow, although modestly. Competition between NALA and its rival, NFPA, helps sharpen the discussion, as their stands on certification are major points of difference between them. The bar associations, in the face of considerable paralegal opposition to certification and even more opposition to bar association involvement in paralegal regulation, appear to have backed off from the issue. Certification of paralegals offers too little in the way of lawyer benefits to justify the bar associations incurring the possible ill-will and financial cost that certification and bar association administration of certification schemes might incur. The certification issue appears likely to continue simmering with no new programs being launched in the near future and no rapid expansion in the numbers seeking qualification under the NALA program. Paralegal certification, a voluntary form of credentialing, is not currently perceived by most paralegals as providing sufficient added prestige or income to merit the very considerable effort required to become certified. The lack of long-term career commitment to the occupation by many paralegals is an added factor reducing interest in certification.

Licensing of paralegals, a possible alternative to certification, has never had any appreciable support.[54] Why is this so when lawyers are licensed in all states and paralegals frequently have sought to emulate lawyers? Many other occupations also are licensed, a form of legal control with monopoly advantages to those licensed and arguable benefits to those they serve. Lack of support for paralegal licensing is attributable to the concern that it would exclude many persons from the occupation or materially cut back on the tasks they are entitled to perform. Licensing poses a potential threat to most of those in the occupation, and also could be disadvantageous to lawyers by restricting their flexibility in use of support staff and perhaps increasing the cost of more skilled paralegals. Furthermore, to some lawyers it is perceived as a threat because of the possibility that it would be used as a means of breaking down unauthorized practice barriers and permitting licensed paralegals independently to represent clients in the practice of law. Nor does the argument often advanced for occupational licensing, that it is a needed means of consumer protection, have much appeal when applied to paralegal licensing. Consumers when dealing with many occupations may need the protection of licensing to give some assurance of competence and trustworthiness in those they select as service providers. But consumers of legal services retain lawyers, not paralegals, and lawyers not only are licensed but there are strong inducements for them to make certain that their paralegal employees perform properly and do not incur the risk of employer liability for paralegal work damaging to clients. Paralegal licensing would add little to this client protection. It also would create extremely troublesome problems of unauthorized practice of paralegalism. Strong support for licensing ultimately may come from highly skilled paralegals, but if so, it will probably meet tremendous opposition from inside and outside the occupation.

Another controversial issue concerning paralegals is the extent to which law offices should develop and use formal systems in handling repeat work.[55] Increasingly, as law offices are under greater pressure to become more efficient and to emulate business enterprises, this issue is being faced as a matter of internal law office policy. Advocates of formal systems for legal work generally favor systems that are reduced to writing and that include such instructional materials as manuals, checklists, and legal forms. These materials are often considered most useful if prepared in-house and reflect the preferred standards of the office and the special needs of its clients. Well-designed and well-implemented in-house systems may also give a competitive edge to an office over its rivals and opponents. Paralegals are not essential to the effective use of formal systems for performing law office work, but an advantage of such systems is that they commonly make feasible more extensive reliance on paralegals, with consequent further possibilities of cost savings. Systems proponents often stress the cost cutting that can result from well-programmed and well-administered systems employing the paralegals to do much of the work. The interest in systems within the legal profession greatly increased with emergence of paralegals as a recognized and expanding occupational group.[56]

Formal written systems have been adopted and are being utilized in some law offices, but the concept has not been as widely or completely accepted and implemented as its proponents believe is needed. Why this reluctance, even opposition, despite the support and rather aggressive promotion formal systems have received? There are a number of apparent reasons. Many law offices do not have a sufficient volume of repeat work to make it worthwhile developing and putting in place a formal system of the kind contemplated by systems proponents. Creating, training for, and monitoring a system is expensive, and a steady and substantial work flow normally is essential to justify these efforts in financial terms. Also, many legal matters are not sufficiently routine to make them suitable for application of formal systems. Doctrinal legal problems presented may be new or untested; the evidence may be complex, difficult to assemble, and its probative value uncertain; and what clients or adjudicators will accept may be unpredictable, making it desirable to develop alternate solutions. Factors of this sort are common in many fields of law and militate against routine handling. Then, too, some matters of a type usually routine may be inappropriate for routine approaches because of their exceptional importance. Their importance may be due to the very large amounts of money involved or to other crucial concerns calling for tactics or procedures beyond the ordinary.

Another deterrent to law office adoption of formal systems is that many lawyers react negatively to the formal systems concept, to the idea that a formally structured regimen should be imposed on how lawyers handle client problems. Some lawyers believe that no client's problems are routine,[57] that the factual detail—including time, place, and personalities—differs with each matter that comes into the office, and each matter deserves individualized consideration. Formal systems encourage routine processing that some lawyers consider an unsatisfactory form of client service. The formal systems approach is also antithetical to many lawyers because by temperament and training these lawyers are not good organizers and administrators, aptitudes normally required in establishing and properly operating formal systems. Such lawyers find their satisfaction in problem solving on a case-by-case basis and hence wish to avoid regularizing and overseeing the flow of routine matters.

Not only do many lawyers consider formal systems unsuitable or undesirable for their law offices and the way they prefer to practice law, but the systems concept as commonly described has been challenged as potentially stultifying to paralegals. William Statsky, a paralegal educator sensitive to the interests of paralegals, argues that systems that make paralegals mere routine assembly line operators and eliminate occasions for paralegals to make independent judgments can be disadvantageous to both paralegals and their employers. Overly mechanical and drudgerous systems can cause paralegal alienation and also deprive the law office of paralegals' judgmental capacities.[58] The systems issue poses problems of the proper role for paralegals and may become a focal point for paralegal dissension within law offices. It is an issue, however, that more and more law offices will resolve by adopting systems in an effort to remain competitive. The trend toward larger and more specialized law offices with enhanced volumes in particular specialty fields will tend to make systems increasingly feasible, acceptable, and necessary.

Still another issue involving paralegals that is proving troublesome and controversial is the extent to which the organized bar, particularly the bar associations, should seek to influence and control the paralegal occupation. The organized bar has been ambivalent about its role in this regard. On the one hand, there are organized bar groups highly favorable to paralegals, principally because they view paralegals as useful adjuncts to lawyers who can increase lawyers' profits and the cost effectiveness of law offices. On the other hand, there is an undercurrent of concern within the organized bar that as paralegals become more numerous, more able, and better organized, they may pose a threat to lawyers. The ultimate threat is that paralegals may in time demand and acquire the right to practice some fields of law independent of lawyer supervision and hence to compete with lawyers in attracting clients. One result of these conflicting concerns over paralegals has been an organized bar policy of limited encouragement to the use and development of paralegals but making it clear that paralegals are lawyers' assistants, a subordinate relationship that is and will continue to be backed by law.

Organized bar groups favorable to paralegals, typified by the ABA's Section of Economics of Law Practice and ABA and state bar committees on legal assistants, have sought to encourage lawyers' use of paralegals, increase the effectiveness of that use, and enhance the competence of paralegals.[59] In furtherance of these objectives, representatives of the organized bar have, in speeches and articles, promoted the use of paralegals;[60] published educational materials on how best to use paralegals;[61] held conferences and seminars for paralegals;[62] and instituted and administered an approval program for paralegal schools. In the ABA, from which much of this support has come, encouraging paralegal use and development has, however, been a modest priority and there recently have been cutbacks in ABA funding of this support, part of an overall effort to contain burgeoning expenditures by the association.

Organized bar opposition to paralegals obtaining the right to practice law independently is reflected in the previously discussed authoritative rules and opinions directed against unauthorized practice of law by nonlawyers, including paralegals. Most of this body of authority was either initially promulgated or strongly backed by bar associations, and enforcement of unauthorized practice laws usually has been instigated by bar associations.

The reaction of paralegals to bar association involvement in paralegal matters has been mixed. Paralegals generally have welcomed efforts by bar organizations to promote the use of paralegals by lawyers and have cooperated in bar association-sponsored seminars and conferences for paralegals and in the bar groups' preparation of educational materials directed at paralegals. Bar association regulation of paralegals, however, has generated doubts, suspicions, and some degree of opposition among paralegals. As an abstract proposition, most paralegal organizations and many paralegals are opposed to their occupation being regulated by the organized bar.[63] Important paralegal groups also have questioned the ABA role in approval of paralegal schools, suggesting that a more broadly based body might be a more appropriate approval or accreditation medium.[64] In addition, a minority of paralegals and their adherents are opposed to bar association-backed unauthorized practice restrictions on paralegals and favor relaxation of those controls that would permit independent paralegal representation of clients in at least some fields of law where such practice is now prohibited.[65] Further, there has been paralegal association opposition to paralegal divisions or associate memberships within bar associations,[66] a co-optation perceived as not only a competitive threat to paralegal associations but as a move that could lead to extended efforts by the organized bar to control paralegals.

Clearly, lines are being drawn between the organized bar and paralegals as to what controls should be imposed on paralegals and by whom. There seems to be a strong preference by those paralegals concerned about the matter for a very considerable measure of occupational self-control in their group endeavors and to avoid, when possible, dominance by the organized bar. Paralegals recognize that in the employment relationship they are subordinate to lawyers, but they want more autonomy in their collective affairs. When and if paralegal organizations attract substantially larger memberships, paralegal resistance to organized bar control efforts is likely to increase.

NOTES

1. The term *social control* has a variety of meanings in scholarly writing. Some of these meanings are discussed in Janowitz, Sociological Theory and Social Control, 81 *American Journal of Sociology* 82 (1975). In this study, the term is used in a broad sense to mean regulation by a society in accord with desired principles and values. For a variety of views on social control, *see also* J. Gibbs (ed.), *Social Control* (1982); and D. Black (ed.), *Toward a General Theory of Social Control* (2 vols. 1984). Participation of lawyers in social control relationships is considered in Tomasic, Lawyers and Social Control, A Preliminary Inquiry, 3 *Windsor Yearbook of Access to Justice* 20 (1983).

2. As yet, there apparently are few such firms and those that exist apparently are concentrated in California. Some of them are available on a subcontract basis to do all of the work in a particular field, such as decedents' estates, for law offices buying their services, whether on an emergency or regular basis. On paralegals as independent contractors, *see* Freelance Paralegals, A Conference Overview, *New Roles in the Law Conference Report* 109–11 (1982); and Speech by Linda Harrington, Freelancer, *id.*, at 117–26. The operation most similar to this in New York City of which we are aware is a freelance paralegal turned up in our small-firm sample who works part-time for several small law firms and has occasionally hired other paralegals to help him. His specialty is litigation.

3. New York Judiciary Law, §478. Another section prohibits persons not admitted to practice law in New York from receiving compensation for appearing for a person other than himself as attorney in any court or for drafting specified legal instruments. New York Judiciary Law, §484.

4. New York Judiciary Law, §495.

5. New York Judiciary Law, §485.

6. New York Judiciary Law, §476 a and b.

7. The Code includes similar provisions; *see* American Bar Association, Code of Professional Responsibility, Canon 3 and DR 3–101A.

8. The South Carolina Supreme Court, in a recent case, expressly directed the attention of the South Carolina bar to EC 3–6 in holding a disbarred attorney in contempt for, after disbarment, preparing, having executed, and recording a deed for another. Respondent's defense was that he merely was performing the services of a paralegal. In its opinion, the court said:

Paralegals are routinely employed by licensed attorneys to assist in the preparation of legal documents such as deeds and mortgages. The activities of a paralegal do not constitute the practice of law as long as they are limited to work of a preparatory nature, such as legal research, investigation, or the composition of legal documents, which enable the licensed attorney-employer to carry a given matter to a conclusion through his own examination, approval or additional effort. . . .

The evidence presently before this Court fails to show that respondent's final work product was subject to the approval of a licensed attorney before recordation or that the parties to the deed conferred with a licensed attorney concerning the deed.

It is therefore adjudged that respondent is in contempt of court for engaging in the practice of law in violation of this Court's Order of disbarment. The South Carolina Law Enforcement

Division is hereby ordered to arrest respondent and imprison him in the Richland County Jail for the term of thirty (30) days.

In the Matter of Easler, 275 S.C. 400, 272 S.E.2d 32 (1980).

In a controversial policy statement, the Chicago Bar Association recently approved paralegal closing of real estate transactions without the employing lawyer being present:

... A paralegal may close a real estate transaction unaccompanied by the employing attorney, only (i) if all documents have been prepared and approved by all parties in advance of the closing, (ii) with prior consent of other counsel, and (iii) with the employing attorney being available for consultation and instructions by telephone. Within the foregoing limitations, the use of a paralegal to close a real estate transaction, unaccompanied by the employing attorney, should be approached with caution, having regard to the skill and experience of the paralegal, the complexity of the transaction and the client-attorney relationship, and bearing in mind that the employing attorney retains ultimate responsibility for the transaction.

1 *Legal Assistant Today* no. 2, at 30 (1984). On the Chicago Bar Association policy statement, *see also* A Risky Stand-In?, 69 *American Bar Association Journal* 1812 (1983).

9. *See* New York State Bar Association, Committee on Professional Ethics, Subcommittee on Legal Assistants (1976), Guidelines for Utilization by Lawyers of the Service of Legal Assistants, Appendix, appearing in P. Ulrich and R. Mucklestone (eds.), *Working with Legal Assistants*, vol. 2, at 323–27 (1981). *See also* Committee on Professional and Judicial Ethics of the Bar Association of the City of New York, opinion 884 (1974), one of the most comprehensive bar association opinions as to the professional ethics responsibilities of attorneys who employ paralegals. In opinion 884, this excerpt from ABA Committee on Professional Ethics Opinion 316 (1967) is quoted with approval:

A lawyer can employ lay secretaries, lay investigators, lay detectives, lay researchers, accountants, lay scriveners, nonlawyer draftsmen or nonlawyer researchers. In fact, he may employ nonlawyers to do any tasks for him except counsel clients about law matters, engage directly in the practice of law, appear in court or appear in formal proceedings a part of the judicial process, so long as it is he who takes the work and vouches for it to the client and becomes responsible for it to the client. In other words, we do not limit the kind of assistants the lawyer can acquire in any way to persons who are admitted to the Bar, so long as the nonlawyers do not do things that lawyers may not do or do the things that lawyers only may do.

Opinion 884 also quotes with approval from New York State Bar Association Ethics Committee Opinion 44 (1967), as follows:

A clerk should not represent a client in litigation before any court or administrative tribunal, nor should he perform any act where he would be expected to exercise independent discretion. A clerk may, however, appear at and answer calendar calls, providing no argument is necessary and so long as his role is properly confined to a purely ministerial activity [citing and quoting Opinion 78 of this Committee].

The clerk may not appear to argue motions, conduct examinations for the purpose of taking the depositions of a witness [*see*, to the same effect, NYSBA Opin. 304 (1973)] or conduct examinations on supplementary proceedings.

A clerk may, without his employer being present, attend mortgage closings and other out-of-court matters, but only so long as his responsibilities are clearly limited to those functions not involving independent discretion or judgment.

Finally, a clerk should never independently advise a client concerning his legal rights and duties. Moreover, if a client requests advice from the clerk, either at a face-to-face conference or on the telephone, the client should be informed that the clerk is not a member of the Bar, but only a clerk without the right to give independent legal advice.

Lawyers' professional responsibility obligations involving paralegals are discussed at some length in Ulrich and Mucklestone, *supra* ch. 14, an adaptation of which appears in 67 *American Bar Association Journal* 992 (1981); W. Statsky, *Introducton to Paralegalism* ch. 4 (2d ed. 1982); Haskell, Issues in Paralegalism: Education, Certification, Licensing, Unauthorized Practice, 15 *Georgia Law Review* 631, at 651–62 (1981); Judd, Beyond the Bar: Legal Assistants and the Unauthorized Practice of Law, *Legal Assistants Update*, vol. 3, at 3 (1983); Lehan, Ethical Considerations of Employing Paralegals in Florida, 20 *Law Office Economics and Management* 87 (1979); Lamont, State by State Survey of Activities Regarding Legal Assistants, *Legal Assistants Update '81*, at 65 (1981); and Comment, Legal Paraprofessionals and Unauthorized Practice, 8 *Harvard Civil Rights-Civil Liberties Law Review* 104 (1973). Illustrative advice paralegals are receiving on unauthorized practice appears in Clark, Unauthorized Practice of Law, 7 *Facts and Findings* no. 2, at 1 (1980); and Weathersby, Ethical Conduct and the Unauthorized Practice of Law, 10 *Facts and Findings* no. 3, at 5 (1983).

In a few states, bar associations or courts have adopted guidelines for utilization of paralegals by lawyers. Those adopted in New Hampshire, New York, and Illinois appear in Ulrich and Mucklestone, *supra* 305–328. Also, *see* Kuckherman, Professional Development Guidelines, 7 *National Paralegal Reporter* no. 3, at 9 (1983), expressing a negative position on guidelines.

Paralegal associations have also developed their own codes of ethics for paralegals, indicating the importance they attach to occupational standards of conduct. These codes, on unauthorized practice and other matters, are consistent with the lawyers' standards of conduct. One of the paralegal associations, the National Association of Legal Assistants, has also adopted guidelines pertaining to unauthorized practice. National Association of Legal Assistants, Model Standards and Guidelines for Utilization of Legal Assistants, 11 *Facts and Findings* no. 1 at 6 (1984). We are unaware of any instance in which courts have as yet cited or relied on paralegal association codes of ethics or guidelines in deciding matters before them. On the paralegal association codes, *see supra* chapter 3, note 8.

The suggestion has been made that the American Bar Association prepare a model code of professional responsibility for paralegals, including procedures for enforcement. Ulrich, Legal Assistants and the Organized Bar—Where Do We Go From Here?, 8 *National Paralegal Reporter* no. 3, at 12 (1983). Such a model code, if prepared, presumably would then be considered for adoption by paralegal associations, bar associations, and courts.

10. American Bar Association, Code of Professional Responsiblity, EC 3–5 states: "The essence of the professional judgment of the lawyer is his educated ability to relate the general body and philosophy of law to a specific legal problem of a client. . . . " Assuming that these professional judgment situations can be identified, what supervisory action by a lawyer will permit a paralegal working for the lawyer to perform tasks calling for professional judgment? Neither the Code nor the Model Rules is helpful in answering this question.

11. On ethical problems when a lawyer hires an independent contractor para-

legal, *see* Brookes, Do Independent Contractors Have Special Ethical Considerations?, 10 *Facts and Findings* no. 3, at 7 (1982).

12. For the general prohibition on lay employees making court appearances for
their corporate employers, *see* Comment, Representation of a Corporation by Its
Lay Employees, 5 *Journal of the Legal Profession* 217 (1980).

In 1983, the Kentucky Supreme Court, in a 4–3 decision, denied a motion of
paralegal associations in Kentucky to authorize paralegals to make court appearances of a ministerial or clerical nature and to vacate Kentucky Bar Association
Advisory Opinion E-266 holding that no such appearances can be made. KBA E-
266 appears in 47 *Kentucky Bench and Bar* no. 1, at 43 (1983); and the motion
and court decision are discussed in Burton, Kentucky Update: Motion for Review
Denied, 8 *National Paralegal Reporter* no. 1, at 10 (1983).

13. Lead unauthorized practice cases pertaining to major occupations were particularly prevalent during the period 1920–1960 and established both grounds for
and limits on legal service work that these occupations could perform. On these
cases, *see* Christensen, The Unauthorized Practice of Law: Do Good Fences Make
Good Neighbors—Or Even Good Sense?, *1980 American Bar Foundation Research
Journal* 159, at 189–97; and Johnstone, The Unauthorized Practice Controversy,
A Struggle Among Power Groups, 4 *Kansas Law Review* 1 (1955). Occasional
unauthorized practice cases still arise, however, brought at the bar's instigation
and involving occupations long competitive with lawyers. *See*, for example, N.J.
State Bar Assn. v. N.J. Assn. of Realtor Boards, 461 A.2d 1112 (N.J. 1983),
brought against real estate brokers; and Bennion, Van Camp, Hagen and Ruhl v.
Kassler Escrow, Inc., 96 Wash. 2d 443, 635 Pac.2d 730 (1981), brought against
escrow agents. Following the above Washington case, the Washington Supreme
Court established a board for testing and certifying closing officers who may perform
limited legal services.

14. For example, Sperry v. State of Florida ex rel. The Florida Bar, 373 U.S.
379 (1963); Conway-Bogue Realty Investment Co. v. Denver Bar Assn., 135 Colo.
398, 312 P.2d 998 (1957); Brotherhood of Railroad Trainmen v. Virginia ex rel.
Virginia State Bar, 377 U.S. 1 (1964); and New York County Lawyers' Assn. v.
Dacey, 21 N.Y.2d 694, 287 N.Y. Supp.2d 422 (1967).

15. Fear of antitrust prosecution also has been the principal reason for statements
of principles being dropped as a meaningful approach to unauthorized practice
problems. Statements of principles are agreements between bar associations and
professional or trade associations of other occupations that set forth activities
properly belonging to each participating occupation. Understandings are added
that each occupation will stay within its agreed-to sphere of activities, not performing services that the statement provides can properly be performed only by
the other signatory occupation. The American Bar Association and some state bar
associations had signed statements of principles with a number of other occupational
associations. These agreements have generally been rescinded or allowed to become
inoperative. On the recent fate of statements of principles, *see* Christensen, *supra*
note 13, at 200; and Podgers, Statements of Principles: Are They on the Way Out?,
66 *American Bar Association Journal* 129 (1980). For a recent analysis by a Federal
Trade Commission official of federal government antitrust policy affecting self-
regulation by the legal profession, *see* Winslow, Regulating the Profession, the
FTC Approach, 9 *Bar Leader* no. 1, at 23 (1983).

16. For attacks from within the legal profession on unauthorized practice laws, *see* Christensen, *supra* note 13, at 159–216; Morgan, The Evolving Concept of Professional Responsibility, 90 *Harvard Law Review* 702, at 707–12 (1977); Rhode, Policing the Professional Monopoly: A Constitutional and Empirical Analysis of Unauthorized Practice Prohibitions, 34 *Stanford Law Review* 1 (1981); Hunter and Klonoff, A Dialogue on the Unauthorized Practice of Law, 25 *Villanova Law Review* 6 (1979–80); Project, The Unauthorized Practice of Law and Pro Se Divorce: An Empirical Analysis, 86 *Yale Law Journal* 104 (1976); Note, Legalizing Nonlawyer Proprietorship in the Legal Clinic Industry: Reform in the Public Interest, 9 *Hosfta Law Review* 625 (1981).

17. Examples of recent appellate opinions holding novel or unusual lay legal service activities to be the unauthorized practice of law are Dauphin County Bar Assn. v. Mazzacaro, 465 Pa. 545, 351 A.2d 229 (1976), lay claims adjuster enjoined from representing accident victims in settlement efforts with tort feasors or their insurers; Oregon State Bar v. Gilchrist, 272 Or. 552, 538 P.2d 913 (1975), lay persons enjoined from assisting parties to divorce proceedings in selecting and filling out divorce kit forms; In re The Florida Bar, 355 So.2d 766 (Fla. 1978), insurance agent enjoined from preparing legal instruments and giving legal advice in pension and corporate planning; Florida Bar v. Carmel, 287 So.2d 305 (Fla. 1974), layman enjoined from providing for others a service of preparing, filing, and releasing mechanics' and materialmens' liens and providing a mechanics' lien kit to customers with information on legal rights.

A recent unauthorized practice case that received nationwide media attention is Florida Bar v. Furman, 376 So.2d 378 (Fla. 1979), appeal dismissed, 444 U.S. 1061 (1980), contempt ordered, 451 So.2d 808 (Fla. 1984). Defendant operated a secretarial service and provided assistance to clients in a variety of legal matters for which she also typed up necessary legal documents. Many of those she worked for were acting pro se in divorce or adoption proceedings. After being enjoined from practicing law, she persisted in the work she had been doing and was held in criminal contempt. Her negative comments about lawyers and judges were widely quoted, and following proceedings being filed against her, she received sympathetic support from many lay sources. It is alleged that Ms. Furman had served 10,000 clients. Murry, Slugging It Out for Justice, 1 *Legal Assistant Today* no. 4, at 20 (1984). For reactions of the Florida State Bar President to the Furman case, *see* Henry, Ms. Furman, 58 *Florida Bar Journal* 269 (1984). A favorable view of Ms. Furman's activities and the significance of her case appear in Murry, The Rosemary Furman Issues That Won't Go Away, 2 *Legal Assistant Today* no. 1, at 10. Toward the end of her article, *id.*, at 36, Murry concludes:

Some say the day may not be too far off when many segments of the public could have legal needs met by corporations of paralegals who hire attorneys to oversee their work.

This wide open look at the practice of law is what the Furman issues are really about. It is not whether she did or did not give legal advice. Isn't it more a question of whether what she says and does needs to be said and done?

For a legal service model in which lawyers would be paraprofessionals' assistants in social action and social reform organizations, *see* American Bar Association, *New Careers in Law II* 40–41 (1971).

18. Richard Abel defines legitimation as follows:

Legitimation is the attempt by those engaged in some realm of social activity to offer a normative justification for their actions. The attempt may be addresssed to an external audience, as in public relations, but it may also be a dialogue among the participants themselves. Participants need not speak with a unified voice; segments can offer different, even inconsistent accounts (in which case legitimation can also be a form of symbolic politics, a competition for status through the declaration of moral superiority). An activity may plausibly be interpreted as an attempt at legitimation even if it does not succeed in that attempt—even if no one, not even those engaged in the enterprise, is satisfied by the result. Despite the pejorative connotations that sometimes attach to the term, the justification may be persuasive and coherent as well as flimsy and illogical, and the person advancing it may be sincere as well as hypocritical. . . .

Abel, Why Does the ABA Promulgate Ethical Rules?, 59 *Texas Law Review* 639, at 668 (1981). He also discusses legitimation in Abel, Toward a Political Economy of Lawyers, 1981 *Wisconsin Law Review* 1117, at 1162–82.

19. Arguments advanced by occupations and their representatives in the process of legitimation may constitute ideology or myth as some social scientists use those terms. For example, *see* H. Lasswell, N. Leites, and associates, *Language of Politics* 9–10 (1949); and R. Merton, *Social Theory and Social Structure* 546–48 (1968).

20. Bower, Can Paralegals Be Profitable?, 54 *Florida Bar Journal* 223 (1980).

21. Fellers, The Economics and Delivery of Legal Services, 58 *Judicature* 114, at 115 (1974). When this was written, James Fellers was president of the American Bar Association.

22. Comment, The Revitalization of the Legal Profession Through Paralegalism, 30 *Baylor Law Review* 841, at 852 (1978).

23. Stevenson, Using Paralegals in the Practice of Law, 62 *Illinois Bar Journal* 432, at 432, 438 (1974). Among many other similar statements are those in R. Kurzman and R. Gilbert, *Paralegals and Successful Law Practice* pt. 1, sec. 1; New York State Bar Association, in Ulrich and Mucklestone, *supra* note 9, at 316; McMenamin, Dawn of the Age of the Legal Assistant, 59 *American Bar Association Journal* 1448 (1973); Sternin, Ten Most Frequently Asked Questions About Paralegals, 3 *Legal Economics* no. 4, at 33 (1978); Kurlander and Wilson, The Paralegals' Role in Law Office Efficiency, 7 *Facts and Findings* no. 6, at 9 (1981).

A California paralegal educator and former paralegal has warned, however, that: "The public is not well served by the development of the lay assistant as another legal specialist who assists the lawyer in the delivery of legal services if the cost of those services continues to increase. It has not been adequately documented that any cost saving resulting from the use of the legal assistant has been effectively passed on to the consuming public." Watenmaker, The Impact of the Legal Assistant on the Delivery of Legal Services, 10 *Journal of the Beverly Hills Bar Association* no. 7, 22, at 49 (1976). In the same vein, *see* comments by Statsky, The Education of Legal Paraprofessionals: Myths, Realities, and Opportunities, 24 *Vanderbilt Law Review* 1083, at 1130 (1971). For an article by a management consultant concluding that many law firms, in terms of billable hour profits, are not making money from their paralegals or as much money as they could be making, *see* Malone, Smart Money, 1 *Legal Assistant Today* no. 1, 26 (1983). Malone attributes low or no profitability to ineffectual paralegal utilization principally.

24. Kurzman and Gilbert, *supra* note 23, at 7; Sparer, Thorkelson, and Weiss, The Lay Advocate, 43 *University of Detroit Law Journal* 493, at 511–12 (1966);

and Ulrich, Organizing, Developing and Managing a Legal Assistant Program, 22 *Law Office Economics and Management* 197, at 198 (1981).

25. Ulrich, *supra* note 24.

26. American Bar Association, *supra* note 17, at 1–4.

27. For example, State v. Sperry, 140 So.2d 587, 595 (Fla. 1962); Resh, The Bar's Duty to Prevent Unauthorized Practice, 30 *Unauthorized Practice News* 177, at 187–88 (1964); Johnstone and Hopson, *Lawyers and Their Work* 173–75 (1967).

28. Dauphin County Bar Assn. v. Mazzacaro, 465 Pa. 545, 551, 351 A.2d 229, 232 (1976). In a similar vein, *see* ABA Standing Committee on Unauthorized Practice of Law Report, 32 *Unauthorized Practice News* no. 2, 47, at 48 (1966).

29. Fry, The Future of Paralegals and Advocacy, *New Roles in the Law Conference Report* 230, at 233–34 (1982). *See also* Baily, Kleeman, and Ring, Paralegal Functions and Legal Restraints, 9 *Clearinghouse Review* 851 (1976); Fry, A Short Review of the Paralegal Movement, 7 *Clearinghouse Review* 463, at 469 (1973); Sparer, Thorkelson, and Weiss, The Lay Advocate, *supra* note 24, at 493–515.

30. Selinger, Functional Division of the American Legal Profession: The Legal Paraprofessional, 22 *Journal of Legal Education* 22 (1969).

31. *See supra*, note 16. Arguments opposing the bar's monopoly are also discussed in Johnstone and Hopson, *supra* note 27, at 175–77 (1967).

32. For an indication of what is likely to happen to any paralegals who might seek to go it alone as private practitioners representing their own lay clients, *see supra* note 17, in which illustrative cases are cited of various lay activities held to be the unauthorized practice of law.

33. This expansive view is also reflected in some paralegal instructional materials. For example, *see* T. Eimermann, *Fundamentals of Paralegalism* 49–55 (1980); and N. Shayne, *The Paralegal Profession* 1–2 (1977).

34. On malpractice liability of lawyers, *see* American Bar Association, Section of Insurance, Negligence, and Compensation Law, *Professional Liability of Trial Lawyers: The Malpractice Question* (1979); R. Mallen and V. Levit, *Legal Malpractice* (2d ed. 1981); C. Kindregan, *Malpractice and the Lawyer* (rev. ed. 1981); D. Stern and J. Felix-Retzke, *A Practical Guide to Preventing Legal Malpractice* (1983); Symposium, Legal Malpractice, 30 *South Carolina Law Review* 201 (1979); Johnston, Legal Malpractice in Estate Planning—Perilous Times Ahead for the Practitioner, 67 *Iowa Law Review* 629 (1982); Pfennigstorf, Types and Causes of Lawyers' Professional Liability Claims: The Search for Facts, *1980 American Bar Foundation Research Journal* 255; Wade, Tort Liability of Paralegals and Lawyers Who Utilize Their Services, 24 *Vanderbilt Law Review* 1133 (1971); Comment, Attorney Professional Responsibility: Competence Through Malpractice Liability, 77 *Northwestern Law Review* 633 (1982); and Comment, On the Question of Negligence: The Paraprofessional, 4 *University of Toledo Law Review* 553 (1973).

35. Wade, *supra* note 34, at 1145–48; and Mallen and Levit, *supra* note 34, at §35. *See also* American Law Institute, *Restatement (Second) of Agency*, §§212, 213, and 219. There are few reported American judicial opinions in which lawyers have been held liable for acts of their paralegals or other lay employees. One such case, however, is In re McGuinness, 69 App. Div. 606, 74 N.Y.S. 1054 (1902), lawyer liable to client for fraud by the lawyer's clerk; and *cf.* Attorney Grievance Commn. v. Goldberg, 441 A.2d 338 (Md. Ct. Apls. 1982), lawyer operating a legal clinic suspended from the practice for failure to supervise adequately an employee func-

tioning essentially as a paralegal who negligently handled many matters, resulting in the lawyer being held to have violated several sections of the Code of Professional Responsibility; Gleason v. Title Guarantee Co., 300 F.2d 813 (1962), lawyer liable to client for defective title examination by an abstract company; Noble v. Sears, Roebuck and Co., 33 Cal. App. 3d 654, 109 Cal. Rptr. 269 (1973), lawyer can be liable to injured party for intentional torts of employee of a private detective agency hired by the lawyer; Vaughn v. State Bar of California, 6 Cal. 3d 847, 494 P.2d 1257 (1972), lawyer disciplined for, among other misconduct, gross negligence in failure properly to supervise his office staff; DeVaux v. American Home Assurance Co., 387 Mass. 814, 444 N.E.2d 355 (1983), summary judgment for defendant reversed and case remanded for trial in malpractice action against lawyer whose secretary misfiled letter requesting legal advice, which letter was not discovered by lawyer until after the statute of limitations had run out. Despite skimpy case authority, it seems probable that there are many unreported situations in which improper paralegal work performance has led lawyers or their insurers to pay off on malpractice claims.

36. W. Statsky, *Torts: Personal Injury Litigation* 462–65 (1982); Wade, *supra* note 34, at 1134.

37. Mallen and Levit, *supra* note 34, at chs. 4 and 5.

38. McCarthy, Insurance Aspects of Legal Malpractice, in American Bar Association, *supra* note 34, at 50. On claims data, including the relatively high frequency of claims, *see also* Pfennigstorf, *supra* note 34, at 255–63.

39. J. Felix, *A Lawyer's Guide to Legal Malpractice Insurance* ix (1982). On malpractice insurance for lawyers, *see also* Mallen and Levit, *supra* note 34, at ch. 22; McCarthy, *supra* note 38; Stern and Felix-Retzke, *supra* note 34, at ch. 9; and Stern and Johnson, Understanding Your Professional Liability Insurance Policy, in American Bar Association, Section of General Practice, 13 *Law Notes* no. 2 (1977).

40. Morrison, Who Sues or Defends Attorneys?, *National Law Journal*, March 28, 1983, at 1.

41. Felix, *supra* note 39, at 19.

42. Mallen and Levit, *supra* note 34, at 881.

43. Stern, Causes of Attorney Malpractice Claims, 3 *Professional Liability Reporter* 199 (1979). Stern reports on a thirteen-state study of malpractice claims that disclosed major causes of such claims to be these: failure to meet procedural deadline, 11.23 percent; faulty research or abstract, 9.02 percent; errors in preparation of document, 8.30 percent; failure to comply with statutes of limitations, 7.19 percent; fraud or conspiracy, 6.03 percent; failure to file required papers, 5.64 percent; malicious prosecution or abuse of process, 4.87 percent; inadequate advice, 4.81 percent; incorrect advice, 3.87 percent; and improper interpretation of law, 3.54 percent. On types of lawyers' malpractice claims, *see also* Pfennigstorf, *supra* note 34, at 271–74.

44. On effective docket controls, *see* K. Strong and D. Stern, *Docket Control Systems for Lawyers* (1981).

45. *Supra* note 43.

46. On lawyer certification, *see* American Bar Association, Standing Committee on Specialization, *Interim Report* (Oct. 1976); Christensen, Toward Improved Legal Service Delivery: A Look at Four Mechanisms, *1979 American Bar Foundation*

Research Journal 277, at 280–83; and Haskell, *supra* note 9, at n. 53. There also is a national certification program for trial lawyers, administered by a private organization, the National Board of Trial Advocacy. Lumbard, Specialty Certification for Lawyers: The National Alternative to the Non-Existent State Programs, 67 *Women Lawyers Journal* no. 1, at 23 (1980). The ABA's Special Committee on Legal Assistants has defined certification and licensure as follows:

Certification is the process by which a nongovernmental agency or association grants recognition to an individual who has met certain pre-determined qualifications specified by that agency or association.

Licensure is the process by which an agency (or branch) of government grants permission to persons meeting predetermined qualifications to engage in a given occupation and/or use a particular title or grants permission to institutions to perform specific functions.

American Bar Association, Special Committee on Legal Assistants, *Certification of Legal Assistants* 10 (1975).

47. On the NALA certification program, *see supra* ch. 3, at notes 13–15 and accompanying text.

The English paralegal association, the Institute of Legal Executives (ILEX), has long had what in effect is a certification program somewhat similar to that of NALA, but a far higher percentage of the nation's paralegals participate in it. There are different gradations of paralegals in the English program, the highest being fellows, and those qualifying as fellows must have substantial work experience and pass a stiff examination mostly on substantive legal subjects. On the ILEX certification program, *see* Johnstone and Flood, Paralegals in English and American Law Offices, 2 *Windsor Yearbook of Access to Justice* 152, at 181–83 (1982); Royal Commission on Legal Services, *Final Report*, vol. 1, at 408–10 (HMSO, cmnd. 7648, 1979); and the Institute of Legal Executives, Memorandum of Evidence to the Royal Commission on Legal Services 18–39 (June 1977).

48. On the Oregon certification program, *see* Oregon State Bar, 1979 Legal Assistant Certification Program, *Legal Assistants Update '80*, at 31 (1980).

49. Farren, Analysis of Findings of State by State Survey of Activities Regarding Legal Assistants, in *Legal Assistants Update '80*, at 19–20 (1980). In 1982, the State Bar of South Dakota proposed that by Supreme Court rule mandatory certification of paralegals be imposed. The South Dakota Supreme Court referred the proposal back to the State Bar for further study. Polsinelli, Certification Proposed in South Dakota, 7 *National Paralegal Reporter* no. 3, at 12 (1983).

50. American Bar Association, Special Committee, *supra* note 46, at 28–29. Also, *see* Report of the Standing Committee on Legal Assistants, 101 *Annual Report of the American Bar Association, 1976*, 313, at 317–22 (1980). This committee recently has indicated that it will restudy the issue of certification. In 1975, the ABA's Standing Committee on Unauthorized Practice of Law also came out against certification of paralegals but apparently for a quite different reason than did the Special Committee on Legal Assistants. The Unauthorized Practice Committee appeared concerned that certification would increase the risk of lay practice of law: "The thought was expressed that the minute it is conceded that paralegals are into the lawful practice of law that you create a second class of lawyer to the disadvantage of the public. . . . In summary, the committee voted that the certification of legal assistants is not in the interest of the public and that the committee should be

opposed to the certification of legal assistants at this time." Report of the August 9, 1975, meeting of the ABA Standing Committee on Unauthorized Practice of Law, 40 *Unauthorized Practice News* 35, at 37–38 (1976). It is unlikely that the Unauthorized Practice Committee's views on paralegals have had any effect on the Legal Assistants Committee.

51. On the arguments for or against paralegal certification, *see* Terhune, The Case for Certification, *Legal Assistants Update '80*, at 5 (1980); Current, The Case Against Certification, *id.*, at 11; NFPA/NALA Focus: Two Perspectives, *Legal Assistants Update*, vol. 3, at 81, 83–85 (1983). On certification, *see also* Kleeman, Limits and Controls, *New Roles in the Law Conference Report* 162, at 167–72 (1982); New York City Paralegal Association Statement on Certification, 6 *Venue* 8 (March 1981), opposed to certification; Sanders-West, Resolved: That legal assistants in Kansas should be able to voluntarily elect to be certified and so recognized, 5 *Facts and Findings*, no. 6, at 9 (1979); American Bar Association, Special Committee, *supra* note 46, at 22–27; Claypool, Regulation of Paralegals Opposed by Mass. Bar Report, 5 *National Paralegal Reporter* no. 1, at 6 (1980); Haskell, *supra* note 9, at 641–51.

In a thoughtful and thorough report by a commission that the Attorney General of Ontario appointed, licensing is opposed for a number of paraprofessional occupations, including paralegals (law clerks and legal secretaries), but a certification system for paraprofessional occupations is recommended. Ministry of the Ontario Attorney General, *The Report of the Professional Organizations Committee* 74–76, 229–33 (1980). Licensure, the committee suggests, "should be reserved for professional markets characterized by high costs of errors by providers, high information costs faced by consumers, and/or substantial and widespread adverse third party effects not fully compensable in damages." *Id.*, at 227. For a generally negative position on mandatory licensure, by an authority on occupational controls, *see* Gellhorn, The Abuse of Occupational Licensing, 44 *University of Chicago Law Review* 6 (1976).

52. Professor Haskell gives a well-reasoned presentation of the case for paralegal specialist certification. Haskell, *supra* note 9, at 648–50. NALA has recently instituted specialty certification in a few fields: litigation, probate and taxation, real estate, corporate, and law office management.

53. Current, *supra* note 51, at 15. On differences between NFPA and NALA on certification, *see also* NFPA/NALA Focus, *supra* note 51. NFPA, however, has had a committee studying the certification issue and this could lead to some shift in that association's position on certification. Peeples, Certification Committee, 8 *National Paralegal Reporter* no. 3, at 13 (1983).

54. There appears to be concern in some paralegal circles, however, that serious efforts to adopt licensing requirements will be made. NALA seems to hope that its Model Standards and Guidelines, with their criteria for minimum paralegal qualifications, will help upgrade the paralegal occupation sufficiently to forestall any licensing efforts. The then president elect of NALA has said:

We recognize that as written these standards and guidelines have no real teeth. They are voluntary only in nature. However, it is the hope of NALA that state bar associations and courts will use these model standards as a guide to development of voluntary standards within their own states. The sole purpose of this document is to aid and provide a service to the legal community, lawyers and legal assistants alike. If standards and guidelines are adopted with some consistency throughout the 50 states there will be no need for licensing. Lacking this, licensing may occur in random instances and we believe our product provides a means of countering unnecessary licensing.

Field, Legal Assistants: Where Do We Go From Here?, 10 *Facts and Findings*, no. 6, 17 at 23 (1984).

55. On systems, *see also supra* ch. 1, notes 9–12 and accompanying text.

56. Two early proponents of systems who had a substantial influence in popularizing this aspect of law office management are Lee Turner and Kline Strong. For their early published comments dealing with systems, *see* Turner, The Effective Use of Lay Personnel, in American Bar Association, *Proceedings of the Third National Conference on Law Office Economics and Management* 27 (1969), abridged version in 11 *Law Office Economics and Management* 73 (1970); and Strong, The "Systems" Approach for Implementing a Program of Providing Legal Assistants for Lawyers, in K. Strong and A. Clark, *Law Office Management* 117 (1974), a paper presented in 1970 to the American Bar Association's Special Committee on Legal Assistants.

57. Chief Justice Burger seems to share this view. In his opinion in Bates v. State Bar of Arizona, 433 U.S. 350, 386 (1977), he says: "Indeed, I find it difficult, if not impossible, to identify categories of legal problems or services which are fungible in nature. For example, Justice Powell persuasively demonstrates [in his Bates opinion] the fallacy of any notion that even an uncontested divorce can be 'standard.' " Both Burger and Powell dissented in part and concurred in part in the Bates case.

58. Statsky writes:

If the result of the systems approach is that paralegals will perform only the routine, mechanical tasks in a law firm, then the result is grossly misguided. This is not to say that the paralegal should have nothing to do with the so-called routine functions of a law practice. In fact, paralegals historically have performed the most routine and standardized tasks in law offices. The mechanical tasks, however, are only the paralegal's starting point from which s/he should move quickly to the more difficult tasks that call for a full range of judgment abilities. If s/he does not make this move, then neither s/he nor his/her employer will tolerate the other very long. . . . In fact, this system will break down if it downplays the role of the paralegal as a significant decision-maker within the law office. The lawyer will find in practice that the most useful paralegal is one who can be trusted to make decisions under general supervision.

Statsky, *supra* note 9, at 114.

59. For a survey of state bar association paralegal activities, *see* 1982 Analysis of State Bar Activities in the Paralegal Profession, *Legal Assistants Update*, vol. 3, at 59 (1983).

60. For example, Fellers, *supra* note 21; McMenamin, *supra* note 23; and Turner, *supra* note 56.

61. For example, Ulrich and Mucklestone, *supra* note 9.

62. *See*, for example, Mason, Personal Observations of the Boston Conference, *Legal Assistants Update '80*, at 89 (1980). Some seminars are held jointly by bar associations and paralegal associations. For materials on one such seminar, *see* Kansas City Bar Association and University of Missouri-Kansas City Law Center in cooperation with the Kansas City Association of Legal Assistants, *Systems for Legal Assistants, Resource Manual* (1980).

63. Illustrative of this view is the following policy position taken at the 1981 Georgetown New Roles in the Law Conference: "The conferees present endorsed the following policy positions on matters of concern to the [paralegal] movement: ... (3) Strongly encouraged self-regulation of the paralegal/lay advocate professions and discouraged the development of guidelines and/or regulation of these professions by state bar organizations...." *New Roles in the Law Conference Report* 237 (1982).

64. *See*, for example, *id.*, at 166–67 and 238; and NFPA/NALA Focus, *supra* note 51, at 91–92. *See also* Gregson, An Explanation of the Federation's Position on Accreditation, 7 *National Paralegal Reporter* no. 3, at 3 (1983), in which the following statement is made:

Paralegal education must remain free of bar domination and evolve and expand in direct response to the public's expressed need for legal services, not to the economic needs of lawyers. The ABA has unilateral control over the accreditation of law schools; it continues to attempt to bring control of our occupation under its umbrella of self-regulation. Historically, self-regulation has been the hallmark of a profession. How we either are or can become a profession in the traditional sense while allowing the ABA to control and accredit our training programs is beyond understanding.

65. *Supra* note 29.

66. On bar association paralegal divisions and associate memberships and opposition to them, *see* ch. 3, *supra*, at notes 28 and 30–32 and accompanying text.

5

PARALEGALS, PROFESSIONS, AND BUREAUCRACY

Most work can be categorized as professional or bureaucratic and most workers as professionals or bureaucrats. A strata of workers can be identified, however, that consists of persons who are neither professionals nor bureaucrats but fall in between and include what can be characterized as paraprofessionals. A paraprofessional is defined by us as a person who performs some of the same work tasks as does a professional, but usually tasks too rudimentary to be most efficiently performed by a professional. In addition, a paraprofessional must have a considerable degree of training and prestige and maintain a substantial measure of collegiality, although to a lesser extent than do professionals. Paraprofessionals are employed or directed by professionals, and commonly are extenders of professional services who, working for or with professionals, enable the professionals to concentrate on what are considered more demanding or more economically essential tasks. Paraprofessionals are to be distinguished from other subprofessional groups, which we refer to as semiprofessionals. Semiprofessionals differ from paraprofessionals in not being substitutes for or extenders of the work of professionals and in not usually being employed or directed by professionals. They do, however, resemble paraprofessionals in their degree of training, prestige, and collegiality. Illustrative semiprofessionals, as we use the term, are social workers, primary and secondary school teachers, librarians, and city planners.[1]

Paraprofessionals are becoming more numerous and more significant, especially where the cost of professional services is high. A growing set of paraprofessionals is apparent in the health field, including nurses, heart-lung machine technicians, physical therapists, and dental assistants. Other examples of paraprofessionals are draftsmen in architects' offices, college teaching assistants, and deacons in some Roman Catholic churches. Most paralegals are paraprofessionals, although the occupation is still so new and somewhat amorphous that there are those labeled as paralegals who are not paraprofessionals. It also should be recognized that persons may have the requisite degree of training, prestige from training and experience, and outside collegial contacts to be paraprofessionals but may not function as such on the job. They may, for example, be assigned by their employers to bureaucratic slots in the organizational hierarchy that are so lacking in prestige, responsibility, and opportunity for collegial relationships with fellow employees that they cannot operate as working paraprofessionals. For a fuller understanding of paraprofessionals, the nature of occupations, professional organizations, and bureaucracy needs to be considered.

THE NATURE OF OCCUPATIONS

Occupations are complex social roles because they combine in very intricate fashion two distinct and basic features of social life. On the one hand, occupations are created sets of obligations and behaviors which have been designed with a unique task in mind: to take on a particular responsibility or fit into a particular division of labor pattern. It is generally understood that most occupations are imposed in the sense that a person is trained to take them on and chooses, in however rudimentary a fashion, to adjust to their perceived constraints.[2] On the other hand, occupations are also expressions of a way of life, a way of supplying a personal identity and living up to the tacit expectations of the people with whom one is significantly associated, such as friends and kin.[3] They are not just means to an end, but ends in themselves, a way of being in a society.[4] Indeed, occupational information is often provided in informal conversation as a way of conveying the sorts of persons who are talking—their preoccupations, their prestige in society, their probable income, and a host of other inferences. To be without an occupation, whether presently working at it or not, is considered a sign of personal crisis going far beyond the financial. It has to do with the purposefulness of a person's life as a whole.

We often lose sight of the designed character of an occupation when we ponder the extent to which it seems the outcropping of a personality or its function for society as a whole. We think it a natural or inherent part of social life, as if we could not imagine a society without preachers or artists, or even the receptionists and waitresses who have become such a neutral and usual part of our mental landscape.

All occupations can be analyzed in terms of the extent to which they have professional or bureaucratic characteristics or some combination of both. Lawyers and physicians are usually perceived of as professionals, clerks and factory workers as bureaucrats. Paralegals are an especially intriguing occupation to analyze in this way not only because they are part of the general development of paraprofessional occupations which makes use of both professional and bureaucratic organizational characteristics, but because they are one instance of the playing out of the conflict between professional and bureaucratic modes of organization that keep vying for dominance in the modern world.[5] A comparative analysis of the roles of paralegals in different settings provides insights as to where and why the paralegal is likely to serve in a bureaucratic role, a professional role, or in a distinctive paraprofessional role that combines characteristics of both bureaucracy and professionalism.

THE ESSENTIALS OF PROFESSIONAL ORGANIZATION

Students of occupations have identified a number of different characteristics of professionals, but three of them we consider of special relevance to the study of law offices and law office utilization of paralegals.[6] These three are collegiality, which resembles identifications in such social communities as tribes and fraternities; occupational prestige, which is largely and usually derived from the prestige of the social class from which occupational members are drawn; and overtraining, the acquisition of excessive learning and skill. The training of professionals is marked by overtraining, far more knowledge acquired by each professional than will ever be needed in any individual professional's practice. Law schools, medical schools, and engineering schools, for instance, all require that each student master vast amounts of subject matter, much of which will turn out to be irrelevant in the particular working career of that student. Overtraining thus is one of the main characteristics of a profession.

All three of these major professional features being stressed by us are contrary to what is commonly found in bureaucratic organizations. Professional overtraining is replaced by bureaucratic specification of the knowledge base needed to perform each task reliably. Prestige is replaced by remuneration as the primary basis for accepting authority and acting authoritatively in work performance. Collegiality, with its independence and autonomy of professionals, is replaced in most bureaucracies by delegation of authority from above to do narrowly specified tasks. In general, bureaucracies are designed social structures, overtly understood as inventions for the achievement of goals, which have a place within our world like so many machines, and like machines, polluting as well as enriching the world of such "natural" social relations as social class. Bureaucracies are hierarchically organized, authority is rigorously imposed downward in a chain of command, there is often a complex division of labor with individual workers assigned narrow roles, incentives for satisfactory role performance are largely monetary, and official conduct is commonly governed by detailed rules.[7] Bureaucracies are organizational forms aimed at rationally and efficiently coordinating the work process, particularly where many individuals and many different skills and aptitudes are needed in carrying out that process. They are extensively adopted in the modern world where pressures for efficiency are strong and where there are many large and complex organizations.

It is to be expected that professionally oriented occupations will often be in conflict with bureaucratically oriented ones. These two kinds of occupations are so different and frequently so competitive with one another, that persons attuned to one commonly find the other threatening, impractical, and even immoral. Conflict can also be expected within organizations over whether they should become more professional or more bureaucratic. In professional organizations such as law offices this conflict can center on the issue of whether to become less professional by taking on more paraprofessionals or even by assigning more responsibility to those already employed.

OVERTRAINING

Overtraining means that before being qualified to practice, each professional is given more knowledge and skills than he is likely to need in his practice.[8] The body of professional knowledge imparted may resemble either tribal lore or scientific principles, and which of the two depends on how one regards the validity of the knowledge. Professional schools all require that each student master vast amounts of subject matter, much of which will turn out to be irrelevant in the working career of that student. In the course of the comprehensive and rigorous education they provide, professional schools also forge a bond of shared traumatic experience among their graduates which gives them a sense of having passed through to another way of life, with its own way of thinking, its own ability to withstand pressure.[9] Professional schools are good examples of places that create a sense of a way of life as an end in itself. The training institution environment, where many of the most talented professionals can be found, also remains a model of what is essential to the occupation and provides a potential focal point from which the occupation can be redirected through the education of a new generation of doctors, lawyers, professors, or other professionals. Each new generation of students sees whatever is done in the professional schools as the essential quality of mind and practice which the occupation should strive to emulate.

A great deal of superfluous training has a number of advantages and disadvantages. It builds up camaraderie and identification with the goals of the profession among those who have gone through the training ordeal; it leads to admiration for those things that are taught and valued in the training institutions, such as careful analysis and hard work; it sorts out many of those who are not likely to be successful practitioners by the crude and coincidental but probably accurate indicator of their ability to master analytic concepts and a great deal of information very rapidly; and it increases the employment options and versatility of professionals by providing them with sufficient exposure to a wide range of background knowledge and skills relevant to practice so that each may choose among many specialty employment possibilities as opportunities present themselves in the future. Furthermore, overtraining often causes professionals to value opportunities for trying out what they feel trained to do.

However, these advantageous features have their disadvantageous complements. People who might make perfectly adequate practitioners are eliminated because they cannot do what only a very selective elite of the occupation ever has to do. Also, the emphasis that many professional school professors give to novel, forefront, and major policy problems may lead to disregard and disparagement of day-to-day professional work and a carryover lack of interest in the ordinary problems of ordinary people when the students become practicing professionals. Moreover, overtraining comes at a very substantial cost in time and money invested by students and schools alike.

But perhaps the most important feature of overtraining, which does not seem to have a negative complement and so is often used to justify the scope and intensity of professional training, is that practitioners will find their day-to-day work so easy in relation to what they are prepared to do that their performance on rudimentary cases is likely to be of so high a caliber, so beyond minimum requirements of the immediate tasks, that they will prove very reliable in doing those routine activities, even without supervision, and without working up to their true capabilities. Even on a bad day, overtired and less than fully attentive, a sufficiently disciplined professional can still handle his practice satisfactorily. A major goal of grueling training is to avoid true horror stories rather than to enable every doctor, lawyer, or other professional to utilize all his skill or knowledge to the maximum.

Overtraining, however, need not be limited to those with full professional credentials. It exists for all those who know considerably more than they need to know to do their jobs. Overtraining in this sense can be of importance to paralegals in how they adjust to their jobs and their sense of satisfaction or dissatisfaction with their work. It also can be of significance to paralegal employers. Our study noted some sharp variations among paralegals in different work settings as to the amount and kind of overtraining they had experienced and in their views and the views of their employers on overtraining.

Most paralegals who attend paralegal school come away with a substantial degree of overtraining in relation to the jobs they are later assigned in law offices and many of them resent the fact that they are not given a chance to make use of much of what they were taught in paralegal school. They interpret their narrow assignments as lack of employer respect for their occupation and lack of employer appreciation of them as individuals. They do not perceive their formal occupational training in a professional sense, as justifiably developing much more knowledge and skill than they will ever need on the job. Instead they are prone to look at their formal training from a bureaucratic point of view: all of their training should be related to the job that each of them takes and failure to assign work broadly enough to require drawing on all major aspects of their training deprives them of work satisfactions and job opportunities that they deserve. Some also are critical of their paralegal school instructors for expressly or implicitly misrepresenting the scope of paralegal work their students later will be doing. Again, they are looking at their formal training in a bureaucratic context—occupational training should be efficient and practical, namely used on the job without wasted learning.

In the large firms, the attitude of paralegals and their employers on the matter of overtraining does not conform to this bureaucratic outlook. These firms pride themselves on hiring paralegals for their superior intellectual quickness and astuteness and often avoid hiring persons who have been to paralegal school. Thus overtraining based on paralegal school experience seldom creates an issue of concern. However, in another sense, many bigfirm paralegals are tremendously overqualified for the work they are expected to perform. Although unquestionably bright and many with degrees from the best universities, these paralegals are often given work far below their capacities. The firms seem pleased with the availability of such qualified people. If the brightest can be secured for rather simple and easy work at a fairly cheap price, why not take advantage of the situation? There are of course risks in terms of morale, performance quality, and turnover, but most big-firm lawyers seem to think that on balance they are coming out ahead by drawing most of their paralegals from this kind of labor pool.

A still different outlook on paralegal overtraining appears to prevail in corporate law departments. Although they draw their new paralegals rather heavily from paralegal schools, there seems little interest in whatever advantages overtrained paralegals may bring to the work situation. Paralegal school background provides persons with some assured occupational commitment and a measure of screening for competence. What the corporate law departments usually seem to want from their paralegals is on-the-job acquired familiarity with relevant company procedures and with the people who must cooperate in implementing those procedures. Corporate paralegals usually become expert in significant aspects of their employer organization and indeed often wonder if this expertise is transferable to other possible employers even in the same industry. Overtraining is of little concern in corporate law departments except as a source of dissatisfaction to some paralegals with paralegal school training who are disappointed that their work assignments are far narrower than what they believe their occupational education qualifies them for. However, from our interviews we were given reason to believe that paralegals who go to work in corporate law departments usually have more realistic expectations as to the scope of their work than those starting with private law firms.

Some of the government law offices included in our study reported that serious undertraining, not overtraining, was typical of many paralegals they took on, especially those hired through civil service. Not only had few of these people been to paralegal school, but in many instances their prior education had not provided a level of knowledge and ability sufficient to do their work well. Some were not diligent in performing their assigned tasks and considered routine work demeaning, seemingly because they did not realize the importance of properly performed routine to the accomplishment of legal objectives. Overtrained paralegals may not like performing routine tasks but they usually appreciate the need for these tasks to be done thoroughly and accurately.

PRESTIGE

Prestige is the renown and respect accorded to members of an occupation within the occupation and in the society at large. Save the case of medicine, where the profession's technical acuity has allowed it to emerge in the past century as the most prestigious of occupations, other professional occupations receive their respect largely from the institutions of which they are a part—such as the church, the military or the university—or from association with prestigeful social classes from which they draw much of their membership. Professional prestige is an occupational characteristic that borrows from society rather than being invented by the professions.

The prestige of a professional occupation not only helps provide a sizable income to its members as rewards for their services but makes those it serves more deferential, less likely to challenge the professionals they have hired or to question or ignore the professional advice they are given. The social class disparity that exists between so many professionals and those they minister to helps in creating this deference and acceptance. Those of higher social class are likely to have an aura of knowledgeability and infallibility to persons of lower-class status. Professional prestige also helps professionals present themselves as more authoritative than they in fact feel themselves to be. However well-trained, professionals commonly must deal with problems concerning which there are too many imponderables and too little information or knowledge to make judgments that are assuredly correct. One way professionals cope with this uncertainty is to take action, give advice, or make recommendations without disclosing the uncertainty entailed to those they serve.[10] Professional prestige makes it easier to mask uncertainty, a tactic that under many circumstances, although obviously not all, can be in the best interests of the patients or clients involved. This prestige on many occasions helps professionals compensate for limitations of the professional knowledge base rather than being the result of that knowledge base.

Occupational prestige is important in the lives of paralegals, although overshadowed by the prestige of lawyers. It does, however, vary considerably in different kinds of paralegal work settings, typical of occupations with prestige, although perhaps more pronounced in the paralegal field than most others because the paralegal occupation has not yet matured and recognition and acceptance are still very uneven in different work settings.

With outsiders, paralegals in all kinds of law offices enjoy the reflected prestige of the office where they work, and some law offices have very high prestige within the legal profession, among clients, and with the public at large.[11] The elite big firms included in this study are high-prestige organizations. So are some of the government law offices, especially those that have reputations for effective criminal prosecution. Legal aid agencies also are high-prestige bodies in many circles, most particularly among the poor, the large segment of society that the agencies serve. There is even considerable prestige reflected on those who are paralegals in law departments of giant corporations, corporations known for their wealth, power, and market influence. Employees of a prestige organization, especially employees holding positions of some apparent significance, are seen by the outside world as having prestige merely from their affiliation with the organization.

Inside the offices where they are employed, paralegal prestige is mixed, although commonly paralegals are at the top of the lawyer support staff prestige ladder, however big the gap between them and their superiors, the lawyers. Internal office prestige is somewhat dependent on the amount of responsibility paralegals are permitted to assume and on the importance attached to the work they are assigned. The more work responsibility and importance, the more prestige. In these respects, legal aid paralegals often gain prestige benefits and so do many of the more experienced and trusted paralegals in medium- and small-sized law firms, those paralegals given broad authority over decendents' estates or real estate closings for example. Seniority usually helps in obtaining work of significance and responsibility, and many paralegals in offices with relatively low paralegal turnover have enhanced prestige. High turnover rates among big-firm paralegals have a reverse influence on paralegal prestige within these offices.

Upward mobility prospects also can enhance the prestige of an occupation, and the dead-end nature of most paralegal jobs has negative prestige consequences for the occupation. Merit raises, formal paralegal grading, and advancement of deserving paralegals to supervisory or management positions in the law office have some effect in enhancing the occupation's prestige. But the usual promotion ceiling that blankets paralegals below the lowest lawyers in the office is a major block to higher paralegal prestige.

Some paralegals seek prestige for themselves by achieving prominence in a paralegal community that extends beyond the office of their employer. Becoming active in paralegal associations and acquiring leadership positions in these organizations is the most obvious means of achieving prestige in the wider paralegal community. It is also a means for individuals of some prominence to emerge from the occupation as role models and figures of respect whose prominence enhances the reputation of the entire occupation. Unlike the professions, the paralegal occupation is severely circumscribed in the possibilities it offers for enhancing its reputation through the medium of respected individuals of prominence identified with the occupation. In a limited way, however, the paralegal associations are enabling some of their members to attain a degree of national or local prominence within the occupation.

COLLEGIALITY

The essence of professional collegiality is a sense of community among members of a profession in which members for many purposes are considered as equals.[12] This equality is based on mutual dependency in which members are expected to preserve the profession's position and prerogatives through service to the society at large. A crucial feature of this equality is that each member has the right, even the obligation, to carry out his work responsibilities as he sees fit in the interests of those he serves.[13] Within a very broad spectrum of what is proper behavior, the professional should be free to use his own best judgment. Such independence supposedly increases effective performance, as professionals are thought to operate best if they have extensive autonomy without interference from their peers. It also reduces friction within the professional community. Once admitted to membership, each member is entitled to his own eccentricities, his own special style of doing things, and his own independent professional judgment. Individuality is permitted and respected.

Collegiality also carries with it a willingness to cooperate with fellow professionals, especially those working in the same organization. It means sharing information with other professionals when this would be helpful and offering aid and assistance to those in trouble or to beginners in need of guidance. Professional collegiality is roughly analogous to the relations among members of extended families. There is a recognized common bond and a felt sense of mutual regard and obligation.

As with overtraining and prestige, collegiality is possible with paralegals but varies among work settings. In law offices with only one or a few paralegals each, there are limited opportunities for developing collegial relations with other paralegals. Local or national paralegal associations can be an outlet for these and other paralegals with strong collegial feelings. Trade unions, to the extent law offices have been unionized, also help in fostering collegiality among paralegals. Even paralegals in small legal aid offices have found that membership in the same trade union encourages interoffice collegial relations among paralegals.

From our interviews, we conclude that collegiality among large-firm paralegals is particularly weak. They seem to enjoy the social congeniality of working with other paralegals but have not developed a group *esprit de corps* as to work obligations or collective responsibility for work performance. Contributing to this lack of perceived stake in how other paralegals in the office perform is the recognition by most of them that their paralegal careers will be very short; they see little social virtue in the work paralegals in the office are asked to do; and their monetary compensation, present or future, is not tied to how well fellow paralegals perform. Deterrents to paralegal collegiality are considerable in all types of law offices, but the net effect of these deterrents in discouraging collegiality among paralegals seems strongest in large elite law firms.

ORGANIZATIONAL FORMATS FOR USING PARALEGALS

Different ways of organizing paralegal work were observed in the legal settings we studied. Some of these methods seem to be relied on more than others in structuring paralegal work along professional rather than bureaucratic lines and encouraging paralegals to assume professional rather than bureaucratic roles. The determination as to whether a paralegal will function more or less like a professional is to a considerable degree up to the employer and how the employer chooses to organize and shape paralegal work.

Ways of organizing paralegal work that we observed were the pool method, the personal assistant method, the caseload method, and the team method. How thoroughly and completely paralegals are supervised can of course vary and can influence how paralegals function under each method.

Under the pool method, which operates similarly to a typing pool, no paralegal is assigned permanently to a particular lawyer but paralegals are drawn from the pool whenever any lawyer in need of help requests it. A lawyer may ask for a particular paralegal if available or assignments may be made by a head paralegal. When an assignment is completed, the paralegal is available for a new assignment from the same or a different lawyer. Paralegals who do low-quality work are likely to be passed over when there is a request for more demanding work. In some offices, those in the pool have desks in a "bullpen" area that may be on a different floor from the lawyers or in an otherwise out of the way part of the office. The pool approach is most likely to be found in large elite law firms and some offices utilizing this form of organization do not allocate all of their paralegals to the pool.

The pool method of paralegal assignment is usually indicative of bureaucratic orientation to paralegals and their work. It is efficient in that paralegal availability is more assured whenever needed, and there is less chance that some paralegals will run out of work and be idle. Properly administered, it may enable an office to obtain the same amount of work from a smaller paralegal staff. As with typing pools, assignment to a paralegal pool usually means lower prestige than other forms of assignment, partly because lawyers are often reluctant to use the pool for more important paralegal-type tasks as there can be doubts about reliability of work performance. In addition, pool assignments provide less opportunity for reflected prestige from close continued association with a prominent lawyer in the office.

The personal assistant method of paralegal organization entails permanent or long-term assignment of a paralegal to a particular lawyer for whatever needed tasks the lawyer believes the paralegal can usefully perform. Depending on the trust the lawyer has in the paralegal and the lawyer's willingness to assign a broad range of tasks, this can evolve into the paralegal becoming a near professional as the alter ego of the lawyer. These alter ego situations seem most likely to develop in overworked and understaffed government and legal aid offices in which lawyers are subject to tremendous work volume pressures. On the other hand, a lawyer may be assigned a paralegal exclusively and use his assistant as merely a bureaucratic appendage to perform highly regimented repeat tasks with no discretion and minimal prestige.

Where the caseload method of paralegal organization is adopted, it too can enable paralegals functionally to be almost indistinguishable from lawyers; in fact, some legal aid clients assigned to paralegals with caseloads think that the paralegals are lawyers. Under the caseload method paralegals are allocated a flow of cases to handle, frequently from beginning to end, with little or no lawyer oversight but with the expectation that lawyer advice will be sought if unusual circumstances are encountered and the paralegal has doubts about how to proceed. Caseload responsibility of this sort is likely to be assigned only very experienced and trusted paralegals. We found some instances of the caseload method being used in most types of law offices, usually with more repetitive and standardized kinds of matters, such as simple real estate closings, welfare and other government benefit claims, and perfunctory corporate documentation. If sufficiently competent paralegals are assigned caseloads, the caseload method can operate very effectively in professional organizations. The independent but subordinate role it provides paralegals can readily be accommodated to the roles of lawyers, the dominant occupation, if the lawyers are willing to grant a substantial measure of independence to paralegals. The caseload method combines professional ideals of knowledge, prestige, and collegiality with a bureaucratic division of labor and recognition of ultimate paralegal subordination.

Under the team approach, a group of paralegals is assigned to a particular project in which efforts of team members must be carefully coordinated successfully to complete the project. Lawyer or lay supervisors or both usually are responsible for the coordination. A good example of the team approach to paralegal organization that we observed in both large firms and corporate law departments is document processing in complex litigation, such as antitrust cases, in which massive volumes of documents must be screened and classified. These teams are likely to be physically separated from the rest of the office and function as a separate unit for as long as it takes for the project to be completed. The teams are often very bureaucratically structured.

The pool and team methods of organizing paralegal work are particularly attractive to some professionals as means of solving, in their interests, conflicts and tensions over the bureaucraticization of law offices. Paralegals are placed in a separate bureaucratic enclave within the professional organization, an enclave that functions as a separate unit, may be physically isolated as a separate operation, and provides the advantages of a bureaucracy without infecting or threatening the professional standards or practices of the rest of the organization. Some of the more rudimentary tasks perceived of as lawyer's work can be shunted off to nonlawyers in the office, can thereby be performed effectively at lower cost and conceivably at greater profit, and the professionalism of most of the lawyers in the organization remains untouched and unchallenged. The enclave phenomenon may become more attractive to lawyers as law offices become larger and more offices find this structural format feasible. It also helps explain why what are generally the most professional of law offices, the large firms, utilize many of their paralegals in the most bureaucratic manner.

One difficulty with separate enclaves for paralegals is that such enclaves are likely to accentuate paralegal dissatisfaction with their work because of the bureaucratic way in which enclave work is usually structured. It has long been a contention in organizational sociology that bureaucratic settings tend to create worker dissatisfaction and that worker satisfaction is generally much greater in professional settings.[14] This seems borne out by our study that found a principal on-the-job satisfaction of paralegals to be working on their own,[15] a feature of work frequently found in professional but not bureaucratic settings. The study also found a principal on-the-job dissatisfaction of paralegals to be boring work,[16] presumably a reaction in part to not enough independence in work assignments. The significance of paralegal independence to paralegal work satisfaction suggests that how paralegal work is organized is more important to achieving job satisfaction, with its positive implications for work effectiveness, than are other morale boosters and incentives. An important antidote to paralegal work dissatisfaction would appear to be allowing paralegals much more opportunity to manage their own time but with responsibility for doing so productively and well. Of course, to be acceptable, this would have to be correlated with competence and only those capable of handling expanded roles should be given them. In addition, complete paralegal independence cannot be granted without incurring risks of unauthorized practice and lawyer violation of professional responsibility obligations.

PARALEGAL RECRUITMENT

The recruitment process has tremendous importance for an occupation as it determines who is hired. It also has an influence on both the kinds of people who seek entry into the occupation and perceptions of employers as to the kinds of persons they want for particular jobs. Then, too, recruitment effectiveness can have significance for how much professionalism is permitted employees in the job setting. The aptitudes, limitations, and interests of those attracted to jobs can be important considerations in how the jobs are shaped. If in background and outlook paralegals who are hired are relatively professional, employers may respond by organizing paralegal work in a more professional manner. Moreover, every incumbent makes some imprint on how a job is structured, and the professionally oriented paralegal is likely to have an effect in making that particular job somewhat more professional.

Occupations are closely meshed with the rest of life because what people bring with them to the job strongly influences how they will perform on the job. People have expectations of what work will be like, what kinds of demands will be made of them, how work will fit into family life, and whether it will provide the satisfactions education and upbringing have led them to expect. Work performance can be supported or diminished by its part in the overall life of a person. Moreover, job performance itself requires skills in dealing with people, in taking on responsibility, in picking up procedures or modifying them when needed, that include but go far beyond what is taught on the job or in job-training courses. How to get along with a boss or when to take initiative or how to know when you know something are very subtle processes, picked up more by emulation and the development of good judgment than by specific instruction. This is an added reason why recruitment of people to an occupation is such a vital part of any occupation. It is at the recruitment stage that those who are favorably inclined and capable of doing the work of the occupation and fitting it into their lives commonly are separated from those who are not. Employers, primarily concerned with getting the job done, are inclined not to take risks but to hire persons they believe can do the work and will readily fit into the organization. Those selected are people who are seen as having the qualities that are thought to make effective workers.

The need for careful selection of workers is particularly difficult and critical with a fledgling occupation, such as that of paralegals, where suitable candidates may know little or nothing about the occupation, or not be willing to take a chance on it, and where stable sources of qualified recruits may not have crystallized. Since the precise duties are still in a state of flux, the adequacy of recruitment procedures developed in the occupation's early days of formation may strongly influence the way the job is modified before it becomes fixed in a job description. The job may be more or less independent of supervision, depending on the people who take on the job and exert some pressure to mold it in their own image, including a relatively professional image if that is their preference. To some extent, this refashioning of jobs to the needs of the people who hold them also occurs in well-established occupations where, for example, the lowering educational level of military recruits can lead to rewriting of manuals and simplification of procedures. But job refashioning is probably more frequent in new occupations, occupations in which expected skills and functions often are still open to question and hence employers are prone to adapt the work to what those hired are most able and willing to do. Because of the significance of recruitment to paralegals and the kind of paraprofessionals they can become, it seems appropriate at this point to explore in greater detail the nature of the recruitment process.

Recruitment of workers for an occupation can be thought of as a combination of sortings in which cruder devices are supplemented by finer ones when the cruder categories of discrimination are considered insufficient.[17] Think of these sets of characteristics as layers of discernment, comparable to what goes on in the sorting of college admission applications. Sometimes a supplementary characteristic like travel experience or an unusual hobby will replace a more usual category, such as college board scores, as an object of notice, and a candidate will be excluded only if the usual criteria are seriously deficient, while at other times supplementary characteristics will play a relatively small role. Occupational recruitment operates similarly.

The selection of paralegals seems to be a process that uses two different sets of criteria to match prospective employees with their setting. Briefly defined, these are "crude tuning," which classifies by social class background, and "fine tuning," which classifies by other criteria. Employers seek some certainty about their employees. They want to make sure that, personality quirks aside, newly recruited workers will fit into the routines of the organization and appreciate its demands and priorities. One of the surest ways that employers sense this can be done in hiring paralegals is to match the social class of paralegals being taken in with the social class of those who have successfully performed the same or comparable jobs in the past. As paralegals perform many of the same functions as do lawyers and interact frequently with lawyers, there also is a preference in many offices for hiring paralegals from the same social class as that of lawyers in the office. But if paralegals have extensive client contacts, the attempt may be made to select paralegals who match the client group's social class.

The social class of the job seeker attests less to technical skills than it does to overall sophistication and familiarity with the kinds of attitudes and responses expected of employees. Reliance only on exhortation to act properly is a very weak reed on which to depend for job assurance. A person whose father worked on an assembly line is often a good candidate for a manufacturing job because all of the needed reactions that go along with that kind of work do not have to be explicated—for example, the need to accept routine and to do what one is told. Similary, the person who grew up in the family of a professional well may have an edge in orienting readily to lawyers and law office work. Recruitment by social class is made easier by employers normally seeking recruits from sources that provide candidates of the desired social class. Wall Street firms have connections with elite colleges, or their employees have connections that reach the kind of people the firms want. Other offices by such means as paralegal school placement contacts, advertising, or in-house promotion generate an acceptable applicant flow of the class they prefer. Candidates for employment are also likely to turn to offices recommended by word of mouth and where they think they will feel comfortable. Recruitment by social class is crude in the sense that it proceeds on the basis of an overall stereotype of who is suitable for employment, with only a cursory look at detailed characteristics. This is similar to the way most people relate to new people when they are first introduced.

Crude tuning can be supplemented or supplanted by what may be called "fine tuning." Fine tuning is the process of more carefully and subtly trying to fill employment slots hard to fill because of special needs or uncertainty as to what the needs are. Any organization may find itself requiring unusual job specifications, like long or irregular hours, or have unusual personnel problems, such as a valued senior staff member who is irascible and hard to get on with. But the recruitment and placement criteria for an occupation still in formation can be particularly unstandardized because job definitions are changing and it may be unclear to the organization as to what its staffing needs are in the way of prior experience and credentials. There is still this inchoate element to paralegal recruitment in many law offices, as there was with computer work a decade or so ago and before formal credentialing took over.

A significant feature of fine tuning is that it makes room for people who otherwise would not be considered by a particular organization or for a particular job. Social class becomes less of a determinant and any of countless other elements may become highy relevant. Persons with unusual, even deviant, career histories or experiences or talents may become preferred recruits because of their unusual characteristics. Thus an ex-convict or ex-drug addict may be hired as a legal aid paralegal, a fluent Spanish speaker as a public defender paralegal, a former courthouse clerk as a paralegal in a litigation firm, and a former insurance adjuster as a paralegal in a personal injury firm. In addition, older people, including older women reentering the job market after many years absence, may be considered attractive paralegal recruits by many law offices, although their age may be a handicap in most employment markets. Older persons often are willing to do routine jobs without complaint and many of them are satisfied with a secure position and not given to job hopping.

Formal education is such an important consideration in job placement that it merits separate consideration, as it can have a tremendous influence on crude tuning and fine tuning as these processes have been described. Moreover, not only does it have a major effect on what kinds of persons employers are seeking to hire but on the sorts of jobs that those in the job market are willing to take. In most paralegal hiring, some college education is an essential prerequisite to employment, and for many law offices a baccalaureate degree has become an essential. How prestigious the college is also can be important, more so with some kinds of offices than others. Most paralegal employers supplement or even substitute college background for class background in their crude initial evaluations of job candidates.[18] This is especially true for those candidates who have attended more prestigious colleges. The American system of higher education may be looked at as a prism that takes a band of roughly similar people and fractionates it into distinct types as to abilities and ambitions, thereby raising some people from lower-class backgrounds and lowering others from higher-class backgrounds. This, of course, can apply only to those who seek and gain entry to college. In addition, there obviously is a strong class influence on who goes to what level of institution in the hierarchy of colleges and whether or not attendance continues until a degree is obtained. But, despite these limitations, higher education results in adjusting class consequences for many persons.

Higher education can also provide special competence and expertise attractive to employers when they resort to fine tuning. Law students obviously offer something special that law offices often react to favorably in paralegal hiring. Occasionally, too, other academic fields of specialization are seen as providing background needed for a particular paralegal slot and are determinative of who gets hired. For example, an applicant who has majored in mathematics or chemistry may be hired if the office is involved in major litigation calling for background in one or the other of these disciplines.

The prism metaphor can be applied as well to paralegal applicants based on whether or not they have had formal paralegal school training and to some extent on what kind of training and where. This educational experience, or lack of it, can provide a further filter for applicants and is a filter that many employers rely on heavily in paralegal recruitment. Formal paralegal school training provides employers with potential recruits who are initially well-disposed to the job and probably even have some relevant training for it, although the actual content of the training may be less relevant than the emotional preparation to deal with the job. The quality of candidates, too, is likely to be more uniform and predictable than if they were selected from more diverse sources. For some paralegal candidates it also helps make up for past career or educational failures and shows a decisiveness of vocational purpose that they previously may have lacked.

In the course of this study we noted extensive reliance on crude tuning by employers in hiring paralegals. The crude tuning approach seems most common in offices where paralegal positions have little professional standing, where there is rapid paralegal turnover, and where there is an assured flow of acceptable replacements. The large firms appear particularly prone to use this approach, but only after a major adjustment of class backgrounds by college backgrounds in their crude evaluations of applicants for paralegal positions. Medium-sized firms and corporate law departments also rely largely on crude tuning in recruiting paralegals, but with frequent adjustments of class based on whether or not an applicant has been to paralegal school, and if so, which one. Most government law offices for much of their paralegal recruitment are required to rely on civil service selection, a system that attempts through fine-tuning requirements to avoid political patronage and to screen applicants carefully and objectively. Cumbersome administration, inadequate criteria, and the inability to attract enough of the best possible candidates have often defeated the laudable goals of the civil service format. Civil service has become a bureaucracy unto itself that has too frequently failed to attract effective paralegals of either a professional or bureaucratic orientation. Legal aid, with its great variety of paralegal jobs, has been much more successful in its paralegal recruitment and has placed more emphasis than most offices on fine tuning and carefully matching those they select with the jobs for which they are selected.

POWER AND PROFESSIONALISM

The interplay between professional and bureaucratic forces in law offices allows us to hazard the following generalization: whatever group is powerful in a legal setting considers itself professsional and adopts professional characteristics, relegating other people in the legal setting to bureaucratic or administrative roles. Professionalism becomes the mode of work organization for those who can get away with it, bureaucracy the mode of work organization for those who have little choice in the matter, and paraprofessionalism increasingly may become the mode of work organization for those who can put up some struggle.

Economic need influences power, and law offices subject to the greatest cost-control pressures are particularly vulnerable to effective power pushes by paraprofessionals to be treated more like professionals. Among New

York City law offices, cost-control pressures currently are strongest on large government law departments and legal aid, with budgets seriously short in relation to demand on these offices for legal services. Many small private law offices are also under acute economic pressure to cut costs, but one way that they respond is by increasing the work load of professionals, especially those of the proprietors, reducing the necessity for financial outlay on support staff. Collective action by paralegals against their employers, as through trade union organizing and bargaining, may help move paralegals toward more professional status. But as we have discussed earlier, unions have had little success in organizing law offices, except in government and legal aid, and this situation seems unlikely to change soon. Moreover, if lawyers and paralegals are both organized, the paralegal fight for more professionalism may occur not just with employers but in the union arena with lawyer employees. Also, union demands usually concentrate on wages and hours, with greater professionalism having a low, if any, priority.

In what is likely to be growing tension between paralegals and lawyers over how much professionalism paralegals may attain in their work, the outcome may be a compromise. In this compromise it is quite possible that an adjustment may be worked out in which paralegals accept subordination to lawyers and do not seek the right to practice on their own in exchange for an enhanced degree of collegial independence within the law office. In any such creative adjustment, paralegals would become entrenched as paraprofessionals, closer to being professionals than many of them are today, but with perpetuation of a major restraint on their upward mobility, subordination to lawyers.

NOTES

1. On semiprofessions, *see* A. Etzioni (ed.), *The Semi-Professions and Their Organization* (1969). This book, however, does not draw a distinction between subprofessions that are professional extenders and those that are not, and in it nurses are considered semiprofessionals. *See also* G. Ritzer, *Working: Conflict and Change* ch. 6 (2d ed. 1977).

2. Stanley Udy argues that social evolution involves the differentiation of work into an institution independent of the customs of the society in which it is embedded. S. Udy, *Work in Traditional and Modern Society* (1970).

3. It is not essential to the concept occupation that there be financial remuneration for the services or other work products rendered. Max Weber defines occupations only as those pursuits which are remunerative, but his analysis of professional "callings" or vocations, which insists on the purely personal rewards of professional life, does not depend on remuneration as a component. M. Weber, *The Theory of Social and Economic Organization* 81 and 250 (T. Parsons ed. 1947). *See also* H. Gerth and C. Mills (eds.), *From Max Weber* 77–158 (1946).

4. This distinction between means and ends is derived from Ferdinand Tonnies,

who thought of traditional societies as ends in themselves while modern societies and the factories which inhabit them are enterprises which are means to the ends of public happiness or profit. *See* F. Tonnies, *Community and Society* (C. Loomis ed. 1957). This seminal distinction is used by classical theorists to characterize any number of social institutions.

5. For a study of the conflict between professional and bureaucratic orientations, *see* S. Cole, *The Unionization of Teachers* (1969).

6. For examples of how professions and professional characteristics are perceived in the sociological literature, *see* H. Becker, *Sociological Work* ch. 6 (1970); E. Freidson (ed.), *The Professions and Their Prospects* (1973); M. Larson, *The Rise of Professionalism* (1977); T. Parsons, *Essays in Sociological Theory* 34–49 (rev. ed. 1954); A. Reiss, *The Police and the Public* 121–24 (1971); H. Vollmer and D. Mills (eds.), *Professionalization* (1966); Goode, Community Within a Community: The Professions, 22 *American Sociological Review* 194 (1957); and Wilensky, The Professionalization of Everyone?, 70 *American Journal of Sociology* 137 (1964).

Professionalism in the military is considered in M. Janowitz, *The Professional Soldier* (1960) and S. Huntington, *The Soldier and the State* (1957). The deviant path of medicine, in which prestige followed upon professionalization, is discussed in P. Starr, *The Social Transformation of Medicine* (1982). In C. Mills, *White Collar* ch. 6 (1951), turn of the century doctors and lawyers are identified as professionals because they were free entrepreneurs, independent of bureaucracies.

7. On the nature of bureaucracies, *see* M. Weber, 3 *Economy and Society* ch. 11 (1968); and Gerth and Mills, *supra* note 3, at 196–244. *See also* P. Blau, *The Dynamics of Bureaucracy* (2d ed. 1963); M. Crozier, *The Bureaucratic Phenomenon* (1964); R. Merton, *Social Theory and Social Structure* 195–224 (rev. ed. 1957); and Hall, The Concept of Bureaucracy: An Empirical Assessment, 69 *American Journal of Sociology* 32 (1963).

8. On professional overtraining, *see* Larson, *supra* note 6, at 230–31; and Goode, The Theoretical Limits of Professionalization, in Etzioni, *supra* note 1, 266 at 282–83.

9. *See*, for example, S. Turow, *One L: An Inside Account of Life in the First Year at Harvard Law School* (1978).

10. *See* R. Fox, *Experiment Perilous* (1974), for a discussion of doctors coping with the risks of uncertainty. *See also* M. Millman, *The Unkindest Cut* ch. 6 (1978); and Horobin, Professional Mystery: The Maintenance of Charisma in General Medical Practice, in R. Dingwall and P. Lewis (eds.) *The Sociology of the Professions* 84 (1983).

11. On prestige rankings within the legal profession, *see* J. Heinz and E. Laumann, *Chicago Lawyers: The Social Structure of the Bar* ch. 4 (1982). For a study of solo practitioners in a large city that comes to the conclusion that these practitioners are at the bottom of the legal profession's ladder, *see* J. Carlin, *Lawyers on Their Own* (1962).

12. Max Weber had little use for collegial bodies, thinking they could rarely serve as more than advisory councils. This is in keeping with his general preference of hierarchical coordination as an effective mechanism for action. *See* Weber, *supra* note 3, at 392–407. On the other hand, sociologists strongly influenced by Emile Durkheim view collegiality as something of a community in the sense of a group

out to preserve its own way of life by proving of service to the society at large. *See* Goode, *supra* note 6. *See also* T. Parsons, *Action Theory and the Human Condition* 42 and 59 (1978).

13. This is reflected in an important canon of the lawyer's Code of Professional Responsibility: "A lawyer should exercise independent professional judgment on behalf of a client." American Bar Association, Code of Professional Responsibility, canon 5.

14. On worker alienation, a strong indication of dissatisfaction, *see* R. Blauner, *Alienation and Freedom* (1964); G. Friedman, *Industrial Society* (1977); Kohn, Occupational Structure and Alienation, 82 *American Journal of Sociology* 111 (1976); Miller, Professionals in Bureaucracy: Alienation Among Industrial Scientists and Engineers, 32 *American Sociological Review* 755 (1967); and Pearlin, Alienation from Work: A Study of Nursing Personnel, 27 *American Sociological Review* 314 (1962).

15. *See* table 21.

16. *See* table 20.

17. There is considerable disagreement among sociologists about the best way to study entry into occupational life. A standard method is to compare a person's occupation to that of his father. *See*, for example, P. Blau and O. Duncan, *The American Occupational Structure* 188–191 (1967); D. Featherman and R. Hauser, *Opportunity and Change* ch. 3 (1978); and Heinz and Laumann, *supra* note 11, at 186–91. Table 17 provides data on father's occupation for those in our questionnaire sample. This father's occupation approach has been criticized on methodological and theoretical grounds. One argument is that the characteristics of organizations influence mobility and not just features of the work force such as class, education, and race. *See* Baron and Bielby, Bringing the Firms Back In: Stratification, Segmentation, and the Organization of Work, 45 *American Sociological Review* 737 (1980). Another argument is that the distinction between upward mobility and stable class position is unfounded, since the standard method based on father's occupation cannot take account of changes in the content or social position of occupations. *See* Sobel, Structural Mobility, Circulation Mobility and the Analysis of Occupational Mobility: A Conceptual Mismatch, 48 *American Sociological Review* 721 (1983).

18. The validity of substituting education for social class as a basis for recruitment is suggested by a survey that demonstrates education is important in determining personal attitudes, but social class "cultures" are not. *See* Davis, Achievement Variables and Class Cultures: Family, Schooling, Job, and Forty-Nine Dependent Variables in the Cumulative G[eneral] S[ocial] S[urvey], 47 *American Sociological Review* 569 (1982). This is contrary to the view of some sociologists of education who see education as a simple sorting mechanism to move people into an occupation appropriate to their social class. *See* S. Bowles and H. Gentis, *Schooling in Capitalist America* (1976); C. Greer, *The Great School Legend* (1976); and C. Jencks et al., *Inequality: A Reassessment of the Effects of Family and Schooling in America* (1972). Further support for the independent effect of education is provided by Kazuo Yamaguchi, who argues that educational attainment is a generalized channel for occupational mobility except in the cases of proprietorship, service work, and farming. Yamaguchi, The Structure of Intergenerational Occupational Mobility: Generality and Specificity in Resources, Channels and Barriers, 88 *American Journal of Sociology* 718 (1983).

6

CONCLUSIONS AND RECOMMENDATIONS

GROWTH AND DEVELOPMENT

The paralegal occupation has made remarkable progress in a very brief period of time. In numbers, a sense of identity, law office reliance, and occupational organization and cohesion, development has been rapid and substantial. This has been true not only in New York City, with the greatest law office concentration in the nation, but in much of the rest of the country as well. Paralegals are also being utilized by many law offices of all kinds: large and small, public and private, profit and nonprofit, ordinary and elite. The occupation has become an important element in the provision of legal services to American consumers of those services. Furthermore, the numbers and importance of paralegals will probably increase, with significant implications for the future of lawyers and the legal order. The occupation is still in the process of growing and maturing.

In its present evolutionary stage, the paralegal occupation consists of a varied and somewhat ill-defined body of law office employees generally located in office hierarchies between the professionals at the top—the lawyers—and the clerical support staff. The status line is normally quite clear between paralegals and lawyers, but it may be fuzzy in some offices between paralegals and secretaries or paralegals and lay office administrators, with paralegal positions sometimes consolidated with one or both of these other positions.

However striking has been the development of the paralegal occupation since the 1960s, paralegals remain subordinate to lawyers in authority and their work roles have principally been as substitutes for lawyers in performing less demanding, less interesting, and less important tasks that lawyers consider can safely be delegated to lay personnel. Paralegals usually do not have useful skills or expertise not possessed or readily attainable by lawyers. They are replacements for lawyers at the lower end of the work scale, with lawyers determining when and how extensive the replacement shall be.

Much of what paralegals do is routine and there is a growing practice of law offices expanding the amount and scope of routine work delegated to paralegals by precise and detailed programming of the work process in highly repetitive fields of law practice. Well-prepared programs of this sort, commonly referred to in the legal literature as systems, are particularly conducive to a division of labor in which less expert persons can satisfactorily take on a greater share of the law office work load. Many paralegals also act as the personal assistants of designated lawyers, performing a miscellany of delegated ad hoc tasks as they arise in the day by day work of the lawyers. These tasks may involve some simple legal drafting and legal research, but more commonly they entail fact investigation or assembly or analysis of factual data, major forms of paralegal work. Clerical tasks are commonly mixed in with other paralegal assignments. Lawyers usually reserve to themselves the diagnosis of client problems, developing strategies and solutions to those problems, negotiation with opposing parties, most client contacts, most legal research and drafting of legal documents, and, of course, court appearances, as these latter are generally restricted by law to lawyers. In any particular office, exceptions may exist to the usually prevailing pattern of lawyer-paralegal division of labor; and paralegal roles are likely to be greater in understaffed law offices. Understaffing is especially prevalent in government and legal aid offices.

Why is it that there has recently been such an explosive growth in numbers of paralegals employed in law offices and in such a short time paralegals have emerged as a relatively cohesive occupational group with its own organizations and with a separate identity recognized inside and outside the group? More particularly, why these developments when at the same time numbers of lawyers in the United States have been increasing rapidly, with many new lawyers having difficulty establishing themselves in the legal profession? Superficially, it seems incongruous that at a time when more lawyers were being admitted to the profession than could be absorbed by it, an occupational group in part competitive with lawyers and with much less in the way of professional training should make such rapid strides. The market for legal services provides a principal explanation for this occupational expansion and development by paralegals. There have been changes in that market subjecting law offices to increased pressures to rationalize economically their modes of operation. Many law offices have been subjected to a cost-income squeeze making them more cost conscious, and paralegals are a means of cutting costs as their labor is usually cheaper than that of lawyers. It is common for beginning paralegals to be paid only one-half or one-third as much as beginning lawyers, and pay disparities between experienced paralegals and experienced lawyers are usually even greater. To the extent that paralegals can do lawyers' work, substituting paralegals for lawyers can offer substantial savings opportunities. The principal attraction of paralegals is their low cost.

The cost-income squeeze is being felt by all types of law offices. Common cost increases are in staff salaries, rent, library upkeep, new equipment and its maintenance, and malpractice and other insurance. Increases have been particularly sharp for experienced legal secretaries and for newly admitted lawyers with degrees from prestige law schools. Law firms of all sorts are also finding that clients are doing more comparison shopping among firms and that major clients are increasingly prone to bargain over fees and to give closer attention to how fees are calculated. Larger corporations are also moving more of their legal work from private firms to in-house law departments, principally to cut their legal service costs, and they are then imposing law department restraints to hold down still further in-house legal expenditures. Legal aid and government law offices have shown similar in-house legal cost concerns, especially pronounced with legal aid agencies given their acute funding problems. Significant weakening of controls that have provided lawyers with a partial but substantial monopoly over legal service work and inhibited competition among lawyers has contributed to the cost-income squeeze on law firms. Provision of legal services is increasingly competitive, both within the profession and between lawyers and such lay occupations as title insurers, banks, and accountants that are authorized to perform certain kinds of legal work for third parties of a kind also performed by lawyers. There is still not as competitive a market for legal work as for many other important services provided by the American economy, but the move has been to reduce controls and open up the legal services market to much greater competition. Even the bar associations, through which lawyers often act collectively on public and professional issues, have been pushing monopoly rights less and enhanced law office efficiency and quality more as their preferred answers to the bar's market problems.

In the increasingly competitive environment in which law offices are operating, paralegals are but one attractive alternative for cutting costs. Others are greater lawyer specialization, adding more lawyers per office so as to offer a wider range of client services, establishing branch offices thereby reaching a broader market, pressuring or enticing lawyers in the office to produce more billable hours of work, advertising in the mass media and by direct mail, participating in prepaid legal insurance plans, installing new labor-saving office technology,[1] and encouraging staff continuing legal education. Expanded use of paralegals is only one aspect of a much broader movement by law offices to become more economically rational. Some of these other developments, furthermore, have been conducive to the use of paralegals by drawing more repeat-type legal work to particular offices, thereby encouraging such economies of scale as more detailed and efficient systems for handling work and the expanded reliance on paralegals that this makes feasible. Volume concentration of repeat-work tasks can be essential to maximizing law office efficiency. Not all legal matters are amenable to mass handling techniques, but many are and many law offices are being restructured to better attract and accommodate work of this sort. This is all part of the increasing bureaucratization of law offices, and concentration of repeat work has been a major factor in bringing about this bureaucratization.

That it has become commonplace for American law offices to try to cut costs by hiring paralegals is quite apparent. But why paralegals? Why have law offices not used recently admitted lawyers who have been unable to find employment as lawyers to fill the slots now occupied by paralegals and at the same salaries paid paralegals? With less-distinguished graduates of less-prestigious law schools frequently having difficulty finding lawyer jobs, would they not be willing to break into the profession by doing what paralegals are doing and should not law offices be willing to hire them for such jobs? Persons professionally qualified with three years of intensive professional training would seem to be preferable to unadmitted and less trained or untrained paralegals. The answer in part is that young lawyers of this sort still are doing much work that paralegals also do. To the extent that paralegals do legal work requiring considerable professional skill or knowledge, young lawyers also do this work. However, as has been seen, the usual paralegal tasks are of a less professionally demanding nature. Are lawyers being used extensively for these tasks in offices where such work must be performed in considerable volume? In some offices they are, in others they are not, but the trend is toward paralegals taking over an increasing percentage of these tasks.

In our interviews with senior lawyers, when we raised the use of lawyers rather than paralegals issue, we found a great deal of reluctance, often refusal, to hire or use young lawyers principally for undemanding law office work of the sort usually assigned to paralegals. Time and time again we were told that the offices of those we interviewed preferred paralegals for such work because they wanted only one class of young lawyers, those on the ladder to partnership or other advanced professional standing in the office, and that on salary and career grounds this group will not long tolerate doing principally routine paralegal kinds of work. The work tasks involved tend to be dull and boring, they do not provide the experience base on which professional upward mobility is usually predicated, the work is of low status, and it normally is low-paid. This view was most strongly expressed by lawyers in offices that recruit the more market-attractive beginning lawyers, those from the top-prestige law schools or the top ranks of other law schools, but it was also expressed by lawyers in other kinds of offices. The opposition we encountered to a dual classification of young lawyers, with those on the promotion ladder doing more interesting and important tasks and those not on this ladder doing routine tasks, seemed based on the fear that dual classification would lead to acute jealousy and dissatisfaction among those in the inferior class, with consequent adverse effect on their work performance. We also had hints that such a dual classification might cause embarrassment over established office recruitment and promotion policies and troublesome questioning of those policies if any of the lower-echelon lawyers showed unusual competency and dedication on the job. These problems, of course, can be avoided by having only one class of young lawyers. Furthermore, hiring paralegals instead of associates, to the extent that paralegals can do associates' work, eases the tensions so common in big firms over making partner and associate-partner ratios.[2] Paralegals, as do associates, can produce profits for firm partners, but there is no risk with paralegals, unlike associates, that partners' profits will be diluted by making new partners from among juniors in the firm. An additional advantage of paralegals over lawyers, some of our informants stressed, is that when and if paralegals shift firms, no danger exists that clients will shift with them. This risk of losing clients when junior lawyers leave can be a real one to firms serving small businesses and individuals of modest means, as some of their clients well may follow young lawyers from one firm to another.

A further advantage that many law offices now recognize paralegals have over lawyers is that paralegal employment can more easily be adapted to uneven work flow. The demand for services made of the individual law office tends to vary, often sharply, with unpredictable ups and downs. A big new lawsuit, an important new client, or a major change in a field of law the office specializes in are illustrative of factors resulting in sudden need for additional staff help to handle the new work. Alternatively, staff needs can precipitously decline with the conclusion of a big case, sudden loss of a major client, or repeal of a law crucial to the firm's work flow. To the extent that paralegals are substitutes for lawyers, many law offices find it simpler and more acceptable to hire paralegals on a temporary basis as a means of meeting work demand fluctuations rather than hiring and then discharging lawyers. One reason for this is that in New York City and other urban centers employment agencies have developed that will provide on a temporary basis any number of paralegals needed for as long as required, usually at an hourly charge and without such job perquisites as accumulated vacation time or sick leave. Also, in some cities, freelance paralegal firms have been formed that will provide services to law offices on a case-by-case or short-term independent contractor basis, a useful means of accommodating to a sudden surge in work demands, and some law offices also maintain their own lists of paralegals available for temporary work. Most big firms and many middle-sized firms and corporate law departments draw on the temporary paralegal market in adjusting to uneven work flow. No comparable well-developed market exists for temporary lawyers.[3] Another reason that law offices find it easier to follow flexible hiring policies for paralegals than for lawyers is that in many law offices there seems to be a greater sense of obligation to lawyers than paralegals when it comes to layoffs. Lawyers, as fellow professionals, are entitled to more consideration than are nonlawyers, it is felt. Frequently, too, compared to paralegals, lawyers are older, have greater career commitments to law, and hence are seen as having more at stake in their jobs and thereby harder to lay off once hired, even when performing similar work to that of paralegals.

As has been seen, a surplus of lawyers, including a steady flow of new admittees to the bar, many with marginal employment prospects in the legal profession, has not prevented the rapid growth in the number of paralegals. But what about legal secretaries; why has not the number of legal secretaries been dramatically increased and their task assignments altered so that they would have absorbed the work that has gone to paralegals? In part, as has been indicated, this too has happened and there are many offices with paralegal-secretaries, whether this is the title given them or not. But the more common development has been for law offices to draw a sharp line between their secretaries and paralegals. Different reasons for this emerged in our interviews. In some offices, good legal secretaries with highly reliable typing, filing, and communication skills and well-attuned to those for whom they work are considered so valuable in this work and so difficult to replace that it is deemed unwise to broaden extensively their mix of duties. It is easier and cheaper to hire paralegals than to turn able secretaries into secretary-paralegals. Another reason is that many offices want paralegals with different educational and cultural backgrounds from those of most secretaries. They want paralegals with college degrees and with much the same interests, values, and aspirations as the lawyers in the office. Although the term is not used, what many offices seem to want is paralegals of the same class as their lawyers, and by this standard most secretaries do not qualify. These feelings seem particularly strong where paralegals are treated much like professional colleagues.

The remarkable short-term growth and development of the paralegal occupation has been aided by other causative factors peripheral to cost considerations. These include the occupation's effectiveness in creating a considerable measure of cohesion and in establishing an organizational base for upgrading the occupation through manipulation of controls internally and externally. Upgrading efforts are common to occupations and are to be expected once there is a sense of identity among those engaged in the occupation. Table 33 indicates the importance paralegals attribute to upgrading the status and influence of the paralegal occupation. Allies who share the occupation's goals or overlap its interests can prove helpful in the upgrading process. Formation of occupational organizations is essential to upgrading, as they provide the medium for necessary collective action and outlets for individual commitment and leadership. Most such organizations are located outside the workplace and provide occupational ties and push occupational interests that cross workplace lines. As these organizations become larger and stronger they provide more career opportunities of their own and attract an increasing number of persons who as volunteers or employees concentrate heavily on furthering occupational interests. Occupational upgrading is often dependent on such individuals for ideas, planning, and implementation; and an occupation that can afford paid staff members is usually more effective in these regards. There are good possibilities of takeoff in occupational development once an occupation establishes its own organizations.

The paralegal occupation's most important organizations are its associations and its schools. Despite their many limitations, they have been of major significance in fostering a sense of occupational identity, creating occupational cohesion, and starting a process of occupational upgrading. They have helped move the occupation somewhat toward professionalism, influenced by the fact that lawyers have so often been their models and reference group. They have been active in the control arenas, more influential in some than in others. They have had a significant impact in establishing the legitimacy of paralegals as lawyer adjuncts and in gaining access by paralegals to the legal services market, again as lawyer adjuncts. The schools have used their considerable control over education to exert major influence on paralegal recruitment, role expectations, and acceptable standards of work performance. They have also imparted to much of the paralegal population some degree of expertise transferable to work settings. None of the paralegal organizations has as yet had much influence on laws pertaining to paralegals, laws that for the most part were well-set before paralegals emerged as a recognized occupational group.

In their efforts to integrate and upgrade the paralegal occupation, paralegal organizations have often had the support of lawyers and the bar associations. Especially in education, many of these lawyers have been co-opted by the paralegal occupation. They remain licensed lawyers but identify so fully with paralegals and their interests are so tied to paralegal organizations that they have become a part of the paralegal occupation. Other lawyers very favorable to paralegals and active in bar associations promoting paralegal interests are paralegal allies. They see paralegals as beneficial to lawyers and support moves to strengthen and upgrade the paralegal occupation so long as in their view lawyers are benefited. Continued lawyer dominance over paralegals is generally favored by this group.

Lawyer dominance of the paralegal occupation poses a problem to the paralegal organizations, but with some ambivalence their approach has been one of cooperation rather than confrontation. They recognize a dependence on lawyers for jobs, work assignments, income, and status. Under these circumstances it is seen as generally better to support the occupation's allies and to encourage expansion in numbers of those friendly to it, rather than taking more independent and potentially divisive positions in trying to strengthen and upgrade the occupation that could risk loss of allies and a harmful backlash from the bar. Paralegals have generally been wary about opposing lawyers on any issue of significance or even of raising issues that could create conflict with lawyers.

The paralegal occupation has had much going for it to enable it to progress as it has. In important respects the environment has been favorable. But the occupation is also faced with fundamental restrictions that have limited the way it has grown and will also limit the form and degree of its future development absent some major restructuring of the legal service delivery system. The dominance of lawyers in the legal services field and dependence of paralegals on lawyers are very basic restrictions. Lawyers comprise a large, powerful, and well-established occupation that, as has been seen, exerts extensive control over paralegals. It will be difficult for paralegals to progress in ways that do not have broad lawyer support.[4] Lawyers' dominance over paralegals is facilitated by extensive acceptance of this dominance among paralegals. Cooperating with lawyers in furthering lawyers' views of what paralegals should be is seen not only as good strategy for upgrading the paralegal occupation, but most paralegals do not seriously challenge their lower position in the occupational hierarchy. They are generally willing to concede lawyer hegemony in providing legal services, including hegemony over nonlawyer support staff.

An added limiting factor to further expansion and development of the paralegal occupation is the opposition to paralegals and their use that still exists within the legal profession. Many lawyers are unconvinced that paralegals should be used as lawyer substitutes even for routine tasks supervised by lawyers. These lawyers refuse to hire paralegals, despite offices similar to theirs doing so, as they consider it unprofessional to use lay persons to perform lawyer tasks. Even though it means less cost-effective office operations that may reduce their own income or the productivity of their offices, they adhere to a view of professionalism that does not permit efficiency to compromise client service. This outlook can lead to lawyers personally performing most all tasks involved in work brought to them, no matter how trivial or boring some of the tasks may be, thereby assuring both clients and themselves of commitment to the sort of personalized consideration and quality work performance that each side expects. Furthermore, if work must be delegated to others, it means that professional tasks will be performed by professionals, not by lay personnel. Such is the traditional concept of professionalism as viewed by many lawyers and a concept they believe should be preserved even though it may mean economic sacrifice. It is a view in decline but still widely enough held to deter hiring of paralegals and support for their organizations in many offices.

Lack of a unique paralegal knowledge base or of unique skills also is a deterrent to development of the paralegal occupation. It can be easier for an occupation to extend its influence and expand its rewards if it exclusively possesses these occupational essentials from which so many other occupational characteristics derive. Not only is there no knowledge or skill sphere exclusively held by paralegals, but their principal knowledge base and skills are those over which lawyers generally have greater mastery. Furthermore, lawyers and organizations largely controlled by lawyers have preempted the field of servicing the crucial knowledge base of legal doctrine and practice through published summaries, commentaries, and critiques. Thus paralegals have moved into an area already competently occupied by others and in which further broadening of the paralegal scope of activities will be difficult.

Quite apart from the power lawyers may have to block paralegal expansion they oppose, the paralegal occupation will have serious problems in developing needed competence if it seeks to expand beyond its present role limits. Not the least of these problems is that access to law school and bar admission is such a viable option for many paralegals that a sizable proportion of those interested in developing greater competence are becoming lawyers. This attrition through crossover will no doubt continue and could accelerate if there is a strong push to increase the lawyerlike competencies of paralegals. Development prospects of paralegals would be better if lawyers were a much smaller and more exclusive occupational group.

Still another restraint on development of the paralegal occupation is lack of strong feelings of commitment and loyalty to the occupation by most paralegals. High occupational turnover and absence of perceived need by many paralegals for affiliation with paralegal organizations help create such feelings. Many paralegals have not even been exposed to paralegal school training, an experience that can create a sense of occupational belonging and obligation. Inducements to participate in continuing legal education programs are normally weak or nonexistent and there is little employer or peer pressure to join or become active in paralegal associations. Nor are on-the-job dissatisfactions often viewed by paralegals as matters that collective occupational action will help resolve. An exception to this may exist where paralegals are members of trade unions. Stated succinctly, paralegals recognize their occupational identity but with rare exceptions their occupational affiliation means less to them and they are less committed to the goals, interests, and organizations of their occupation than is true of lawyers, physicians, and other professionals.

To date, what has been the impact of the paralegal occupation? Given its rapid growth and development in recent years, what effect has it had on the legal service delivery system, on consumers of those services, and on lawyers and law offices? It seems obvious that paralegals have had an appreciable effect in holding down or reducing law office costs where paralegals have been employed. However, there are no studies of what savings there have been and whether or not cost-cutting benefits have been passed through to firm clients of for-profit operations and have resulted in more clients served and matters handled in not-for-profit operations. The strongest indication of cost savings from paralegal employment is probably the continuing and expanding utilization of paralegals when the principal motivation for their use is cost reduction. If paralegals were not saving their employers money it seems unlikely that they would long remain on the payroll. However, it should be recognized that law offices have not reached that stage of economic rationality at which careful cost-benefit studies are made to determine relative merits of using one type of personnel rather than another. Such studies would be useful and there are doubts that paralegals always save an office money, especially in offices where the disparity between paralegal and lawyer salaries is comparatively small.

Another apparent impact of paralegals is on the role of lawyers. From our interviews it is clear that paralegals have often replaced lawyers, performing less professionally demanding work that without the presence of paralegals usually would be assigned to lawyers. This has tended to upgrade the work of lawyers, especially those who are very junior, and may have accentuated orientation and learning pressures on many young lawyers by taking from them the more simple tasks formerly assigned beginners breaking into the practice. We also heard from some young lawyers that they feel less well-grounded in routine fundamentals than their seniors because paralegals have now taken over so much of the routine work in the office. Paralegal takeover of lawyer work presumably has also reduced somewhat employment prospects of marginal new lawyers, those least attractive in the market for legal talent. Some offices would have hired this type of lawyer if paralegals were not an accepted alternative, although, as indicated earlier, there has long been reluctance, even refusal, of many law offices to take on such marginal lawyers and be faced with the unsatisfactory situation of a dual classification of junior lawyers, those on the promotion ladder and those not.

The addition of paralegals to law offices has had the further effect of adding to law office personnel problems by inserting a new level of employee, paralegals, with uncertainties and tensions as to how those in this level should be treated and what role they should be assigned. Secretaries, particularly those who are more senior, may resent paralegals as a threat to secretarial role and status positions. If paralegals are treated much like lawyers, junior lawyers may take offense at persons they see as inferior in training and qualifications being given positions approximating theirs. But if paralegals are treated like clericals, this is likely to be deeply resented by the paralegals.

The problem of law offices in accommodating to paralegals and locating them in stable role and status positions that will maximize their usefulness with a minimum of tension is made more troublesome by the decentralized management patterns prevailing in most law offices and the inept supervision that many lawyers give to paralegals and other support staff. Through lack of interest, training, and capacity many lawyers are poor administrators, yet lawyers usually have responsibility for directing the work of support staff, and with rare exceptions paralegals' immediate supervisors are lawyers. As supervisors, lawyers are frequently insensitive to the needs and desires of their subordinates and to the subtleties of human interactions in close working relationships. Often they are not even very thoughtful or discerning in what work they delegate and to whom. Personnel management is hardly a high law office art.

Looked at in broad perspective, paralegals have been an important contributing element in the increased bureaucratization of law offices. Given their heavy involvement in routine procedures and their subordinate and often carefully directed law office roles, they have been closely involved in the more bureaucratic aspects of law office operations. They have facilitated law office bureaucratization by providing a cheap labor pool willing if not eager to work under bureaucratic restraints that many professionals would reject. This has made the move toward law office bureaucratization more acceptable to the professionals by reserving to them the more satisfying and remunerative tasks and continued dominance of the workplace while shunting off to others much of the drudgery and low-paid work that a bureaucracy can require. However, this pattern of work allocation has contributed to extensive paralegal apathy, discontent, and occupational dropout, conditions that in their own self-interest lawyers should be more concerned about. There is a risk that the more efficiently paralegals are sought to be used, the more chance that costly attitudinal dysfunctions will emerge.

FUTURE POSSIBILITIES

Over the relatively near term, the next generation or so, it is possible to forecast with considerable prospect of accuracy what will happen to the paralegal occupation. The occupation is now firmly enough established and there are enough relevant trends apparent that short-term estimates of the future can be fairly reliable. Also, paralegals are heavily dependent on what happens to lawyers, and while this latter occupational group is going through some important changes, it is so well-implanted in American society that drastic alterations in its structure and operations seem unlikely in the near future. Over the longer term, of course, predictions for paralegals, for lawyers, and for the system of delivering legal services are far more conjectural.

In the short run it seems certain that the number of paralegals will continue to increase: the supply is there and demand is strong, with indications that demand will become stronger. The labor pool from which most new paralegals are drawn will remain massive. It consists principally of young people with at least some college education, undecided about their futures but drawn to white-collar employment. To many in this group, paralegal work has a strong initial appeal. But the occupation abandonment rate by experienced paralegals will probably remain high, caused mostly by monotonous work assignments and dead-end career prospects, requiring an unusually heavy flow of new recruits to replace those who leave. The paralegal schools, with effective recruitment and placement programs, are geared to channeling large numbers of beginners into the occupation. In many communities, there are schools with a sufficient variety of program offerings in terms of education and experience prerequisites, cost, required time commitments, and academic difficulty to draw a wide range of potential paralegals. However, one of the most attractive types of paralegals, those that have been employed by large firms in particular and without prior paralegal school training, will probably be available in far fewer numbers in the future. These are the graduate school dropouts suddenly in need of work upon giving up their studies because of dim employment prospects in their field of academic concentration, especially the lack of jobs in college and university teaching. As graduate student enrollments in the arts and sciences are pared back to more employable numbers, fewer graduate school refugees will be seeking employment as paralegals.

The paralegal occupation shows every sign of remaining mostly populated by women, especially in middle- and small-sized firms. As with most other law office support staff jobs, this seems set and once set is likely to remain. Opportunities in paralegal work for economically disadvantaged persons with modest educational backgrounds, on the other hand, do not appear very promising. Early programs to recruit and train poor people from low-income racial communities for paralegal jobs faded away, although a number of such persons have been hired as paralegals by legal aid, and the CETA program added some to government law offices. An upturn in legal aid employment, which eventually will probably occur, no doubt will provide further paralegal job opportunities for these kinds of people. In hiring paralegals, private sector law offices have shown little interest in affirmative action for the minority poor or the educationally disadvantaged, a situation that seems unlikely to change.

Another factor conducive to increase in paralegal numbers over at least the short-run is the continuing trend toward further economic rationalization and bureaucratization of law offices. As this trend persists into the future, conditions should be even more favorable to paralegal employment, including still larger law offices, more concentrated routine work, more competition for clients, and more cost-conscious law office management. Resistance among lawyers to employing paralegals will dwindle and reliance on paralegals increase. Many of the offices that now refuse to hire paralegals will become convinced that it is wise to do so and will add them to their staffs. However, as law offices become increasingly bureaucratized they will encounter greater pressure from paralegals not only to ease what are seen as the excesses of bureaucracy but to be treated in many respects as professionals. The sentiment of a large and important body of paralegals seems to be that paralegals will accept subordination to lawyers and lower pay than lawyers but in return want a considerable measure of professional independence, responsibility, and respect. This sentiment will become more explicit and more pervasive and be more emphatically expressed in paralegal school training, in programs of the paralegal associations, during paralegal recruitment, and in pressures exerted by paralegals on the job. Paralegals can be expected to try to enhance their position in that grey area between professionals and bureaucrats where so many of them find themselves. In so doing, they will be behaving as typical paraprofessionals.

With anticipated expansion in the American population and continued rapid social and legal change, the demand for legal services will also probably expand, with consequent need for more paralegals. Some fields of law practice will decline but others will grow and new fields emerge. Complex heavily documented litigation, an important field for paralegal employment, currently is in decline but will revive as government regulation of business again intensifies, a likely prospect. If there is a continued easing of federal regulation of economic activity, state and local government controls well may increase, with added need for lawyers and paralegals. New and expanded state and local taxes will produce similar needs. Then, too, it is widely recognized that the American criminal justice system is so seriously overburdened at the trial level that in most large urban communities and many smaller ones there are intolerable delays and far too many ill-considered and plea-bargained dispositions. One reason for this deplorable situation is insufficient staffing of courts, prosecutors' offices, and public defenders' offices. As the criminal justice system becomes more of a public scandal, major steps conceivably will be taken to ease staffing shortages, and given the severe economic constraints involved, this could mean more reliance on paralegals and more paralegal jobs. Similar crippling staff shortages exist in many state and big-city government law offices responsible for civil matters and gradual alleviation of these shortages is quite possible, also with added utilization of paralegals. Legal aid, as well, has severe economic restraints and staff shortages and these could become much more serious if legal aid funding is defederalized. The result might then be a stretching of resources by legal aid offices hiring a larger percentage of paralegals in lieu of more expensive lawyer personnel.

Another factor that has an important bearing on the near-term future of paralegals is the favorable prospect for continued upgrading of the paralegal occupation. Upgrading can contribute not only to increases in paralegal numbers but to the roles and responsibilities entrusted to paralegals by their employers. Paralegals generally consider upgrading an important priority, a facilitating consideration. With more experience, paralegal schools should be able to improve the education they provide, more useful paralegal CLE programs should evolve, the paralegal associations should become stronger and more action-effective, and despite a high career abandonment rate there should be more paralegals who through aptitude and diligence in time have become essential to their employers. The occupation has developed so rapidly that its full potential has yet to be realized. That potential, however, will encounter a ceiling beyond which upgrading will be extremely difficult. The ceiling results from the restrictions and deterrents previously discussed, of which lawyer dominance and paralegal dependence on lawyers are crucial. Inability of the much older and better established English paralegal occupation to upgrade itself after reaching a certain plateau of development is illustrative of what the American profession will probably experience.[5]

As paralegals become better integrated and frustration grows from their limited upgrading possibilities, stronger support for trade union affiliation may develop. The benefits that union membership have brought to paralegals in some legal aid offices and to a lesser extent in some government law offices will be used as arguments in support of paralegal organizing efforts elsewhere. But it may prove impossible to organize paralegals successfully unless junior lawyers are also organized, as otherwise paralegals can too easily be replaced by junior lawyers. There seems little chance in the foreseeable future of associate attorneys on the partnership ladder of private firms accepting trade union affiliation, but possibilities of such affiliation by junior lawyers in corporate law departments may be slightly better. Prospects for union organizing also are more promising if most of those in the target group have working-class backgrounds or if unions already have organized competing enterprises. In these terms, private law firms and corporate law departments are likely to remain particularly difficult enterprises to organize.[6] For paralegals to be organized in most private law offices will also require considerable reorientation of values and attitudes on their part, and many current paralegals apparently do not wish to be involved with the confrontational tactics of trade unions. Because of their usual cooperative rather than confrontational approach, the paralegal associations also would probably oppose any major union attempts to organize paralegals in private law firms, the principal base of the associations' membership. The associations would also quite likely see a major effort at paralegal unionization as a threat to their power and influence, unless the associations themselves became union bargaining agencies, an improbable but not impossible role shift.

A trend that seems likely to persist and that has some benefit potential for paralegals is the continued chipping away at the lawyers' monopoly by lay businesses and professions that have, with or without clear legal authorization, moved into the legal services field. Contributing to this trend has been a weakening of the lawyers' aggressive stand against unauthorized practice of law. Benefits to paralegals that these moves into legal services by lay organizations and professions may bring is that the lay enterprises involved can use persons with paralegal training or experience; and as these enterprises generally are not dominated by lawyers, they commonly offer those performing paralegal-type functions more expanded roles and more favorable promotional opportunities than are available in law offices. This is evident, for example, with such business enterprises as title insurance companies and bank trust departments. Lay workers performing lawyerlike services may even become proprietors, common, for instance, in real estate brokerage, debt collection, and independent insurance adjusting. In the near term, lay businesses and professions will probably take over even more legal service work for others, especially in real estate title searching and examination, real estate closings, tax return preparation and advice, and estate planning and administration of decedents' estates. Another field vulnerable to greater lay encroachment is divorce, with non-lawyer mediators already assuming an expanded role in many communities.

There is some prospect, as well, that unauthorized practice restraints will largely be repealed or invalidated as means of preventing large corporate enterprises from providing legal services on a vastly expanded scale. This could mean a major collapse of the lawyers' monopoly, not just a chipping away at it. Funded perhaps by prepaid insurance schemes or government subsidies and aided by the overlap of so many legal and business services, we may see banks, insurance companies, accounting firms, brokerage houses, department stores, or entirely new types of business entities selling a much broader range of legal services to the American public on a dramatically expanded scale. Furthermore, many of these corporations may be nationally integrated, adding to their market penetration power. Models already exist; for example, the national title insurance companies and the national, even international, accounting firms. Medicine also provides examples of nationally or regionally integrated professional service organizations in the recent development of large for-profit hospital and nursing home chains, a development that is weakening the traditional professional independence of physicians.[7] Vast expansion of private corporation legal service functions could result in major legal service personnel modifications, including a possible blurring of distinctions between lawyers and paralegals.

There is also the strong possibility that the future will see more individuals representing themselves before courts and administrative agencies.[8] But for this pro se representation to expand substantially, it is essential that many of the parties have guidance in procedures and document preparation[9] or have much of the needed detail work taken over by court or agency staff members. Paralegal types can provide needed guidance, such as the help now being provided by private lay groups in some communities to parties appearing pro se in divorce cases. Pro se assistance could also be a means for trade unions to expand their legal services to members at low cost. Employees of courts or other agencies of government could greatly facilitate pro se representation by expanding their pro se guidance roles or actually taking over most of the requisite routine tasks needed for the pro se parties to achieve their ends. Even if the adjudicatory process is streamlined, a pro se system will not work for most individual citizens without specialists available to guide the parties or in considerable part take over for them.

Still another trend with some promise of increasing opportunities for those with paralegal training or experience is growth in demand for lay advocates, that amorphous group of persons not under the general supervision or control of lawyers who, usually as employees of public service agencies, provide legal assistance to disadvantaged persons. Some of those discussed above who assist pro se litigants fall in this category. Many paralegals are well-equipped to become lay advocates but there has so far been little movement by paralegals into lay advocacy, partly because paralegals are not familiar with opportunities in that direction and partly because many lay advocate positions are poorly paid. Also, there are lay advocates whose legal advocacy is incidental to their principal occupation, such as social work or the ministry, and it is rare for paralegals to be qualified in related service occupations. Given the inadequate resources of legal aid and public defender organizations to service properly many of the legal needs of disadvantaged persons, there is a major void that lay advocates can usefully fill. Some lay advocates operate in the uncertain zone of possible illegal law practice; but if their principal thrust is as educators on legal rights, generators of pro se action, community organizers, lobbyists, or referrers to legal aid law offices, they run little risk of conduct that would be considered the unauthorized practice of law.

As can be seen, in these volatile times many changes are possible in the short term that could have significant consequences for the American paralegal occupation. Over a longer period, of course, even more fundamental changes and consequences of changes can be conceived without becoming overly fanciful. For example, drastic long-run shifts may occur in the demand for legal services, with resultant effects on paralegals and other legal service occupations. Legal service demand may drop sharply if the society becomes more stable, if law becomes a less important means of social control, if most private wealth is nationalized, or if power becomes concentrated in a more authoritarian government. Demand for legal services is inordinately high in the United States compared to most every other country in the contemporary world, but this could change with advent of new conditions drastically reducing this demand. Nor is there any assurance that the present degree of heavy reliance in the United States on the

principal legal service intermediaries—lawyers and their support staffs—
will continue indefinitely. It is possible, for example, that over the long
term nonadversarial modes of dispute resolution will become so prominent
that present-day types of law offices will in major respects become obsolete.
It is also possible that eventually, with a more enlightened and better
educated citizenry, pro se representation will expand tremendously with
far less need than today for representation by legal service intermediaries.
It is conceivable, too, that new kinds of adversarial representatives will
replace lawyers and their aides in important conflict arenas.[10]

Of great significance to paralegals also could be long-run changes in the
structure of their occupation and that of lawyers, and some very fundamental structural changes in both occupations are likely to occur in due
course. More formal and sharply delineated fragmentation is one obvious
possibility. Law offices are becoming increasingly diverse in such respects
as size, clientele, work performed, recruitment sources, staff capabilities,
status, organizational affiliations, and income. This diversity is creating
occupational segments whose goals and interests often conflict, with fewer
common concerns and less common identity than formerly. It is doubtful
if uniformities in traditions, education, licensing, and standards of professional conduct can keep the lawyers' profession from fragmenting to a
point of becoming separate professions. Furthermore, even the law schools
and bar associations are feeling the pull of diversity, with individual law
schools increasingly specialized as to which segments of the profession they
channel their graduates[11] and most major bar associations becoming umbrella organizations for different sections and committees with appeal to
different professional segments and with association positions on issues of
professional importance increasingly difficult to attain. Diversity of interest
and outlook among bar segments was highlighted recently by the long and
often acrimonious efforts by the American Bar Association to develop new
standards of professional responsibility, resulting eventually in adoption
of the heavily compromised Model Rules of Professional Conduct, rules
that face an uncertain future at the state and local level. The fragmenting
trend among lawyers is highly relevant to paralegals because the degrees
of cohesion among paralegals is strongly influenced by the degree of cohesion, or lack of it, among lawyers. A more fragmented bar can mean a
more fragmented paralegal occupation.

In time it is possible that the bar will split into two professions, formally
and functionally separate, one profession that takes care of largely routine
legal service needs and the other that deals with novel and difficult legal
problems having important policy implications for the society.[12] In a very
rough sense this split might resemble the present division between English
barristers and solicitors, with less emphasis on litigation differences. If such
a division among lawyers takes place, paralegals are likely to fragment
similarly, with most paralegals employed by and oriented toward the

profession that concentrates on routine work. Conceivably, this latter profession would also be downgraded sufficiently in entry requirements that many paralegals could readily qualify for admission to it, in effect a merger of paralegals and this less elite professional group. Fragmentation by the bar thus could lead to enhanced bar-paralegal merger prospects.

Forecasting in a less speculative vein, it seems probable that on its own the paralegal occupation will eventually become formally fragmented, irrespective of further fragmentation by the bar. As presently constituted, the occupation consists of groups too diverse in function, ability, and commitment to remain indefinitely within the same occupational tent. Those who are more competent and dedicated are likely to insist ultimately on becoming licensed in hopes of improving their lot and giving them more of a competitive edge over the less-qualified and over the transients who quickly move in and out of the occupation. Law office administrators may fully separate themselves from paralegals by becoming licensed, certified, or developing unique and essential occupational association ties that exclude paralegals. Then, too, most law student employees of law offices may take on a unique standing from that of paralegals. Law students working in law offices, other than summer clerks and summer interns, have commonly been treated as paralegals but this may change. With costs of attending law school expected to continue escalating and with widespread dissatisfaction over readiness of recent law school graduates to practice law, a combining of law office experience with law school training may become the traditional route to qualifying as a lawyer. Students would then become paid interns, their work would be integrated with their course of study, and law office employers would be expected to assume some instructional responsibilities, monitored by law school teachers. Interns might frequently become apprentices being looked over for permanent job offers as lawyers upon completion of law school. A program similar to that outlined may even be necessary if private law schools, those without state university affiliation and support, are to survive financially. Their students must be able to pay mounting fees; and paid internships, widely available, may be an answer to this problem, but with the law office experience being integrated into the law school educational program to provide more assurance of professional development. Some movement in the direction indicated is apparent, and as law school costs increase, more such movement may occur.[13]

Despite the many uncertainties as to how and when the paralegal occupation will change, that it will change substantially is inevitable. All occupations change and this one is subject to particularly strong and persistent change pressures, even in the short term.

RECOMMENDATIONS

Recommendations should seek to further desirable goals and an obvious and important goal that recommendations pertaining to paralegals should generally aim to achieve is providing better legal service to clients. Better in this context usually is measured in terms of lowered cost or higher quality, although additional criteria can be relevant, such as lowered levels of client consternation and inconvenience. Among other goals worthy of consideration in making recommendations about paralegals are insuring appropriate remuneration and other rewards to those providing legal services; increasing the cost-effectiveness of government in the administration of justice; and increasing the extent to which legal process decision makers, such as lawyers and judges, act knowledgeably and fairly.

We have recommendations pertaining to paralegals that we believe are not only consistent with the goals outlined but should prove sufficiently appealing to have realistic possibilities of implementation. Our recommendations appear below.

1. *Recruitment.* Although we favor continued recruitment into paralegal ranks of varied sorts of persons, dissatisfaction among paralegals and their high job turnover and career abandonment rate are such serious problems that we recommend more emphasis be given to recruiting those likely to find paralegal work rewarding and fulfilling. This may mean recruiting persons with lower expectations and ambitions than the typical young college graduate and should include more persons interested in paralegal work from such groups as high school graduates or those with only a year or two of college not planning on more education, those whose main interests are an outside avocation or the home and who have limited vocational ambition, and some of the more vigorous retired persons who wish to continue working. To these groups might be added some of the unemployed industrial blue-collar workers whose jobs are gone for good and who must be retrained in new directions if they are again to be employable. In intelligence, education, and adaptability many of the blue-collar unemployed are capable of becoming paralegals. It would also help in recruiting more persons likely to be contented with the paralegal occupation if a more accurate picture were given paralegal school students and other prospective paralegals as to what are the work roles and career prospects in the occupation. Less puffing by the schools would mean fewer high-risk-of-discontentment recruits being drawn into the occupation.

2. *Education and training.* We recommend that there be fewer but larger paralegal schools with more staff and resources available to each school. In some communities this could best be attained by school mergers. There also is a need for more full-time paralegal school teachers without substantial administrative duties who can concentrate on teaching, research, and preparation of teaching materials. Larger schools in terms of students should be helpful in providing funds required to employ more full-time teachers as well as to improve library resources, placement services, and physical space needs. Our recommendation also is that most paralegal schools, in their programs for students without prior paralegal experience, focus on providing a required core curriculum for each beginner, plus

courses in specialty areas of the law presented in some depth, with each student required to become proficient in at least one specialty area. Such a program would assure a basic background plus knowledge of a specialty area and exposure in how one goes about mastering a new specialty.

For paralegals who later move into specialty fields for which they have not received academic training, extended continuing legal education courses in specialty fields should be offered by the schools on a classroom or correspondence basis. Paralegal schools cannot be expected to provide each student prior to starting work with the range of specialty area familiarity that law schools provide each of their students by graduation time. But lack of specialty knowledge can seriously restrict a paralegal's flexibility of movement in or between law offices, a problem best dealt with by post-employment training once the need arises. Paralegal schools should be much more than training centers for initial occupational entry. They should be equally important and equally relied on in helping paralegals to shift specialties later in their careers. However, the quality and usefulness of CLE training, as perceived by both paralegals and their employers, must be improved considerably if such training is to assure the enhanced significance we recommend. Nor can CLE education take over the full burden of paralegal training. The law office should assume a substantial training obligation for both beginning paralegals and those switching specialties if the unique needs and demands of the employing office are to be met most effectively. As with lawyers, paralegals have much to learn from supervisors and fellow workers in the office employing them.[14] Care should be taken to perform this law office training function more consciously and intelligently. Paralegal school continuing legal education course offerings should require substantial part-time student effort over a semester or other protracted period of time, with class sessions held in the evening or late afternoon. Well-conceived and well-monitored correspondence courses also are needed to make instruction available to paralegals who lack convenient access to paralegal classes. Because of their potential for drawing students statewide and even nationally, correspondence courses have the added possibility of increasing the number and variety of course offerings. Cassettes can increase the appeal of correspondence instruction, and audio-visual or closed circuit television presentations to groups also are possibilities, although generally upping costs.

Another of our recommendations is that paralegal schools experiment more consciously and thoughtfully with curriculums, course coverage, and course materials. There should be less copying of law school models and more concern with adapting courses and course materials to paralegal needs and interests. Undue attention should not be given to how-to-do-it aspects of law practice, and there should be recognition that paralegal students will be more proficient and more interested in their studies and their jobs if exposed in their courses to subject matter at a respectable intellectual level. A special effort also should be made to provide groundwork preparation in those aspects of paralegal work in which lawyers often show little interest or ability. In addition, special effort should be given to improving student writing. All paralegals should be capable of writing good expository English, but many are seriously deficient in writing skills, as are many if not most paralegal students. The paralegal schools can do much to remedy this deficiency in their students if the schools are willing to give writing the emphasis it deserves and to employ teachers qualified to take on this difficult and burdensome task. The paralegal writing problem will not go away by the paralegal schools taking the position that responsibility for developing competence in writing lies with the high schools and colleges.

If the paralegal schools step up their pedagogical experimentation as we recommend, an added burden will be placed on the program for approving or accrediting paralegal schools. The risk in any approval or accrediting scheme for academic institutions is that in trying to impose and sustain high standards, needed experimentation will be penalized and excessive conformity encouraged. Paralegal education is so beset with problems and is in such an early evolutionary stage that this risk must be minimized and it can be minimized only by standards flexible enough to encourage extensive experimentation and enforced in a manner tolerant of creativity.

3. *Expertise.* It is our recommendation that the paralegal occupation stress far more than it has in the past development of expertise and competence unique from that generally possessed by lawyers. This will increase the stature of the occupation and enhance career opportunities for paralegals. Most paralegals presumably will continue performing lawyerlike tasks that differ from what lawyers do principally in being simpler and more routine. But there are other law office tasks and subjects of useful knowledge less within lawyers' special sphere of competence. Among these are law office management; computer technology; marketing of legal services; public relations specialized to law offices; and formal work programming or systems formulation, with or without use of computers. These are not subjects lawyers learn much about in law school and if they have picked up any knowledge of them in practice it is usually random and haphazard. They are all areas in which paralegals could stake out claims of systematic expertise that would make paralegals more useful and to some employers even indispensable.

Another form of valuable law office expertise sufficiently unique from what lawyers normally possess and that a paralegal could acquire systematically and in depth is knowledge of the nonlegal aspects of a field in which the paralegal's employer concentrates. Those with such knowledge also are likely to have developed personal contacts useful in factual investigation, referrals, and even in attracting clients. There are endless possibilities of fields in which paralegals can develop valuable expertise, varying with the specialties of any particular office, but examples are the local real estate market, securities investment, accounting theory and practice, lending practices of commercial lending institutions, insurance company claims investigation and adjustment practices, family counseling techniques, prison administration, and welfare administration. In essence what we are recommending is greater emphasis on paralegals becoming in-house law office experts with nonlegal competence and knowledge highly relevant to the particular office hiring them.[15] Frequently this will make paralegals more effective in performing their lawyerlike work and also give the office more in-house capacity to perform nonlawyer tasks, as well as providing readily available sources of advice on matters of relevance to the office. This recommendation envisions a paralegal type somewhat upgraded from the usual paralegal found in law offices today, but with larger and more specialized offices particularly, we believe there is a need for more lay experts of the sort described. In some instances, paralegals can acquire the necessary expertise in college, university, or paralegal school courses. In other instances, it is best acquired by working in another field prior to becoming a paralegal.

4. *Supervision and incentives.* Frequent poor supervision and inadequate incentives in law offices make many paralegals more discontented and less productive than they should be. Supervision and incentives commonly are related, as how persons are directed can both create and shape work incentives. In their overseeing role, supervisors often have the power to grant or withhold rewards, and able supervisors can help develop in their subordinates a sense of collegial achievement and pride in work well done that themselves can be important work incentives. We believe that there are steps that most law offices employing paralegals can and should take to improve working relations with their paralegals. Furthermore, it should be realized that paralegals generally have quite different career prospects and expectations from those of junior lawyers and that directives and inducements effective with young lawyers may fail with paralegals. For example, the severe work demands placed on large-firm associates in terms of long hours, intense application, and assumption of responsibility will normally be unacceptable if applied to paralegals. Paralegals, after all, are not striving for partnership and their pay and other incentives are not commensurate with those of big-firm associates.

Steps that we recommend be taken by law offices to improve working relations with their paralegals are better communication; more task rotation; a formal ranking of paralegal positions; and, where possible, more promotion opportunities up and out of paralegal work. There should also be more willingness on the part of some offices to fire paralegals with poor performance records rather than waiting for such persons to quit of their own accord. Of greatest importance, however, should be increased opportunity for paralegals to work on their own and assume responsibility for important work, consistent with the individual paralegal's competence and sense of responsibility. This, as table 21 indicates, would probably do more than anything else to improve the often low paralegal morale, with favorable consequences for work quality and productivity.

Better communication should include informing paralegals of how their work on particular matters fits into the overall service being provided clients, where this is not self-evident. Paralegals are less likely to be enthused about tasks they are performing or to do quality work if they have little or no idea of what the product of their efforts will be used for or why what they are doing is important. Other means of improving communication are periodically evaluating in some detail each paralegal's performance and discussing the evaluation with the paralegal; asking for, and adopting when merited, paralegal suggestions for improvements in office procedures or work practices; being sensitive to paralegal complaints about their work and work setting and making reasonable efforts to eliminate the grounds for these complaints or at least make clear to the paralegals why corrective changes cannot be made; and when paralegals are supervised by intermediate-level staff personnel, making certain that those at the top who set office policy are made aware of the problems and suggestions pertaining to paralegals uncovered by the supervisor.

Task rotation has the obvious advantage of reducing boredom and it also enhances a paralegal's capabilities, something potentially of value both to employer and employee. Advantages of frequent task rotation can more than make up for the added training cost of breaking in a paralegal to new tasks. The often stultifying and dead-end nature of paralegal employment can also be broken for many paralegals if upward mobility possibilities are increased. This can be done by more law offices establishing a ranking of paralegal positions in a hierarchy of classifications, with each step up the ladder bringing more pay, status, and responsibility. Some offices are doing this, more should, and the upper positions should not be restricted to supervisors.

Needed upward mobility would also be encouraged if more employers promoted from within up and out of their paralegal ranks. Most possibilities of this sort are in large government and corporate enterprises that can advance promising personnel to nonlegal positions outside law departments. But they may exist in any kind of law office; for example, the possibility of promoting law student paralegals to lawyer positions upon admission to the bar or of promoting paralegals to office manager positions where these jobs carry higher than paralegal ratings. In offices with enough paralegals to justify employing an experienced paralegal as paralegal coordinator or supervisor, consideration should be given to expanding the responsibilities of this position to include case planning, cost monitoring, quality controls, and preparation of systems for performing routine work.

5. *Cohesion.* A better integrated and more cohesive paralegal occupation is still needed and no doubt will come with time. However, there is one

move that we recommend be taken as soon as possible that we believe would enhance considerably chances for greater occupational cohesion, and that is merger of the two major national paralegal associations: the National Association of Legal Assistants and the National Federation of Paralegal Associations.[16] Differences between the two associations in outlook and purpose are relatively minor and consolidation of the two bodies should provide enough resources to enable the new organization to accomplish more than is possible from the two bodies acting separately. A single strong national organization would also contribute to occupational unity. Further, it would make more authoritative any association decisions and pronouncements, as one national body is more likely to be perceived as acting and speaking for the entire occupation. In the trade and professional association world, there are great advantages to an occupation having but one clearly paramount national organization.

We recognize how difficult it is to achieve a merger of two rival organizations with somewhat different traditions and with the risk to the power base of individual leaders, but we believe that with enough good will, a consolidation can be achieved. There is no need to wait until one body is clearly dominant over the other or has forced the other out of existence. It would also be of value to paralegals and to other occupations providing legal services if a consortium of occupational associations in the legal services field were formed that held meetings of members at least once a year to discuss common interests, differences, and problems. Among associations that might usefully be brought together in such a consortium would be associations of lawyers, paralegals, legal administrators, social workers, law enforcement officials, judges, law schools, and paralegal schools. Every few years the consortium might organize and sponsor a national conference open to all interested parties, with the 1981 Georgetown New Roles in the Law Conference as a possible model. Delivery of legal services has become a multioccupational endeavor and no single occupational association, even one as large as the American Bar Association, can adequately raise all the issues or consider all the diverse viewpoints that are significant in the legal services field today. A more comprehensive and overarching organizational structure is needed to assure adequate exchange of ideas among occupations active in the legal services field and to provide more understanding of what each occupation can contribute to the legal order.

It will be fascinating to see how the paralegal occupation evolves from now on. It appears to have completed its initial burst of growth, organization, and recognition as a separate occupation. The next stage presumably will be one of strengthening its organizational structure and determining more precisely who does and does not belong in the occupation. Further adjustments can be expected in its satellite relationship to lawyers and in its accommodation to the often conflicting forces of professionalism and bureaucracy. How well it fares in this next stage will be dependent in part on its leadership. Occupations often have difficulty in developing effective leaders and this seems especially true of paraprofessions. Unless paralegal trade union membership becomes more extensive than seems likely, the most promising sources for vigorous paralegal leaders probably are the paralegal associations and the paralegal schools. But paralegal leaders should be more than vigorous, they should be knowledgeable and perceptive and in addition well-known and respected within the occupation and with those outside the occupation that they must deal with. Highly desirable are leaders up from the ranks who are seen as fully identifying with the occupation and who have personally experienced the hopes and frustrations of working as paralegals. Only leaders of this sort may be able to generate the credibility and support required to provide the necessary guidance to an occupation that is very much in need of guidance.

NOTES

1. New and expanded use of computers in law offices is opening additional opportunities for paralegals, but eventually the increased standardization and greater efficiency that computers make possible may diminish the role of both lawyers and paralegals. On these points, *see* Fry, The Impact of Technology on the Practice of Law, 1 *Legal Assistant Today* no. 2, at 9 (1984); and Mason, Establishing a Computer Component: A User's Guide, 2 *Journal of Paralegal Education* no. 1, at 35 (1984).

2. On the significance of associate-partner ratios in large firms, *see* R. Nelson, Practice and Privilege: The Social Organization of Large Firms 139–41 (unpublished Ph.D. dissertation, Northwestern University, Department of Sociology, 1983).

3. Other means for dealing with sudden and apparently temporary surges in demand for law office services are requiring existing staff to work overtime, delaying work on some matters, and turning down clients or closing intake, perhaps with referral to other law offices.

4. Nurses have been similarly restricted by the dominant entrenchment of physicians. *See*, for example, Katz, Nurses, in A. Etzioni (ed.), *The Semi-Professions and Their Organization* ch. 2 (1969). Progress of social workers, on the other hand, has been favored by having no strongly entrenched opposing or competing occupation. Goode, The Theoretical Limits of Professionalization, in Etzioni, *id.*, 266, at 290.

5. On upgrading difficulties encountered by English paralegals, *see* Johnstone and Flood, Paralegals in English and American Law Offices, 2 *Windsor Yearbook of Access to Justice* 152, at 187 (1982).

6. It is somewhat relevant here to the possibility of organizing private law offices that both lawyers and paralegals are organized and members of the same union in a large New York City prepaid legal service operation that is not a legal aid agency. However, the precedent significance of this example for prospects of organizing other private law offices is lessened considerably when it is noted that the office in question is itself a trade union instrumentality and serves municipal employees pursuant to a collective bargaining agreement between the union and the City of

New York. On this office, Municipal Employees Legal Services, *see supra* ch. 3, at note 99.

7. For the dramatic changes occurring in the structure of medicine, *see* P. Starr, *The Social Transformation of American Medicine* book 2, at ch. 5 (1982).

8. On trends in pro se representation, *see* Business Trend Analysts, Inc., *The U.S. Market for Legal Services* 166–69 (1984).

9. For a guide to self-representation, *see* K. Lasson et al., *Representing Yourself* (1983).

10. Advocate planners are illustrative of potential nonlawyer intermediaries of this sort. The advocate planner proposal attracted considerable attention a few years ago. This proposal is well-described by one of its major proponents in Davidoff, Advocacy and Pluralism in Planning, 31 *Journal of the American Institute of Planners* 331 (1965). Proposals for somewhat similar groups, with strong grass roots orientations and less top-down professional control than exists where lawyers are the principal legal service intermediaries, have been suggested for servicing the legal needs of the poor in developing countries. *See* Dias and Paul, Lawyers, Legal Resources and Alternative Approaches to Development, in C. Dias et al. (eds.), *Lawyers in the Third World: Comparative and Developmental Perspectives* 362, at 375–78 (1981).

11. On the relation of law school attended to the status and context of law practice, *see* F. Zemans and V. Rosenblum, *The Making of a Public Profession* ch. 5 (1981).

12. Heinz and Laumann conclude that lawyers in Chicago, and presumably other large urban centers, already consist of two professions "to an extent that is quite striking." J. Heinz and E. Laumann, *Chicago Lawyers: The Social Structure of the Bar* 380 (1982). Their division of lawyers, however, is different from what we suggest may evolve, as their two hemispheres of lawyers are those serving corporations and other large organizations and those serving individuals and small business. *Id.*, at 317 and ch. 10 generally. This split is also discussed in A Divided Profession: The Law's Two Worlds, *National Law Journal*, August 6, 1984, at 42. We see the possibility of a more formal division of lawyers, with each group separately licensed.

13. What may develop is a merging of the present paid summer clerkship concept with the practice of some law school clinics in assigning students to legal aid and other types of law offices to assist practicing lawyers. What may become prevalent is a program resembling the one at Northeastern University School of Law, in which four of eleven quarters of the student's enrollment are spent in full-time law office employment. This possibility also is somewhat similar to articled clerkship arrangements for prospective English solicitors.

14. The importance of law office contacts for the education of lawyers, as perceived by lawyers, is considered in Zemans and Rosenblum, *supra* note 11, at 152–55.

15. An occasional law office now has one or more full-time lay experts on nonlegal subjects, such as an engineer, economist, or writing and in-house education instructor. *See* Lauter, Using Non-Lawyers, *National Law Journal*, Feb. 6, 1984, at 1.

16. The two associations apparently are beginning to recognize that there would be substantial advantages to their cooperating more extensively with one another

and there have been some efforts to discuss differences and enhance areas of cooperation. *See*, for example, a joint article by the presidents of the two associations, NFPA/NALA Focus: Two Perspectives, *Legal Assistants Update*, vol. 3, at 81 (1983).

BIBLIOGRAPHIC ESSAY

This review of the literature does not include all sources cited in the text or footnotes to this work and at a few points does include sources not previously cited in the book.

Most of the literature on paralegals in the United States appears in publications of paralegal associations or was prepared as teaching materials for paralegal instruction. The paralegal association literature consists mostly of newsletters and journals containing articles and news items about association activities and personalities, association positions on occupational issues, and substantive legal matters of concern to paralegals. On occasion the paralegal associations have published books or monographs intended as aids in formal educational instruction. Much of the paralegal instructional material, however, consists of books put out by commercial publishers, the West Publishing Company of St. Paul, Minnesota, a major publisher of law school texts and casebooks, being the most active in the field.

As many of the paralegal journals and newsletters are not readily available in libraries, a listing of the principal ones may be useful. They are *Facts and Findings* (National Association of Legal Assistants, 1420 S. Utica, Tulsa, Oklahoma 74104), published bimonthly; *Journal of Paralegal Education* (American Association for Paralegal Education, Quinnipiac College, Legal Studies Department, Hamden, Connecticut 06518), published biannually; *Legal Assistant Today* (6060 N. Central Expressway, Dallas, Texas 75206), published quarterly; *Legal Assistants Update*, published annually by the American Bar Association Standing Committee on Legal Assistants; *National Paralegal Reporter* (National Federation of Paralegal Associations, P.O. Box 14103, Ben Franklin Station, Washington, DC 20044), published quarterly; and *The Paralegal* (National Paralegal Association, P.O. Box 629, Doylestown, Pennsylvania 18901), published bimonthly. A number of local and state paralegal associations publish informative newsletters, examples of which are *Venue* (New York City Paralegal Association, P.O. Box 5143, FDR Station, New York, NY 10150) and *On Point* (National Capital Area Paralegal Association, 910 Seventeenth Street, NW, Suite 617, Washington, DC 20006).

There is a numerically substantial literature on paralegals also appearing in publications of lawyers' associations, especially the American Bar Association, and in law reviews published by law schools, articles in the latter usually being more scholarly in approach. Other lawyer publications that include occasional articles and news items about paralegals are *Law Office Economics and Management* (Wilmette, Illinois: Callaghan & Co.), published quarterly; *National Law Journal* (New York: New York Law Publishing Company), a weekly newspaper of national circulation; and *New York Law Journal* (New York: New York Law Publishing Company), a weekday daily publication circulating in the New York City area. Other localities have lawyer newspapers similar to the *New York Law Journal* that also occasionally include items about paralegals.

A. Deserving of special comment is the *New Roles in the Law Conference Report*, the proceedings of a conference held at Georgetown University June 7–10, 1981. The co-chairpersons of the conference were William Fry of the National Public Law Training Center and May Yonayama of the National Capital Area Paralegal Association. The advising and steering committees for the conference included lawyers, paralegals, lay advocates, and legal educators from a diversity of organizations active in legal services and legal education. The *Report* reflects the varied outlooks and functions of paralegals and lay advocates and highlights many of the problems of these occupations as perceived by insiders. An excellent, almost book-length, early article also merits special comment. It is Brickman, Expansion of the Lawyering Process Through a New Delivery System: The Emergence and State of Legal Paraprofessionalism, 71 *Columbia Law Review* 1153 (1971).

B. Bibliographies on paralegals, comprehensive as of the time they were prepared, appear in W. Statsky, *Introduction to Paralegalism*, Appendix A, 2d ed. (St. Paul: West, 1982); and Brickman, Legal Paraprofessionalism and Its Implications: A Bibliography, 24 *Vanderbilt Law Review* 1213 (1971). Bibliographies of books and articles that may be helpful in paralegal instruction or in assembling a paralegal school library are Bibliography of Selected Materials, 2 *Journal of Paralegal Education* no. 1, at 85 (1984); and Pener, Results of Survey of Legal Assistant Programs, *Journal of the American Association for Paralegal Education, Retrospective 1983*, at 11 (1983).

C. On the work of paralegals, what they do on the job, the literature is substantial, much of it urging expanded use of paralegals by law offices or offering career guidance to prospective paralegals. Examples are Statsky, *supra* B. at ch. 2; P. Ulrich and R. Mucklestone (eds.), *Working with Legal Assistants*, 2 vols. (Chicago: ABA, 1980), a publication of the American Bar Association Section of Economics of Law Practice and the Standing Committee on Legal Assistants; R. Berkey, *New Career Opportunities in the Paralegal Profession* chs. 3 and 4 (New York: Arco, 1983); R. Kurzman and R. Gilbert, *Paralegals and Successful Law Practice* chs. 6–10 (Englewood Cliffs, NJ: Institute for Business Planning, 1981); N. Shayne, *The Paralegal Profession* 2–6 (Dobbs Ferry, NY: Oceana, 1977); T. Eimermann, *Fundamentals of Paralegalism* 49–54 (Boston: Little, Brown, 1980); American Bar Association, Special Committee on Legal Assistants, *Liberating the Lawyer: The Utilization of Legal Assistants by Law Firms in the United States* (Chicago: ABA, 1971); Law Poll, 69 *American Bar Association Journal* 1626 (1983); Fairbanks, Assistants in the Personal Injury Case, 10 *Trial*, no. 5, at 38 (1974), a publication of the Association of Trial Lawyers of America; Guinan, Paralegals in Administration, *National Law Journal*, Jan. 2, 1984, at 14; Guinan and Ferguson, The Changing Role of Paralegals, 40 *Unauthorized Practice News* 280 (1977), an American Bar Association publication; Schaumburger, Role of the Legal Assistant, 10 *Facts and Findings*, no. 2, at 19 (1983); and Stevenson, Using Paralegals in the Practice of Law, 62 *Ilinois Bar Journal* 432 (1974).

D. On the paralegal work force, the kinds of persons who are paralegals, there is a scattering of surveys, some of them with serious sampling problems. Among these surveys are San Francisco Association of Legal Assistants, *1978 Survey* (1978); and Washington [State] Legal Assistants' Association, 1977 Survey Results, in Kansas City Bar Association and University of Missouri-Kansas City Law Center, in cooperation with the Kansas City Association of Legal Assistants, *Systems for Legal Assistants, Resource Manual* 209 (1980). On paralegal job satisfaction and dissatisfaction, generally pointing up the high incidence of job dissatisfaction among paralegals, these sources are helpful: Larson and Templeton, Job Satisfaction of Legal Assistants, in *Legal Assistants Update '80*, at 55 (1980); Templeton, Legal Assistant Job Satisfaction, A Further Analysis, in *Legal Assistants Update '81*, at 37 (1981); San Francisco Association of Legal Assistants, *supra* at 51–83; S. Cramer, Study of Preferences in Continuing Legal Education Programs for Paralegals (unpublished study by the Chair of the Education Committee, Illinois Paralegal Association, 1979); and Childers and Jennings, Paralegal Salary and Job Function Survey, 21 *Law Office Economics and Management* 506 (1981).

E. The organization and activities of the paralegal associations are covered in each association's journal or newsletter, with *Facts and Findings, supra*, and the *National Paralegal Reporter, supra*, being particularly informative. A good comparison of the two major paralegal associations, the National Association of Legal Assistants and the National Federation of Paralegal Associations, appears in NFPA-NALA Focus: Two Perspectives, *Legal Assistants Update*, vol. 3, at 81 (1983). Origins of the American Association for Paralegal Education are described in Kaiser, American Association for Paralegal Education—A History, *Journal of the American Association for Paralegal Education, Retrospective 1983*, at 3 (1983).

F. Paralegal education and educational programs are surprisingly well-documented. Much of the early writing on these subjects was generated by American Bar Association interest in paralegal training and the ABA's formal approval process for paralegal educational programs. Among early ABA monographs on paralegal education are these publications of the American Bar Association's Special Committee on Legal Assistants: *Proposed Curriculum for Training of Law Office Personnel* (1971); *Training for Legal Assistants: San Francisco Pilot Project Report* (1971); and *New Careers in Law II*, at 45–88 (1971). Excellent early articles on paralegal education also include Statsky, The Education of Legal Paraprofessionals: Myths, Realities, and Opportunities, 24 *Vanderbilt Law Review* 1083 (1971); and Brickman, *supra* B, at 1219–48. Some of the other ABA legal education publications by its Special or Standing Committee on Legal Assistants are *Survey of Non-Degree Legal Assistant Training in the United States* (1976); *Legal Assistant Education and Utilization: A 1978 Status Report* (1978); and Ulrich and Mucklestone, *supra* C. Also important is American Bar Association, *Guidelines and Procedures for Obtaining ABA Approval of Legal Assistant Education Programs* (amended 1983). Results of recent surveys of paralegal educational programs are Pener, *supra* B; and Hill, Results of School Survey Announced, 10 *Facts and Findings* no. 2, at 8. Many student texts are now available for paralegal instruction, of which Statsky, *supra* B, is particularly good. Other paralegal instructional texts are cited *supra* ch. 3, notes 61–64. Paralegal educators as promoters of paralegals and their employment are considered in Kaiser, Promoting a New Field: The Educator's Role, 2 *Journal of Paralegal Education* no. 1, at 1 (1984). A good brief review of paralegal training programs is Berkey, *supra* C, at ch. 2, and much can be learned about individual paralegal schools from their catalogs and promotional literature.

G. Codes of professional responsibility and malpractice laws impose limits on lawyers as to how extensively and safely law offices may use paralegals. The professional responsibility limitations are considered in Ulrich and Mucklestone, *supra* C, at ch. 14; and Haskell, Issues in Paralegalism: Education, Certification, Licensing, Unauthorized Practice, 15 *Georgia Law Review* 631, at 651–62 (1981). Other citations on this subject appear *supra* ch. 4, note 9. Paralegal association codes of ethics or guidelines for ethical conduct are discussed in National Association of Legal Assistants, Model Standards and Guidelines for Utilization of Legal Assistants, 11 *Facts and Findings* no. 1, at 6 (1984); W. Park (ed.), *Manual for Legal Assistants* ch. 2 (1979), a publication of the National Association of Legal Assistants; and NFPA's Affirmation of Professional Responsibility, *Legal Assistants Update '81* at 137–39 (1981). Troublesome problems of paralegals as to professional conduct are dealt with in Brookes, Do Independent Contractors Have Special Ethical Considerations?, 9 *Facts and Findings* no. 3, at 7 (1982); and Marquardt, Running with the Hares and Chasing with the Hounds: The Emerging Dilemma in Paralegal Mobility, 2 *Journal of Paralegal Education* no. 1, at 57 (1984), conflict of interest problems when paralegals shift employment. Legal limits on the work paralegals may perform is part of the larger and often controversial subject of unauthorized practice of law. An introduction to this subject is provided by M. Pirsig and K. Kirwin, *Cases and Materials on Professional Responsibility* 77–110, 4th ed. (St. Paul: West, 1984). Other sources on unauthorized practice of law are cited *supra* ch. 4, at note 13, and attacks from within the legal profession on unauthorized practice laws are cited *supra* ch. 4, at note 16. The American Bar Association for many years published a separate journal on unauthorized practice, the *Unauthorized Practice News*. Tort liability of paralegals and lawyers is considered in Wade, Tort Liability of Paralegals and Lawyers Who Utilize Their Services, 24 *Vanderbilt Law Review* 1133 (1971); and W. Statsky, *Torts: Personal Injury Litigation* 462–65 (St. Paul: West, 1982). Other citations on malpractice liability appear *supra* ch. 4, notes 34 and 35. Lawyer's malpractice insurance is discussed in R. Mallen and V. Levit, *Legal Malpractice* ch. 2, 2d ed. (St. Paul: West, 1981) and types of lawyer malpractice claims in Stern, Causes of Attorney Malpractice Claims, 3 *Professional Liability Reporter* 199 (1979); and Pfennigstorf, Types and Causes of Lawyers' Professional Liability Claims: The Search for Facts, *1980 American Bar Foundation Research Journal* 255.

H. The issue of paralegal certification has been a lively one for some time and sources on the topic include American Bar Association, Special Committee on Legal Assistants, *Certification of Legal Assistants* (1975); and Haskell, *supra* G, at 641–51. Arguments for and against paralegal certification are discussed in the sources cited *supra* ch. 4, note 51. The paralegal licensing issue is also dealt with in Haskell *supra*.

I. In this book, systems are stressed as important means of organizing work in law offices, means that are especially conducive to use of paralegals. An influential early description of systems use is Turner, The Effective Use of Lay Personnel, in American Bar Association, *Proceedings of the Third National Conference on Law Office Economics and Management* 27 (1969), abridged version in 11 *Law Office Economics and Management* 73 (1970). Systems are also described in Israel, Systems in Law Practice: Planning for Quality and Efficiency, 26 *Wayne Law Review* 1159 (1980); and R. Ramo, *How to Create-A-System for the Law Office* (Chicago: ABA, 1975). Additional citations on systems appear *supra* ch. 1, note 9, and ch. 4, note 56.

J. As is to be expected, there is a vastly larger literature on lawyers than on paralegals. A major research organization that concentrates heavily on lawyers and the legal profession is the Chicago-based American Bar Foundation, which also publishes books, monographs, and the excellent quarterly journal, the *American Bar Foundation Research Journal*. Articles on lawyers and on organizations and institutions that lawyers control or administer also commonly appear in law school law reviews, bar association journals and monographs, and a miscellany of journals and newspapers such as the Law and Society Association's *Law and Society Review*, published quarterly; *Law Office Economics and Management*; the *National Law Journal*; the *American Lawyer* (New York: AM-LAW Publishing Corporation), a monthly newspaper with a national circulation; and the Association of American Law School's *Journal of Legal Education*, published quarterly. One law review is devoted exclusively to coverage of the legal profession. This is the *Journal of the Legal Profession*, published annually by the University of Alabama School of Law. There are many books about lawyers, examples of which are A. Blaustein and C. Porter, *The American Lawyer: A Summary of the Survey of the Legal Profession* (Chicago: University of Chicago Press, 1954); B. Christensen, *Lawyers for People of Moderate Means* (Chicago: ABF, 1970); L. Friedman, *A History of American Law* chs. 8, 11, and 12 (New York: Simon and Schuster, 1973); J. Heinz and E. Laumann, *Chicago Lawyers: The Social Structure of the Bar* (New York: Russell Sage, 1982); J. Hurst, *The Growth of American Law* chs. 12 and 13 (Boston: Little, Brown, 1950); Q. Johnstone and J. Hopson, *Lawyers and Their Work* (Indianapolis: Bobbs-Merrill, 1967); R. Nader and M. Green (eds.), *Verdicts on Lawyers* (New York: Thomas Crowell, 1976); and D. Rueschemeyer, *Lawyers and Their Society* (Cambridge: Harvard University Press, 1973). There also is a literature on various types of law offices, for example: big firms, *supra* ch. 1, note 23; small firms, *supra* ch. 1, note 28; legal clinics, *supra* ch. 1, note 34; corporate law departments, *supra* ch. 1, note 37; government law offices, *supra* ch. 1, note 42; and legal aid and public defender offices, *supra* ch. 1, note 43. The American Bar Foundation has published censuslike statistical studies of lawyers: *The 1984 Lawyer Statistical Report* (Chicago: ABF, 1984) and *The 1971 Lawyer Statistical Report* (Chicago: ABF, 1972). Law school student texts or casebooks on the legal profession include, among others, L. Brown and E. Dauer, *Planning by Lawyers: Materials on a Nonadversarial Legal Process* (Mineola, NY: Foundation, 1978); V. Countryman, T. Finman, and T. Schneyer, *The Lawyer in Modern Society*, 2d ed. (Boston: Little, Brown, 1976); and M. Schwartz, *Lawyers and the Legal Profession* (Indianapolis: Bobbs-Merrill, 1979). Some of the other books of significance on lawyers and the legal profession in the United States are H. O'Gorman, *Lawyers and Matrimonial Cases* (New York: Free Press, 1963); D. Rosenthal, *Lawyer and Client, Who's In Charge?* (New York: Russell Sage, 1974); R. Stevens, *Law School: Legal Education in*

America from the 1850s to the 1980s (Chapel Hill: University of North Carolina Press, 1983); and F. Zemans and V. Rosenblum, *The Making of a Public Profession* (Chicago: ABF, 1981). A bibliography on lawyers has been prepared by Professor Richard Abel, The Sociology of American Lawyers: A Bibliographic Guide, 2 *Law and Policy Quarterly* 335 (1980).

K. Bureaucracy and professionalism are important concepts in sociology on which there is an extensive literature. On bureaucracy, Max Weber, the great German sociologist, has had tremendous influence. For his views on bureaucracy, *see* M. Weber, 3 *Economy and Society* ch. 11 (New York: Bedminster, 1968); H. Gerth and C. Mills (eds.), *From Max Weber* 196–244 (New York: Oxford University Press, 1946); D. Wrong, *Max Weber* 32–36 (Englewood Cliffs, NJ: Prentice-Hall, 1970); and Ritzer, Professionalization, Bureaucratization and Rationalization: The Views of Max Weber, 53 *Social Forces* 627 (1975). A sampling of other sociologists' observations on bureaucracy includes P. Blau, *Bureaucracy in Modern Society* (New York: Random House, 1956) and *The Dynamics of Bureaucracy* rev. ed. (Chicago: University of Chicago Press, 1963); M. Crozier, *The Bureaucratic Phenomenon* (Chicago: University of Chicago Press, 1967); R. Merton, *Social Theory and Social Structure* rev. ed. (New York: Free Press, 1957); Hall, The Concept of Bureaucracy: An Empirical Assessment, 69 *American Journal of Sociology* 32 (1963); and Riggs, Shifting Meanings of the Term "Bureaucracy," 31 *International Social Sciences Journal* 563 (1979).

The concepts of professionalism and professionals have received diverse treatment by sociologists. Illustrative publications on these concepts are H. Becker, *Sociological Work* ch. 6 (Chicago: Aldine, 1970); R. Dingwall and P. Lewis (eds.), *The Sociology of the Professions* (London: Macmillan, 1983); E. Freidson (ed.), *The Professions and Their Prospects* (Beverly Hills, CA: Sage, 1973); E. Freidson, *The Profession of Medicine* (New York: Dodd, Mead, 1970); T. Johnson, *Professions and Power* (London: Macmillan, 1972); M. Larson, *The Rise of Professionalism* (Berkeley: University of California Press, 1977); T. Parsons, *Essays in Sociological Theory* 34–49, rev. ed. (New York: Free Press, 1964); H. Vollmer and D. Mills (eds.), *Professionalization* (Englewood Cliffs, NJ: Prentice-Hall, 1966); Hughes, Professions, 92 *Daedalus* 655 (1963); Goode, Community Within a Community: The Professions, 22 *American Sociological Review* 194 (1957); Klegon, The Sociology of Professions, 6 *Sociology of Work and Occupations* 259 (1978); Ritzer, *supra*; Toren, Deprofessionalization and Its Sources: A Preliminary Analysis, 2 *Sociology of Work and Occupations* 323 (1975); and Wilensky, The Professionalization of Everyone?, 70 *American Journal of Sociology* 137 (1964). Subprofessions have also received some scholarly attention, for example, A. Etzioni (ed.), *The Semi-Professions and Their Organization* (New York: Free Press, 1969); G. Ritzer, *Working: Conflict and Change* ch. 6, 2d ed. (Englewood Cliffs, NJ: Prentice-Hall, 1977); and S. Robin and M. Wagenfeld (eds.), *Paraprofessionals in the Human Services* (New York: Human Sciences Press, 1980).

APPENDIX: PARALEGAL
RESEARCH STUDY
QUESTIONNAIRE

Your cooperation in filling-out this questionnaire is greatly appreciated. The questionnaire is part of an extensive study of paralegals in New York City being conducted by Professor Quintin Johnstone of Yale Law School and Professor Martin Wenglinsky of Quinnipiac College. It is hoped that the significance, aspirations, and problems of paralegals and the contributions paralegals are making to the American legal system will be better understood upon conclusion of this study. A select sample of paralegals is being asked to complete the questionnaire, and the study is interested in analyzing not how any one person responds to the questions asked but in obtaining a composite picture of paralegals and statistically what generalizations can be drawn from the aggregate of responses. No individual questionnaire will be shown to any paralegal employer nor to anyone else other than those of us conducting the study.

Quintin Johnstone
Martin Wenglinsky

Your name _____

1. Firm name _____

2. Department (if applies) _____

3. Sex: Male ____ Female ____

4. Age _____

5. Marital status: Single ____ Married ____

6. Any children living at home? Yes ____ No ____

7. How do you classify yourself as to religion and ethnicity (For example, "Irish Catholic," "Black Protestant," "Jewish.") _____

8. Father's occupation (last occupation if retired or deceased) _____

9. Your home town (and state) when you completed high school _____

10. Education

    a. Undergraduate college attended, if any _____

        (1) Degree obtained _____

        (2) Years attended if no degree _____

        (3) Major field of study _____

    b. Paralegal school attended, if any. (For example, Adelphi University Legal Assistant's Program or the New York Paralegal Institute.) Also, give approximate dates of attendance (month and year) _____

(1) Paralegal courses taken at paralegal school (check as many as apply)

____ Introduction to Law   ____ Litigation

____ Introduction to the Para-   ____ Real Estate
     legal Profession

____ Legal Research   ____ Matrimonial Law

____ Corporations   ____ Criminal Law

____ Employee Benefits   ____ Contracts

____ Estates and Trusts   ____ Securities Regulation

                                                 ____ Other (list courses)
                                                 _____

(2) Did you receive a paralegal certificate or diploma from the school?

Yes ____   No ____

(3) Did your paralegal school attendance help substantially in (check as many
    as apply):

____ securing a paralegal job

____ securing a job promotion

____ increasing your salary

____ enabling you to become a more competent paralegal

(4) What is the most important way in which your paralegal school program could
    have been improved? (check one):

____ More how-to-do-it emphasis

____ Broader background on the nature of law and the legal system

____ More on helping the poor and disadvantaged

____ Coverage of more fields of law

____ More intense coverage of fewer fields of law

____ More coverage of law office management

____ More instruction on electronic data retrieval systems

____ Better teachers

____ Other, and state what: _____

c. Short seminars or workshops for paralegals or lawyers that you have attended, not organized by your employer. Also, list name of organization putting on the program. (For example, PLI, bar association, paralegal association.) Briefly state subject and length of seminars or workshops. _____

d. In your first full-time paralegal job, what training within the firm were you provided, other than learning by doing with help when needed? (Check as many as apply)

_____ (1) A special orientation program of a day or less

_____ (2) A special orientation program of more than a day to a week or less

_____ (3) A special orientation program of more than a week

_____ (4) Short seminars or workshops organized by your employer

_____ (5) Occasional post-orientation group lectures by office lawyers or others

_____ (6) Other, and state what _____

e. Secretarial school attended, if any, and give approximate dates of attendance _____

f. Law school attended, if any, with dates and years completed _____

g. Any other post-high school education with degrees, if any _____

11. Just prior to becoming a paralegal, your long-term occupational objective was to (check one):

_____ a. remain a paralegal

_____ b. become a professional assistant in another occupation (for example, a nurse or dental assistant)

_____ c. become a lawyer

_____ d. become a professional in another occupation (for example, accountant, doctor, or teacher)

_____ e. become a law office administrator

_____ f. become a secretary, receptionist, or other clerical worker

_____ g. acquire an executive-level position in business or finance

_____ h. other, and state what _____

12. List job titles and approximate dates of service with your current and all previous employers. Exclude summer or part-time jobs except when they involved working in a law office or law department.

Job Title   Dates

_____   _____

_____   _____

13. Your first job as a paralegal was obtained (check one):

____ a. through a paralegal school's placement service

____ b. through a friend or family member

____ c. through advancement from secretarial or clerical job with same employer

____ d. through contacts made on previous job

____ e. through an employment agency

____ f. through newspaper advertisement

____ g. through another method and state what: _____

14. Work is assigned to you (check one):

____ a. as specific assignments by a particular lawyer

____ b. as specific assignments by any lawyer in need of help

____ c. as specific assignments by a nonlawyer paralegal

____ d. by automatic routing to you

____ e. in some other manner and state what _____

15. Your work is usually supervised (check as many as apply):

____ a. regularly on a fixed time schedule

____ b. in irregular conferences

____ c. for accuracy, but not until work is completed

____ d. for thoroughness, but not until work is completed

____ e. for accuracy, during the course of your work

____ f. for thoroughness, during the course of your work

(Question continued next page)

_____ g. to ascertain if work is completed

_____ h. when something goes wrong

_____ i. to educate your supervisor or superior on the content of your work

_____ j. other, and state what _____

16. In your present job, what are your three major work duties? (Rank from "1" for most time consuming to "3" for least time consuming of the three.)

_____ a. Legal drafting, including filling-out forms, exclusive of typing. Include preparation of interrogatories

_____ b. Legal research. (For example, shepardizing, case digesting, and preparation of memoranda on the law.)

_____ c. Acquiring factual information directly from others: in-person interviews, telephone or correspondence inquiries

_____ d. Acquiring factual information from books, records and files. (For example, nonlegal research and analysis.)

_____ e. Keeping clients' books and records. (For example, corporate minutes.)

_____ f. Keeping your employer's books and records. (For example, dockets, firm payroll records, billing records.)

_____ g. Organizing, indexing, or filing masses of financial or other documents (excluding e and f above)

_____ h. Attending court or administrative hearings or the taking of depositions

_____ i. Supervision of paralegals and other office staff

_____ j. Running errands outside the office. (For example, delivery and filing of legal documents.)

_____ k. Typing

_____ l. Office or personnel management

   Other, for example, negotiations with adverse parties; client counseling; maintaining library; proofreading. State what they are.

_____ m. _____

17. Which of the above duties do you not perform in your present job but think you are now competent to do and would like to do? (Check as many as apply.)

_____ a. Legal drafting, including filling-out forms, exclusive of typing. Include preparation of interrogatories.

_____ b. Legal research. (For example, shepardizing, case digesting, and preparation of memoranda on the law.)

____ c. Acquiring factual information directly from others: in-person interviews, telephone or correspondence inquiries.

____ d. Acquiring factual information from books, records and files. (For example, nonlegal research and analysis.)

____ e. Keeping clients' books and records. (For example, corporate minutes.)

____ f. Keeping your employer's books and records. (For example, dockets, firm payroll records, billing records.)

____ g. Organizing, indexing, or filing masses of financial or other documents (excluding e and f above)

____ h. Attending court or administrative hearings or the taking of depositions

____ i. Supervision of paralegals and other office staff

____ j. Running errands outside the office. (For example, delivery and filing of legal documents.)

____ k. Typing

____ l. Office or personnel management

Other, for example, negotiations with adverse parties; client counseling; maintaining library; proofreading. State what they are.

____ m. _____

18. If you do considerable typing on the job, is it mostly of (check one if applicable):

____ work prepared by you

____ work prepared by others

19. In your present job, most of your work is in the fields of (check no more than two):

____ a. litigation   ____ f. criminal

____ b. corporate law and/or   ____ g. pensions and other employee
        securities law   benefits

____ c. real estate   ____ h. antitrust

____ d. estates and trusts   ____ i. taxation

____ e. matrimonial   ____ j. other and list what field

                                           _____

20. What is the average number of overtime hours you work per month? _____

21. Are you paid extra for overtime work? Yes ____ No ____

22. The single major source of satisfaction with your present job comes from (check one):

____ a. being part of important work

____ b. the intellectual challenge

____ c. working in a pleasant environment

____ d. having responsibility for important work

____ e. working on my own with minimal direction

____ f. friendships with fellow workers

____ g. being of service to others

____ h. making a good salary

____ i. having job security

____ j. other and state what _____

23. The single major source of dissatisfaction with your present job comes from (check one):

____ a. boring work   ____ f. no room for advancement

____ b. work of little significance   ____ g. work has no social usefulness

____ c. overly supervised   ____ h. too much snobbery and social
                                                ranking within office
____ d. work is too hectic
                                        ____ i. other and state what _____
____ e. long hours
                                        _____

24. In your opinion what is the most important attribute of a good paralegal?
(check one)

____ a. Knowledge of the law

____ b. Willingness to follow directions

____ c. Ability to get on with others

____ d. Willinginess to work long hard hours

____ e. Ability to take on responsibility for important tasks

____ f. Capacity to learn quickly

____ g. Ability to keep performing dull and boring tasks

____ h. Other, and state what _____

25. In what important respects for working in a law office are paralegals often superior to lawyers? (Check as many as apply)

____ a. None

____ b. Ability to communicate effectively with nonlawyers

____ c. Patience

____ d. Cooperativeness

____ e. Subservience

____ f. Considerateness of others

____ g. Knowledge of office routines and procedures

____ h. Ability to type or operate other kinds of office equipment

____ i. Other, and state what they are _____

26. Are you a member of any of these organizations? (Check all that apply)

____ a. New York City Paralegal Association

____ b. National Association of Legal Assistants

____ c. A trade union local that includes paralegals

____ d. Any other association of paralegals, law office administrators, legal secretaries or other law office personnel, and indicate which ones

_____

27. The main priority of paralegal organizations should be (check one):

____ a. continuing education

____ b. employment service

____ c. developing friendships and social contacts

____ d. pushing for improved paralegal salaries and working conditions

____ e. upgrading the status and influence of the paralegal profession

28. Are you invited to most office social functions? (Check as many as apply)

____ a. At which all lawyers but not clerical staff are invited

____ b. At which associate lawyers or junior lawyers but not clerical staff are invited

(Question continued next page)

____ c. At which clerical staff but not lawyers are invited

____ d. There are no office social functions

29. With whom do you usually eat lunch? (Check as many as apply)

____ a. Other paralegals from the office

____ b. Associate lawyers or junior lawyers from the office

____ c. Partners or senior lawyers from the office

____ d. Secretarial or clerical personnel from the office

____ e. Paralegals from other firms

____ f. Others from outside the office

____ g. Alone

30. With which of the following persons do you regularly socialize after work or on week-ends?

____ a. Other paralegals from the office

____ b. Associate lawyers or junior lawyers from the office

____ c. Partners or senior lawyers from the office

____ d. Secretarial or clerical personnel from the office

____ e. Paralegals from other firms

31. You intend to stay at your present job until (check one):

____ a. go to law school

____ b. finish law school

____ c. go to a college or university program in business

____ d. go to some other college or university program

____ e. become sufficiently trained and experienced to find a better paralegal job elsewhere

____ f. find a better paralegal job for which I am now qualified

____ g. become sufficiently trained and experienced to find a better job in business or finance

____ h. find a better job in business or finance for which I am now qualified

____ i. get married

(Question continued on next page)

_____ j. have a baby

_____ k. children are raised

_____ l. satisfied with present job and intend to stay indefinitely

_____ m. other, and indicate what: _____

32. If you are planning to go to law school, why did you first become a paralegal? (check one)

_____ To determine if you really wanted to become a lawyer

_____ To save money until you could afford to go to law school

_____ You failed to gain admission to the law school of your choice and hoped that paralegal experience would strengthen your law school admission prospects

_____ For reasons unrelated to going to law school, as your interest in attending law school developed after you became a paralegal

_____ Other, and state what your reason was _____

INDEX

38, 39, 42, 44, 45, 48, 50–52, 54,
204, 223–24
Paraprofessionals
defined, 183
difficulty in developing effective
leaders, 227
distinguished from semiprofessionals, 183
examples of, 183
in fields other than law, 5–6, 183
growth relation to fields they serve,
5
paralegals as, 183–84, 200, 215
relation to power and economic
need, 199–200
Patent registrars, 59 (n. 14)
Physicians, dominance of nurses, 227
(n. 4)
Practicing Law Institute (PLI), 132,
135
Prepaid legal services offices, 32, 45–
46, 135
Pro se representation
defined, 157
future prospects of, 217–18
legality of, 157, 158
need for specialist assistance in, 218
paralegal role in, 217–18
Professional school training, 186
Professionalism
influence of power on, 199–200
interplay with bureaucratic forces, 5,
184–85, 199, 200, 215
paralegal demands for, 215
Professionals
characteristics of, 185
lawyers as, 184
overtraining of, 186–87
professional organization, essentials
of, 185–86
Public defender offices, 8, 52

Questionnaire
distribution of, 7–8
return rate, 7

Recommendations concerning
paralegals

as to education and training, 221–23
as to expertise and competence development, 223–24
as to occupational cohesion, 225–26
as to recruitment, 221–22
relation to goals, 220–21
as to supervision and incentives,
224–25
Recruitment of paralegals
affirmative action hiring policies,
lack of, 72
civil service, disadvantages of, 101,
199
criteria for hiring, 101, 196–99
employment agencies, placements
by, 102, 137–38, 207
importance of the recruitment process, 195–96
in-house promotion, advantages of,
101, 102
minority poor or economically disadvantaged, opportunities for,
166, 214
paralegal school attendance, importance of, 123
paralegal schools, reliance on, 101–
102
recommendations as to, 220–21
selection pool, 214
sources of prospects, 98, 100
temporary placements, 138, 207
Routine paralegal work
common assignments to paralegals,
29
computer use in, 30, 31
examples: corporate documentation,
38–39; divorce, 32–34; document
processing in heavily documented
complex litigation, 30–32, 42, 48–
49, 55, 194, 215; estates, 37–38;
government benefits, 34–35; sale
or loan closing, 35–37; other examples, 29–30, 49
frequency of, 19, 21
government paralegals attitude toward, 189
growth of, 204

About the Authors

QUINTIN JOHNSTONE is Justus S. Hotchkiss Professor of Law Emeritus at Yale Law School and Visiting Professor of Law at New York Law School. Prior to entering law school teaching, he practiced law in Chicago. A frequent contributor to scholarly journals, he is the co-author of *Lawyers and Their Work* and *Land Transfer and Finance*.

MARTIN WENGLINSKY is Professor of Sociology at Quinnipiac College in Hamden Connecticut. He has served as a consultant on social problems for various public agencies in New York City and has authored several articles on education and social theory.